WILD BILL AND INTREPID

To Bill Stephenson whose friendship, knowledge and continuing assistance contributed so richly to the establishment and the maintenance of an American intelligence service in World War II —

Bill Donovan

Wild Bill

Donovan, Stephenson,

and the Origin of CIA

Intrepid

THOMAS F. TROY

-.-- ..- .---.

Yale University Press   New Haven & London

To the memory of "the two Bills":
Big Bill Donovan and Little Bill Stephenson

Frontispiece: Bill Stephenson
(Courtesy of Elizabeth Stephenson)

Part 2, "The Coordinator of Information
and British Intelligence," was originally
produced as a government or public
document.

Designed by James J. Johnson and set in
Goudy Roman types by Tseng Information
Systems, Durham, North Carolina.
Printed in the United States of America by
Vail-Ballou Press, Binghamton, New York.

*Library of Congress
Cataloging-in-Publication Data*

Troy, Thomas F.
  Wild Bill and Intrepid : Donovan,
Stephenson, and the origin of CIA /
Thomas F. Troy.
    p. cm.
Includes bibliographical references
and index.
ISBN 0-300-06563-9 (alk. paper)

  1. Donovan, William J. (William Joseph),
1883–1959. 2. Intelligence officers—
United States—Biography. 3. United
States. Central Intelligence Agency—
History. I. Title.
JK468.16T76 1996
327.1273′ 092—dc20   95-43946
[B]

A catalogue record for this book is
available from the British Library.
The paper in this book meets the guidelines
for permanence and durability of the
Committee on Production Guidelines for
Book Longevity of the Council on Library
Resources.

10 9 8 7 6 5 4 3 2 1

Contents

Preface   vii

Acknowledgments   ix

List of Abbreviations   xi

PART ONE
INTREPID IN BERMUDA

Introduction: A Quiet Canadian in Bermuda   3

PART TWO
**THE COORDINATOR OF INFORMATION AND
BRITISH INTELLIGENCE: AN *ESSAY ON ORIGINS***

1. The Coordinator of Information and British Intelligence   19

2. Frank Knox: A Friend at Court   22

3. Stephenson, Hoover, and Donovan   31

4. Donovan: To and from London   48

5. Stephenson's British Security Coordination   62

6. Donovan: In London and the Mediterranean 77

7. Roosevelt and the Intelligence Agencies 93

8. A Green Light on COI 111

9. A Postscript 132

PART THREE
QUESTIONS AND CONTROVERSIES

10. The FBI: Run by the British? 137

11. Three Books: From Obscurity to Fame 150

12. Donovan: A British Agent During World War I? 165

13. Churchill's "Personal Representative" 178

14. Thirty-Seven Years of Deception? 192

15. Too Much Gratitude? 202

16. Twenty-Five Years Later 209

Notes 213

Bibliography 243

Index 253

Preface

PART 2, "THE COORDINATOR OF INFORMATION AND BRITISH INTELLI-
gence: An Essay on Origins," was written while I was a staff officer in the
Central Intelligence Agency. It was classified secret and circulated in CIA
in typescript in January 1970. Still classified, it was published in 1974 as a
special issue of CIA's *Studies in Intelligence* (SII). It was declassified on 17 February 1976 but not publicly released until 28 January 1987. It is now publicly
published for the first time. Meanwhile, the favorable reception of the essay
within CIA led to my continuing the story by writing a full-length book.
*Donovan and the CIA: A History of the Establishment of the Central Intelligence
Agency* was completed in 1976 and then declassified and published by CIA
and then by University Publications of America, both in 1981.

When Part 2 was declassified, the original text lost twenty-four lines
and their accompanying footnotes. That declassified text has been un-
changed here except for a few words here and there to take account of
such events as the death of Sir William Stephenson. A few notes have been
supplemented with matter and references to take account of material published since 1970. The bibliography has been enlarged to take account of
material used in writing Parts 1 and 3. No substantive material, other than
five illustrations (which had been omitted from the SII edition and are re-
stored here), has been added to or subtracted from the text.

Acknowledgments

PART 2 OF THIS BOOK WAS WRITTEN TWENTY-FIVE YEARS AGO, BUT I remember with pleasure and gratitude the people who were so helpful to me. First in the order of time was my boss, CIA's director of training (DTR), John H. Richardson, who encouraged me in my interest and research on CIA's origin and set me on the trail of Sir William S. Stephenson. Next was Sir William himself, who had aroused my curiosity and who, then seventy-four, made digging into his wartime career such a pleasant enterprise. What began as an interview turned into a friendship of twenty years. Third was a quartet of agency officials who made my research and writing possible: Walter L. Pforzheimer, the founding curator of CIA's Historical Intelligence Collection, Hugh Cunningham, a second DTR, Lawrence Houston, CIA's first general counsel, and Richard Helms, then Director of Central Intelligence. Next was my secretary, Jane Early, who typed all my papers with skill and equanimity. John G. Fantucchio made my map of Donovan's travels in 1940–41, and Thomas A. Donlon made a colorful cover for the first edition of my essay.

For many years I have enjoyed the assistance and friendship at the National Archives and Records Administration in Washington of the archivists John Taylor and Lawrence H. McDonald. Recently I have also appreciated the cooperation of Shelley Sweeney at the University of Regina in Saskatchewan, Moira MacKay at the Churchill Archives Centre in

Cambridge, England, and David A. Keogh and Pamela A. Cheney at the Military History Institute, Carlisle Barracks, Pennsylvania. Three friends —George C. Constantinides, Ward Warren, and John Shepardson—gave helpful advice on some of the text. The helpfulness and hospitality of Elizabeth Stephenson, Sir William's daughter, have been much appreciated.

I am particularly indebted to H. Bradford Westerfield of Yale University. His interest in Part 2 set its publication in motion. Completing the process owes much to the friendly cooperation of Charles Grench, executive editor at Yale University Press, and his very capable staff.

I cannot say enough about the patience, support, and love of my wife, Elizabeth. As our eight children and ten grandchildren will agree, she has been one of God's choicest blessings in our lives. And finally it would be base ingratitude, indeed, were I not to acknowledge my indebtedness in my every endeavor to God the Father, the Son, and the Holy Spirit.

Abbreviations

AMCI	*A Man Called Intrepid*
BSC	British Security Coordination
CCC	Caribbean Cement Company
COI	Coordinator of Information
CSS	Chief of the Secret (Intelligence) Service
DCI	Director of Central Intelligence
DNI	Director of Naval Intelligence
DTR	Director of Training
FILS	*Foreign Intelligence Literary Scene*
G-2	Assistant Chief of Staff, Intelligence (MID)
IIC	Interdepartmental Intelligence Conference
JIC	Joint Intelligence Committee
MID	Military Intelligence Division (G-2)
MI-5	Military Intelligence, Section Five
MI-6	Military Intelligence, Section Six (SIS)
NARA	National Archives and Records Administration
ONI	Office of Naval Intelligence
OSS	Office of Strategic Services
OTR	Office of Training
PCO	Passport Control Office (Officer)
PWE	Political Warfare Executive

QC	*The Quiet Canadian*
RCMP	Royal Canadian Mounted Police
RG	Record Group
SE	Security Executive
SII	*Studies in Intelligence*
SIS	Secret Intelligence Service (MI-6)
SIS	(FBI) Special Intelligence Service
SIS	(Navy) Special Intelligence Service
SOE	Special Operations Executive
WCC	World Commerce Corporation
WSP	William Stevenson Papers

PART ONE

Intrepid
in
Bermuda

Introduction:
A Quiet Canadian in
Bermuda

"FOR US, IN THE UNITED STATES," DECLARED WILLIAM J. CASEY IN 1974, "it all began with a New York lawyer who saw his country facing a deadly menace and knew that it was unprepared and uninformed. It's hard for us to realize today that there was a time in 1940 and 1941 when William J. Donovan was a one-man CIA for President Roosevelt."[1]

What Casey told his audience, fellow veterans of the Office of Strategic Services (OSS), surprised none of them; they had heard it before. It had been spelled out many times, notably in 1959 on the occasion of Donovan's death, by OSS veteran Allen W. Dulles, then Director of Central Intelligence (DCI).

It all began, recounted Dulles, when Col. "Wild Bill" Donovan of World War I fame was "called into action" in mid-1940 by President Roosevelt, who sent him first to London on a "fact-finding mission" and then, at the end of 1940, to the Mediterranean and Middle East. As a result of those trips, Donovan urged Roosevelt to establish a central intelligence organization and discussed the proposal with several cabinet officers. The "seeds which Bill planted," continued Dulles, "bore fruit" in July 1941, when FDR established the Coordinator of Information (COI) and "called Donovan to Washington to head it." From COI came OSS and eventually in 1947 the Central Intelligence Agency, "Bill Donovan's dream."[2]

Why this version of CIA's origin held sway is not hard to explain. For

3

one thing, it is not all wrong. Donovan did make those trips; he did report to FDR; he did urge the establishment of COI; he did lead COI and OSS during World War II; and as Major General Donovan he did inspire the establishment of the postwar CIA. His record was impressive.

Moreover, the man thousands of OSS veterans knew as Bill Donovan fitted the Casey-Dulles account perfectly. When the veterans gathered to make their annual or biannual William J. Donovan Award, as when they gave it in 1974 to Bill Casey, they did so against the backdrop of a giant, brilliantly lighted portrait of the general. His superintending blue eyes reminded them of the man they knew as a mild-mannered, imaginative, energetic, innovative, ambitious, and inspiring leader of men and women. They took so easily to singing his praises that no OSS veteran has ever broken ranks, at least publicly. They never questioned how "it all began."

The Donovan story lived on in the new CIA. While Donovan himself never joined the agency, hundreds, if not thousands, of his people eventually did. Allen Dulles, Richard Helms, William E. Colby, and William Casey were four such men who ran the agency for twenty-five years—half of the agency's history. (Helms and Colby, between them, served as deputy director for another four years.) Those and other OSS veterans brought with them all their wartime experiences, lessons, attitudes, and memories. While they were quickly joined by newcomers who had never served in OSS, the latter quickly and happily accepted the OSS version of CIA's origins. It explained everything, featured a hero, and was a good story easily told.

Unknown at CIA

It so happened in the late 1950s that it became my story to tell. As a staff officer in CIA's Office of Training (OTR), I was assigned the job of briefing various employees and outsiders on the history, mission, and functions of the agency. Knowing little of the subject—I had joined CIA as an analyst of Middle Eastern affairs—I sought enlightenment in, inter alia, a book that surprised and intrigued me. It was *The Quiet Canadian: The Secret Service Story of Sir William Stephenson* by H. Montgomery Hyde, who had served under Stephenson.[3]

The reader will recognize Sir William Stephenson as the man made famous much later as "Intrepid." However, at the time he first crossed my path he was only a "quiet Canadian," a characterization bestowed upon him in 1948 by Robert E. Sherwood, Roosevelt's speechwriter and the author of *Roosevelt and Hopkins*.[4] What surprised me in Hyde's story of "the quiet Canadian" was the revelation of a hitherto unknown British dimension to the story of CIA's origin. What intrigued me was the oh so subtle suggestion that, at least initially, Donovan, our CIA hero, had been London's "man in Washington."

As revealed by Montgomery Hyde, it all began quite differently than in the Casey and Dulles account. The creative role was played not by Donovan but by "the quiet Canadian," whose prewar career as a decorated fighter pilot, boxing champion, inventor, and international financier-industrialist is well told by Hyde and sketched here in Part 2. What Stephenson did, as the New York representative both of Britain's Secret Intelligence Service (SIS) or Military Intelligence, Section Six (MI-6) and of Prime Minister Winston Churchill, was to look up his old friend Bill Donovan, whom he saw as the right man for the job he had in mind. Then Stephenson laid on that Donovan trip to London, had the royal red carpet rolled out for him, and helped arrange for the second trip, wherein Donovan received an introductory course in British intelligence and unconventional warfare. Then Stephenson, under his SIS cover as director of British Security Coordination (BSC), convinced both Donovan and FDR of the need for establishing COI, maneuvered Donovan into heading the new agency, and thereafter played intelligence schoolmaster to him and his fledgling organization.

More surprising than this story was the discovery that Stephenson's name was not known to otherwise knowledgeable agency people whom I queried. Much later I would discover, however, that I should have asked CIA's inspector general, Lyman B. Kirkpatrick, Jr., who joined COI in 1942. Reviewing Hyde in 1983 in CIA's scholarly quarterly, *Studies in Intelligence*, Kirkpatrick noted that Hyde gave "the British version" of COI's establishment, which he supposed was "relatively accurate." But Kirkpatrick wrote that publishing it was "extremely questionable." In fact, he found it "shocking indeed."[5]

Nevertheless, in 1968 I did not find Stephenson's name in any CIA documents that were either readily available or uncovered by a little digging. Thus, it never appeared in the U.S. War Department's two-volume top secret history of OSS, which was completed as close to events as 1946–47. Nor did it appear in Arthur B. Darling's CIA history, which was written in 1953, still not too long after the events, but which was shortly thereafter deep-sixed because of official displeasure with it.[6]

This strange ignorance struck me later as having a simple explanation: the Stephenson-Donovan collaboration in the year leading up to the establishment of COI was truly a clandestine affair, one to which very, very few outsiders, if any, were personally privy. Kirkpatrick's attitude shows how sensitive that subject was. It was so clandestine that, more than any other factor, it left the field clear for the rise and sway of the Casey and Dulles version of history.

When queried on this subject in 1969, Stephenson replied from Bermuda, where he was living in retirement, that he had already tape-recorded an account of his early relations with Donovan for another CIA historian. This unexpected response, and the subsequent receipt of a transcript of the tape, meant that someone else in CIA had already been on Stephenson's trail.[7] This pioneer was Whitney H. Shepardson, who had been given access to CIA in mid-1958 to write a history of Donovan and OSS. Shepardson was a distinguished businessman, educator, and editor who joined OSS in 1942, handled British intelligence matters, and knew Stephenson well. However, neither the tape nor transcript could be located in CIA records. Also, Shepardson never moved past the research stage before reported frustration over limited access to documents caused him to throw in the sponge. Hence, Stephenson's name was still lost to CIA history.

In any case, Stephenson's transcript was a memoir, recorded in an easy chair in Bermuda. It told the Stephenson-Donovan story much as Hyde had told it, but of course did not reconcile the American and British versions of CIA's origin. Also, it did not offer any supporting documents. Hence, after more correspondence, reading, and research, and after it was pointed out that General Donovan had died in 1959 and Stephenson was both seventy-three and an invalid, as the result of one or two strokes, I was sent to Bermuda in 1969 to visit him before it was too late (as it turned out, he survived another twenty years). Before recounting that visit, however, let us see what had happened to him since the war.

Out of the Cold

Stephenson ended the war as other veterans did. He left the service and went on to other things. However, he also stopped long enough to pick up honors from both the British and American governments. The only significant difference between the two events was the subdued character of British recognition.

On 1 January 1945 Stephenson's name appeared as a "Knight Bachelor" in a list of forty-one names on the New Year Honours List. The sole identification was a line denoting those in his line of work: "Employed in a department of the Foreign Office." In the British style, that line was adequate recognition for one who performed for his country what Nathan Hale had aptly termed "a peculiar service." It was so even if the service had lasted six years, had been done without salary, and had cost Stephenson $3 million to $9 million of his own money.[8]

That low-key recognition of Stephenson had in the United States little replay beyond the observation by columnist Leonard Lyons that "the name of William Stephenson . . . appeared in the news for the first time in this week." Lyons identified Stephenson as "one of the most active and silent principals of this war." He was "known to the top command," continued Lyons, "as 'Little Bill' . . . member of the 'Two Bills' team, the other being 'Wild Bill' Donovan."[9] The reference to Donovan, whose oss was publicly known as an engine of unconventional warfare, was a sure sign of what Stephenson had been doing when "employed in a department of the Foreign Office."

The British style was not the American style. Thousands of men had been knighted by kings and queens, but never in the United States had a foreigner been awarded the highest civilian decoration given by the United States, the Medal for Merit. Never, that is, until 30 November 1946, when the medal, approved by President Truman, was pinned by General Donovan on Sir William at a publicized ceremony in Manhattan. With Lady Mary Stephenson, Robert Sherwood, and others looking on, Donovan's oss deputy, Edward Buxton, read the citation's recognition of Stephenson's "invaluable" assistance to the United States in the "fields of intelligence and special operations."[10]

The award ceremony was so well reported in American, British, and Canadian papers that it was the most publicity ever garnered by the relatively unknown Canadian. As one London paper reported, it even told the British what Whitehall refused to tell them. Stephenson's BSC, the paper complained, "included a multitude of activities which are already known in the United States but none of which, for security reasons, may be revealed to a long-suffering, liberty-shorn British public."[11]

Two days after receiving the medal, Sir William and his Tennessee-born Lady Mary, his life-long peacetime traveling companion, took off for their winter home in Jamaica so he could "sit in the sun for a while."[12] During the war he had undoubtedly spent as much of himself—in twenty-hour days—as he had of his money. At "Hillowton" in Montego Bay, the Stephensons once again became leaders in the island's social life. They liked Jamaica's scenery and climate so much that they persuaded such friends as Lord Beaverbrook, Noel Coward, Ian Fleming, and Sir William Wiseman, who was his MI-6 predecessor in New York in World War I, to build homes nearby.

Though sitting in the sun, Stephenson, a trim fifty, had already taken up where the war had first found him. Six months earlier he and Bill Donovan, long close personal friends, and several prominent American, British, and Canadian industrialists and bankers had organized what became known as the World Commerce Corporation (WCC). It aimed at enabling Britain and the Empire, short of dollars because of the war, to gain foreign exchange by increasing exports to the United States. The wcc idea, said *Time*, long antedated Harry S. Truman's famous Point Four plan of assistance to economically underdeveloped areas.[13]

For Donovan, active participation in business, aside from lawyering, was foreign territory. He had tired of the law and returned to it only as a way of making a living. His avocations were public service, politics, and public policy, especially questions of national security during the Cold War. While equally anti-communist, Stephenson, who had played a major entrepreneurial role in the interwar years in leading companies in steel, automobiles, aircraft, communications, films, cement, and plastics, business was a milieu to which he had returned like a swallow to Capistrano.

Even so, it was business colored by the wcc idea. Although he had a multitude of investments, corporate affiliations, and business associates clamoring for attention, Stephenson chose the wcc as the vehicle for action. One of his first interests was Bermuda, where he had collaborated with British Imperial Censorship. The island's lifeblood was tourism, and rejuvenating it after its wartime shutdown was imperative. Hence, in August 1947 Stephenson, Donovan, Conrad Hilton the innkeeper, Col. Rex Benson the London banker, and others formed the Bermuda Development Company, with Stephenson as chairman. Among the properties they purchased— which made up five percent of the island—were three of its leading hotels. Announcing the purchase, and eyeing the American tourist, Stephenson said that with this project "we must start the drive for dollars."[14]

Meanwhile, Stephenson had begun working on Jamaica's twenty-year dream of making itself independent of foreign cement, so important to island construction and development. Wintering there made his involvement natural. With other wcc associates, notably Edward R. Stettinius, Jr., former U.S. secretary of state and chairman of the United States Steel Corporation, and three prominent local Jamaicans he formed and chaired the Caribbean Cement Company in 1947. The ccc started clearing ground in mid-1949 for a 100,000-ton plant—Jamaica's first heavy industry—and Stephenson was on hand in 1952 for its formal opening. Caribbean Cement, still operating, remained his interest until his death in 1989.

Stephenson spent the last half of 1952 dealing with the problems of an entirely different part of the Western Hemisphere, Canada's Newfoundland and Labrador. Larger, colder, and richer in natural resources, the area had mismanaged some investments and hence called on Stephenson to serve as chairman of a crown, or public, corporation to lure capital into the area for mining, exploration, and expansion. Refusing compensation, he headed the Newfoundland and Labrador Corporation, Ltd. Arriving in Gander, the wartime base for transatlantic flights, he was hailed as no stranger: he had made forty-three wartime trips.[15] By year's end, when he turned the job over to local talent, he had brought in eight major mining, industrial, and banking interests.

By early 1954 he was back home, in Winnipeg, Manitoba. The first time he had returned, immediately after World War I, he had found Winnipeg unpromising for his business interests and so betook himself to London, which became his center of operations for the next twenty years. Now, in 1954, he returned to a province that had long since begun to develop a balanced industrial-agricultural economy to replace its traditional dependence on the production of wheat but, like Newfoundland and Labrador, was in need of outside capital to establish new industries. Already founder of a Canadian company representing Manitoba in the United States, he responded to a call to establish and chair the Manitoba Economic Advisory Board, the only one of its kind in Canada. His contacts in New York and London gave Manitoba more access to the financial world.

Retired in Bermuda

Manitoba seems to have marked a watershed for Stephenson. One local paper, narrating his career, said at fifty-eight the "slightly greying Winnipegger" was "tak[ing] it easy" in New York where he was residing. Some months later his status was characterized as "semi-retirement."[16] Was it so? And if so, why? Certainly the record shows that Stephenson became less active in such enterprises as I just described. On the other hand he was deeply and regularly involved in the management of the Caribbean Cement Company. Still a traveler, he visited Jamaica regularly. His correspondence shows him intimately familiar with the day-to-day financial, managerial, and technical aspects of the ccc business. His writing style was straightforward, forceful, candid, and constructive.

If Stephenson was semi-retired, he might have become so as the result of the first of two strokes that he allegedly suffered (and which will figure later in these pages). According to researcher Timothy J. Naftali, Stephenson suffered a "serious stroke . . . in 1950" and decades later "stressed the power of this attack" and blamed it on wartime stress. Naftali quoted Stephenson's adopted daughter Elizabeth as saying he had his first stroke "in the early fifties."[17] Unfortunately there is no documentation for any of these claims.

Moreover, the facts noted earlier make us wonder. Bermuda, Jamaica, Newfoundland, and Manitoba showed a first-class entrepreneur in fast action. A 1954 photograph showed no sign of a disabling stroke. Correspondence to and from Stephenson through 1961 shows no concern for his health.[18] The conclusion here is that if he suffered a stroke "in the early fifties," it was not disabling and dictated at most only a more moderate pace of activity.

However, evidence of a stroke in the early sixties is unmistakable. A close wartime friend, Ernest Cuneo, confirmed that Stephenson suffered a "major stroke" about this time—he visited Sir William in the hospital and was dismayed by what he saw. In February 1963 Montgomery Hyde, whose book had just been published, reported that Stephenson "has been and is in very poor health." In June a friend of both Hyde and Stephenson, Col. Charles H. ("Dick") Ellis, of whom more will be heard shortly, reported that Stephenson "has been ill, and is no longer the same man." Naftali wrote that Stephenson was an invalid by 1964.[19] My own first meeting with Sir William in 1969 revealed obvious physical disabilities. The public saw the same evidence in 1983 during his highly publicized reception of the Donovan award in New York.[20]

In any event, semi-retirement had become retirement. By 1960 he had begun spending regular vacations in Bermuda. In September 1964—with the stroke just behind him—he arrived in Bermuda, announced his retirement, said he was taking up permanent residence there, and moved into a suite on the sixth floor of the Princess Hotel. In a few years he built a home to his own specifications, a modest rambler on two to three acres called "Camden House." A mile from Hamilton, Bermuda's capital, it scans the Atlantic to the south. It became his home and the office in which he received visitors and from which he maintained numerous contacts with friends and strangers via mail, telephone, and telex. It was there we first met, in February 1969.

Stephenson had booked me at the Princess Hotel, which he called "our local caravanserai"—an apparent hangover from his time in India in 1934 when he shot game with the Nawab of Bhopal. At the Princess, which had housed wartime Imperial Censorship offices, and where he was then often found, the desk manager startled me when she said: "You will be in Room 658, and Colonel Ellis is in Room 656."[21] The name of Colonel Ellis was familiar to me, but his presence there and then was a very great but very welcome surprise. An sis (or MI-6) professional, Colonel Ellis had been Stephenson's deputy in New York and had been as close to events of interest to me as anybody other than Stephenson himself. How lucky could I be? I didn't realize at the time, however, that a black cloud, formed out of British security concerns, threatened to drown the hopes I suddenly had of a second meeting with Dick Ellis in London.

Meanwhile, back in Room 658 and assuming Ellis would soon appear, I left my door open. He was there within three minutes. A short (5′ 5″ in his prime), slightly rounded, white-haired, proper person, Ellis the SIS veteran, then seventy-five, softly introduced himself. Then we taxied out to Camden House.

Only in imagination could one see in the man who met us at the door the former fighter pilot, lightweight pugilist, and man of action. Thinner than Ellis, also 5' 5", also white haired, and two years younger, Stephenson was warmly dressed, held a cane, but stood erect. His left eye seemed half-closed, and the right corner of his mouth was slightly contorted, especially when he spoke. Like Ellis's, his voice was soft but less audible and distinct. His smile and handshake bespoke "Welcome!" Instead of walking, he shuffled about and tired easily, and was "slightly forgetful," as I noted at the time.[22] Nevertheless, he was fully alert and coherent, in obvious control of his own affairs, and fully immersed in world politics.

When we three sat down in his living room, a nurse brought out drinks, and except for a refill, that was the last seen of her or anyone else—Lady Mary was not well. We sat talking for four hours and, as no light was turned on, deep into the gathering darkness—until Ellis, who was en route from Australia to London, had to leave to catch a flight to Heathrow.

What we three, and then Stephenson and I, discussed during the next four days—himself, Donovan, and COI—are fully developed in Part 2 and will be revisited in Part 3. Suffice it to add here some comments made pertinent by the passage of time, the appearance of new material, and subsequent controversies. Colonel Ellis is a case in point.

His Hand Still in the Great Game

Like Stephenson, Ellis served at the front in France in World War I. As a British army man, he served in Egypt, Persia, and Afghanistan, and then in the early 1920s joined MI-6 and spent the interwar years in Berlin, Constantinople, Paris, and Geneva. Thus an intelligence professional in 1940, he became deputy to Stephenson, whose intelligence career had begun the year before. Ellis, said Stephenson, was the tradecraft expert, the organization man, the one who furnished Bill Donovan with charts and memoranda on running an intelligence organization. He was therefore my best source of answers about BSC's organization and operations.

At the time there also seemed to me another reason for Stephenson's deference to Ellis—namely, Stephenson's occasional inability to recall things that struck me as ordinarily memorable. In this respect he had more noticeable trouble than Ellis. Stephenson's forgetfulness, possibly an effect of his illness, would later loom more important when his complicity in the extravagances of A Man Called Intrepid by William Stevenson brought scorn and condemnation down on his head. In any case, since I wanted to see Ellis again, we agreed on a meeting in London. As will be shown, however, that arrangement was rudely spiked by a higher authority.

Another example of controversy is a book that had been published in 1968 and that greatly annoyed both Stephenson and Ellis. This was Donald McLachlan's *Room 39: A Study in Naval Intelligence*. Its offense was touting the influence on both Donovan and FDR of two British naval officers, Adm. John H. Godfrey, Director of Naval Intelligence (DNI) and his aide, Comdr. Ian Fleming, the future author of the James Bond books, who together had visited the States in May and June of 1941. Ellis said he had objected to many passages in a draft of McLachlan's manuscript, was not given a second look, and only succeeded in getting McLachlan to insert the following: "It is clear that Stephenson had made remarkable progress in *finding and backing a man [Colonel Donovan] with whom the British could work as head of a proper secret organization.*"[23] (My emphasis.) That insertion did not mollify Stephenson, who clearly did not think his year-long cultivation of Donovan was brought to a successful climax by Godfrey's last-minute intervention. But it certainly made Bill Donovan look like London's man in Washington.

When I interviewed Godfrey in London later in 1969, he made it clear that that late intervention, namely, an hour and a half with FDR, had had "some effect," because, he pointed out, "COI was established within three weeks." While he generally spoke well of Stephenson, an acquaintance only, he remarked a few times that Stephenson had "a streak of ambition" that caused him to think of himself as "a kingmaker."[24] The two men never seemed to agree on the credit due each for finding and backing the man "with whom the British could work." For my part, Godfrey's intervention was, like that of many persons other than Stephenson, helpful but not decisive.

Four hours with Godfrey, on a hotel porch in seaside Eastbourne, had proceeded so well that he suddenly asked if I would like to see his memoirs. Such a question! He had only completed them about three years earlier, and very few others had seen them. "You will," he continued, "be sure to return them to me?" The question itself should have told me I already had the memoirs, but instead of settling for "Of course, Admiral," I added what I thought was a clincher, what a British admiral would appreciate about the chain of command, even for a CIA officer. "In case I don't," I said confidently, "all you have to do is call Sir Burke Trend [Secretary to the Cabinet]," and through my mind flashed the rest of the sentence: "he will call the U.S. Embassy, which will cable CIA headquarters, which will call my boss, who will confront me with a simple question: 'What are YOU doing with Admiral Godfrey's memoirs?'" But I never finished the sentence, because Godfrey interjected harshly: "You mean the GOVERNMENT?! I've had forty [actually forty-three] years with the GOVERNMENT, and that's enough!"

At eighty-one, Admiral Godfrey, long since known as a strong, often ruthless, disciplinarian, as well as an outstanding intelligence officer, was immovable. Only later, obviously too late, did I learn that in World War II he was the only British admiral who received absolutely no recognition for his services. His treatment, wrote the British naval historian Capt. Stephen Roskill, was "a disgraceful act of prejudice." After rebuilding naval intelligence, Godfrey was summarily dismissed in 1942 as DNI because of alleged incompatibility with his army and air force counterparts. Then, in 1946, he was held responsible for a mutiny while he headed the Royal Indian Navy. While Roskill added that Godfrey had never made "any complaint about the harsh way he was treated,"[25] I knew that he had erupted angrily at least once.

A third bit of intrigue centers on, once again, Colonel Ellis and that planned meeting in London. Like the entire trip, it had been thoroughly coordinated with all CIA's baronies, including counterintelligence under the redoubtable James Jesus ("Jim") Angleton. Hence, on the eve of my departure I was surprised by a telephone call from Angleton's deputy, Raymond Rocca. His message? "We've been asked on the highest authority to tell you: 'Don't see Ellis.'" Of course, I began to expostulate: "Whaddya mean 'Don't see Ellis.'? It's all been laid on. He knows I'm coming." Then another voice came on the line: "This is Jim Angleton. Do you need higher authority?" That was the time when CIA often seemed to have no higher authority. "No" was my prompt, and proper, response. "And," he continued, "don't tell the chief of station [in London]." Yes, sir. That was Angleton, running operations about which others knew nothing. With Ellis awaiting me, I had a problem.[26]

Compounding the problem was Stephenson, whom I saw on the way over but to whom I did not reveal my predicament. Ever helpful, but despite my demurrer, he cabled Ellis my ETA. Hence in London I immediately found his invitation for lunch the next day. Weaseling out of that—leaving regrets at his club—was not difficult, but a later message set another luncheon five days hence. Meanwhile, I had skirted Angleton's ban enough to send a Mayday message to my friend Walter Pforzheimer in headquarters. That obviously produced some scurrying around, because the station chief, Bronson Tweedy, called me in: "What are you doing about Ellis?" My response was short: "Nothing." His rejoinder, dutifully echoing Angleton, was shorter: "Don't." when I started to explain the ridiculous situation, he cut me off. "He'll understand." Understand what?

Before answering that question, let me dispose of the second luncheon. Because Ellis was then moving out of London, we had no direct communication. I could only leave another "regrets only" message at his club and then, like a fugitive from justice, clear out of my hotel from 8:00 A.M. to 10:00 P.M. lest he come looking for me. Which he did. And he left a package—a long note and 193 typescript pages of a projected book about Stephenson and BSC, which will be discussed in Chapter 11.

Now, understand what? Stephenson told me, on my return trip, that "they"—presumably men from MI-6 or MI-5 (Military Intelligence, Section Five or the Security Service) had questioned him about Ellis's loyalty. There had been some "fuss," they said, about Ellis having allegedly worked for the Germans before the war. Stephenson, who thought highly of Ellis, angrily recalled asking his visitors: "Why tell me this now—twenty-five years after the events? I took him to New York with me, would not have gone without him." Ellis, he said, was "only one of a few in MI-6 [I] would have hired even as a clerk." Ellis, he said he told them, could have, should have, moved up to the number two, or even the number one, spot in MI-6. Blaming the "fuss"on secret fighting between MI-5 and MI-6, he told his visitors he would not believe the charges unless he heard a tape of Ellis's alleged confession or could see his signature on the transcript.[27]

All of that, of course, was surprising news, but as it turned out, it was also only half the story. Ellis was also suspected of having been a Soviet agent as well. The Ellis case, for which the word "fuss" is inadequate, is too complex to try to synthesize here. Suffice it to say that by 1966 it had become a very contentious issue within MI-5 and MI-6 and led to what the experts call a "hostile" interrogation of Ellis. Out of that came, reportedly, his admission of Nazi, but denial of Soviet, espionage, even though he had been offered immunity on the latter charge. Even so, his interrogators were convinced he was "a long-term [Soviet] agent" and "a traitor of major proportions." None of this was known publicly until journalist Chapman Pincher broke the story in 1981 and Peter Wright, the chief interrogator, gave his account in 1987 in the much argued *Spycatcher* case.[28]

While the charges against Ellis have never been judicially proven, they have carried the day. The British government has certainly allowed Ellis, who died in 1975, to twist slowly in the wind. The United States, an interested—possibly an injured—party, has likewise said nothing.

Meanwhile, the relevant point for the Stephenson story is that his wartime deputy in New York, from 1940 to 1944, is widely believed to have been both a Nazi and a Soviet agent. Surprisingly enough, no British or American authorities or authors have ever even hinted at any evidence of treachery on Ellis's part in those New York years. Nor has anyone speculated on the possible damage done by Ellis to SIS, COI, and OSS. Likewise, no trace of Ellis is found in Pavel and Anatoli Sudaplatov's account of Soviet espionage in the United States during the war years.[29] Still, one must wonder what seismic secrets, such as Ellis's actual confession, are locked up in British and American intelligence vaults.

One final case in point: "Olds." Not the automobile, and not a personal name, the word struck me as unusual. It came into my lexicon, however, in my first meeting with Stephenson, after Ellis had left for London. While I had my agenda, I found Sir William had his own. He wanted to involve me in an intelligence network he called "Olds." Explaining that it was out of my job description, I said I could only listen and report back home. Only half hearing me, the old spymaster described "Olds" as an "L.O.C." or line of communications between an "entity" in Bermuda, the British in Washington, and hopefully CIA. The "entity" consisted of three persons in Bermuda—namely, Sir William, a local banker, and "a professional, a former Bermuda chief inspector who does the work". Colonel Ellis was also somehow involved. The purpose of "Olds" was monitoring and frustrating, when necessary, the movement between the Caribbean and Washington via Bermuda of the then worrisome "Black Power" activists.[30]

Whatever, if anything, became of "Olds" thereafter, two things about it always stuck with me. First was the persistence with which Sir William appealed to both my patriotism and self-interest in advancing it. "It's to your own advantage and the good of your country that you do this." To that twofold argument he returned the next three days. He even brought the local banker to see me twice and set up a Washington meeting with him. The hard sell, close on talking about Donovan and COI, evoked the picture, crystal clear in The Quiet Canadian and the Shepardson transcript, of Stephenson discussing, arguing, and maneuvering Donovan into accepting the COI job for his own and the country's good. I could hardly doubt the British version of how "it all began."

Secondly, while "Olds" unveiled the old spymaster as wanting to keep his hand in the Great Game—undoubtedly to the annoyance of a new generation of spies and counterspies—it also showed him as the watchman at the city gate, the defender of the stability and security of his country, the Empire, the West, and all they represented. For them he had risked his life, been wounded twice, and was imprisoned in the first World War—and had been ready to do likewise in the second. In the interwar years, he had secretly furnished vital intelligence on German steel production to Winston Churchill, who vainly warned London about German rearmament, and in the Cold War years he had alerted Britain about the threat of Communist aggression. His standard bearers were Prime Minister Margaret Thatcher and Presidents Ronald Reagan and George Bush.

Unlike Donovan, however, Stephenson was basically not a public man.

He had given only a few public addresses, written no articles or books, given only a few brief interviews, and had never sought elective or appointive office. Instead, he had always worked, as in "Olds," behind the scenes, helping, directing, prodding, and energizing others.

Thus, Stephenson had had little press. He had been given a paragraph in *Roosevelt and Hopkins,* made *Time* twice, been written up flatteringly in a Canadian magazine, garnered modest coverage in the business sections of the press, and been given full-blown treatment in only one book, *The Quiet Canadian.* Until he became "Intrepid," he was hardly known beyond business and intelligence circles. Only his wartime friends knew him as Little Bill Stephenson. That nickname had none of the éclat of Wild Bill, by which Big Bill Donovan was much longer and much more widely known. Stephenson was truly a "quiet Canadian" when I met him in 1969.

A year later Stephenson was still quiet when the essay in Part 2 was completed. Its beginning repeats parts of this chapter. But please bear with me; it will not happen again.

PART TWO

The Coordinator of Information and British Intelligence: An Essay on Origins

I

·—·—·—

The Coordinator of Information and British Intelligence

WRESTLING PHILOSOPHICALLY WITH THE QUESTION "WHAT IS TIME?" St. Augustine observed, in his *Confessions*: "If no one asks me, I know: if I wish to explain it to one that asks, I know not."[1] This insight into the problem of knowing is, perhaps, only slightly less applicable in the order of historical reality, in particular, to the origins of human organizations. The Who, Where, When, What, How, and Why of these developments are rarely as clear-cut and definitive as habitual knowledge would have them. Is this true of the Central Intelligence Agency?

It is generally accepted that CIA, which was established in 1947, evolved, after the usual zigs and zags, from the wartime Office of Strategic Services. This, in turn, is generally known, at least to the older or more informed, to have replaced the Office of the Coordinator of Information on 13 June 1942. Still moving backward in time, it is accepted that COI was set up on 11 July 1941, as the result of a recommendation made to President Roosevelt by Colonel William J. ("Wild Bill") Donovan, which, in its own turn, was the outgrowth of two trips to London and the Middle East taken by Donovan in 1940–41. Finally, as with a firm grasp on the ultimate beginnings, the public knows that this sequence of events was initiated when Donovan was asked by the President, after the collapse of France and the British withdrawal from Dunkirk, to visit London in order to investigate the nature of the Fifth Column and to determine the ability of Britain to withstand the expected imminent assault of the Nazis on England.

This account of Donovan and the establishment of the Coordinator of Information has become a tradition within the CIA. With additional and, in some cases, only slight variations in details, it appears in the classified "Origins of Central Intelligence" by Arthur B. Darling and in such public works as *Sub Rosa* by Alsop and Braden, *The Secret Surrender* by Allen Dulles, and Lyman Kirkpatrick's *The Real* CIA.[2]

Yet few realize apparently that the British have a version of these same events which is significantly different although not necessarily contradictory. This version was put forth most fully by H. Montgomery Hyde in *The Quiet Canadian*, whose American edition is entitled *Room 3603*.[3] This is the biography of William S. Stephenson, who was the chief of British intelligence in the United States during the war and a close friend and collaborator of Donovan's. Some twists to this British account appear in *Room 39*, Donald McLachlan's story of British wartime naval intelligence, and in *The Life of Ian Fleming* by John Pearson.[4]

According to this British account, which has the disconcerting merit of pushing the question of origins one step farther back, Stephenson was personally asked by Winston Churchill, intent on obtaining the fullest American assistance in the dark hours of 1940, to take over the intelligence post in New York. In that capacity, first as passport control officer, later as director of British Security Coordination (BSC), Stephenson renewed an acquaintanceship with Donovan, inspired and arranged both trips in 1940 to acquaint Donovan with Britain's capabilities and needs, urged upon Donovan the idea of the establishment of a new American intelligence organization with which Stephenson's outfit could effectively cooperate, and then finally brought about the appointment of Donovan as the Coordinator of Information. The Fleming angle in this account is his alleged authorship of the memorandum written by Donovan to President Roosevelt recommending the establishment of COI.

Without endeavoring here to assay the respective merits of these accounts or to anticipate the conclusions of this study, suffice it to say that the British account, on its face, is no less plausible than the American version. Indeed, the British account of Stephenson's role, for which he was knighted by King George and awarded the Medal for Merit by President Truman — the first foreigner so honored by the United States government — has the additional merit of revealing the inadequacies of the American tradition. The Stephenson story is prima facie evidence for undertaking a new examination into the origins of the Coordinator of Information.

This study aims not at the mere bare bones of organizational history but seeks to provide an intellectually satisfying answer to the question of how William J. Donovan—lawyer, soldier, publicist, and public servant—came to espouse the idea of an organization for the coordination of American intelligence. In particular, it seeks to answer three basic questions: (1) What was the origin of Donovan's trip to London in July 1940? (2) How did the idea of an organization develop and take hold of Donovan? and (3) How was Donovan's appointment as head of the new organization effected?

In answering these questions, attention will be focused, first, on Donovan himself and his association with the Roosevelt administration, then on Stephenson and his role in advancing British interests in the United States in the field of security and intelligence, and next, on the efforts of the United States government (especially President Roosevelt, army and navy intelligence, and the Federal Bureau of Investigation) to organize itself, in terms of information, intelligence and counterintelligence, and special operations, in the face of the growing needs and problems posed by the threat of war. Finally, it will be shown how out of the activities of these men and organizations a new organization—COI—was born, an organization which was to be part, indeed the *point de départ*, of a larger evolutionary process.

While a search for origins, this study has its own limits; and the time frame must perforce be 1939–41. The beginning is the outbreak of war in Europe in 1939, because it was the war which caused President Roosevelt to bring into his cabinet two outstanding Republicans, Frank Knox as secretary of the navy and Henry L. Stimson as secretary of war; and because in bringing them into the government, he thereby brought into the machinery of his administration another staunch Republican and very close friend of the new navy secretary, Colonel (later Major General) Donovan.

Another reason makes the outbreak of war and the "coalition" cabinet a fitting place to begin this narrative. For Donovan, who had been the hero of New York's "Fighting 69th" in World War I, who had been highly decorated by his own and the French and Italian governments, who in the interwar period had continued to study military experiences and operations in Europe and Africa, and who told an American Legion audience on Armistice Day 1939 that the United States might have to send men to fight in Europe[5] the outbreak of war posed the problem of the area of his own involvement. Secretary of War Stimson, a personal friend of Donovan's, was to observe in August 1940 that Donovan "was determined to get into the war some way or other."[6] Just how? This was the question, and the pages that follow will show that, in Donovan's case, Nasser's famous line about a role in search of a hero must be reversed.[7]

2

Frank Knox: A Friend at Court

EVEN PRIOR TO THE OUTBREAK OF WAR, PRESIDENT ROOSEVELT HAD
given some thought to the formation of a coalition cabinet. Whenever he
did so, he usually thought of the Republican candidates for president and
vice president in 1936, the titular leaders of the party, Alfred M. Landon
and Frank Knox.[1] The latter, the publisher of the *Chicago Daily News,* was
reportedly asked by the President in 1937 to become secretary of the navy,
but this account conflicts so sharply with Knox's own direct statement as to
suggest someone's faulty memory at work.[2]

Landon and Knox were apparently first linked in this fashion by Louis
Brownlow, the University of Chicago professor who was the President's
advisor on governmental reorganization. About the time of Munich, September 1938, he endeavored to pass on to Roosevelt, through others, the
suggestion that if war should come and it should seem necessary for him to
bring Republicans into the cabinet, he should select not "tame-cat" Republicans or "halfway Democrats" but "the particular Republicans who have
been chosen as leaders by the Republican party itself." Since the suggestion
was not passed on, Brownlow, in the spring of 1939, about the time of the
march on Prague, himself proposed it to the President, whose response was,
"You are right. If the time comes, that is what I intend to do, if there is any
practicable way to do it."[3]

That time came in September after the German move on Poland, when the British government was reorganized and a coalition war cabinet was formed with Winston Churchill back after twenty-five years as the First Lord of the Admiralty and Anthony Eden as Secretary for the Dominions. This prompted comments in the American press about the desirability of a similar reorganization in Roosevelt's cabinet. Discussing this with Harold Ickes, the secretary of the interior, on 9 September 1939, the President observed that the columnists "had been harping on the idea that there should be taken into the Administration such men as Herbert Hoover, Arthur H. Vandenberg, Robert A. Taft, young Lodge, and 'even Dewey.'" Both the President and Ickes agreed that such comments were a Republican move to build up a candidate for the 1940 presidential election, because "they do not say anything about Landon and Knox, the titular heads of the Republican party."[4]

Roosevelt, at the time, had many cabinet problems, and he was notoriously reluctant to tackle any of them. The war and navy posts were particularly vexing. In the former, Secretary Harry Woodring, who had been appointed in 1937, apparently on a temporary basis, was not only openly opposed to the President's foreign policy but was also openly at war with his assistant secretary, Louis Johnson. At the navy, Secretary Charles Edison was so deaf he occasionally misunderstood instructions. Replacing both men now took on added urgency, and the need for strength at home made a coalition cabinet, though politically difficult, very desirable.

Knox Pushes Donovan

Negotiations, which were on and off for nine months, initially centered on Landon and Knox, but then, when Landon became unavailable, shifted to Knox and Stimson. In the meantime, Knox tried mightily to get his close friend and political colleague, Colonel Donovan, appointed secretary of war.

The first step in these negotiations was taken on 20 September when Landon and Knox were brought to the White House along with a number of legislative leaders to discuss plans for repealing the arms embargo in the forthcoming special session of Congress. The Republican Speaker of the House, Joe Martin, noting the people in attendance, observed in a stage whisper to Alf Landon, "I don't know what we're doing here. This is a conference of his legislative leaders."[5] The reason for their presence had already been given to Brownlow, who reports that Roosevelt had told him of his invitation to Landon and Knox as providing him with an opportunity "to look them over" and also an opportunity for them "to look me over from a little different angle than they used in 1936." The upshot of this encounter, in which no mention of cabinet posts was made, was that Roosevelt was favorably impressed by Knox but observed that Landon had "acted like a bad little boy," apparently a reference to Landon's alleged uncooperative attitude on plans for effecting repeal of the embargo.[6]

After this disappointment, nothing much happened until the name of Colonel Donovan provoked the White House's first public statement on the possibility of a coalition. On 9 December, the White House discounted a report that Donovan would be made secretary of war in place of Woodring. "I don't think it is likely," said the President's secretary, Stephen T. Early, that "the President will put a Republican in as a member of his cabinet."[7] As a matter of fact, the President made just such a proposal the next day, 10 December, when he had a lengthy Sunday afternoon review of the world situation with Frank Knox.

According to Knox's memorandum of conversation, the President rather abruptly said, in the midst of a discussion of the bad relations between Woodring and Secretary Johnson, "I would like to have you come with me as Secretary of the Navy. I think the crisis in international affairs would justify your doing so." Knox's immediate reaction to this invitation was one of surprise that the President should extend such an offer to one like himself who had been so strong a critic of the President, at least on domestic affairs. Knox went on, however, to say that since recent events had somewhat lessened "the sense of gravity" felt by the general public, his entry into the cabinet would be considered "treasonable to my party, and I would be classified from one end of the country to the other as a political Benedict Arnold." To this Roosevelt entered a demurrer, but Knox held to his conviction that the time was not ripe for public acceptance of such bipartisanship. The publisher then suggested that several Republicans should be brought into the cabinet, and he particularly "urged that a strong man be found for the War Department."[8]

Knox's memorandum does not mention the name of Donovan, and perhaps it did not come up in this Sunday conversation. It did appear, however, in the Roosevelt-Knox correspondence which resulted from this meeting. Back in Chicago, Knox put in writing some of what he had said in person, and then added:

> I have heard during the month even more rumors of your taking my good friend, Colonel William J. Donovan, into your Cabinet as Secretary of War than I have heard of your thinking of me in connection with a cabinet post. I have no means of knowing whether you have even considered this just as I lacked any slightest confirmation of your having thought of me until our talk last Sunday.
>
> I know Bill Donovan very well and he is a very dear friend. He not

only made a magnificent record in the world war, but he has every decoration which the American government can bestow for bravery under fire. In addition, he is an outstanding member of his profession.

Frankly, if your proposal contemplated Donovan for the War Department and myself for the Navy, I think the appointments could be put solely upon the basis of a nonpartisan, nonpolitical measure of putting our national defense departments in such a state of preparedness as to protect the United States against any danger to our security that might come from the war in Europe or in Asia.[9]

This strong testimonial evoked from FDR his own appreciation of Donovan: "Bill Donovan is also an old friend of mine—we were in the [Columbia] law school together—and frankly, I should like to have him in the cabinet, not only for his own ability, but also to repair in a sense the very great injustice done him by President Hoover in the winter of 1929. Here again the question of motive must be considered, and I fear that to put two Republicans in charge of the armed forces might be misunderstood in both parties."[10]

Actually, it is very doubtful that Roosevelt and Donovan were anywhere near as close as Knox and Donovan. Years later, Donovan was to observe that "Roosevelt used to say he was a friend of mine, knew me in law school. But I always reminded people that Roosevelt never knew me in law school."[11] Significant also is the fact that the Roosevelt papers at Hyde Park show little evidence of any contact between the two prior to 1940.[12] Likewise, the White House presidential diaries, which are a catalogue of the names of the many people visiting, dining and overnighting at the White House, show no entry for Donovan in 1940–41.[13] While most Britishers stressed the closeness of Donovan to Roosevelt, one, writing in February 1941, cautioned, "Whilst we have every reason to think that he enjoys the confidence of the President, Colonel Donovan is not one of his intimate associates. Indeed, he only came over to the side of the administration when Colonel Knox joined the cabinet."[14]

Roosevelt could well have wanted to repair the "injustice" done Donovan, that is, the unexpected failure of Hoover to make as his attorney general the man who had served Coolidge as an assistant attorney general, but again there is no indication that Roosevelt ever really contemplated Donovan in the cabinet. At this particular juncture in history, Roosevelt seemed intent on bringing the Republican leaders into his administration.

Putting two Republicans "in charge of the armed forces" may have seemed unwise to Roosevelt at the time, but that, of course, is just what he did when he announced the appointment of Knox and Stimson on 20 June 1940.

Knox returned to the subject of Donovan when, many days later, he

wrote the President: "I am delighted to learn that you, like myself, hold Bill
Donovan in high esteem and can readily understand the point you make
concerning my suggestion in that direction."[15] With this letter, nothing more
is heard of the coalition idea until spring. Knox and Roosevelt did exchange
several pieces of correspondence touching on the war, but none is pertinent
to this study. The correspondence does suggest that there was developing
between the two men a rapport that strengthened the President's resolve to
bring Knox into the cabinet when the time favored it. This does not mean
that Roosevelt was not toying with other candidates or possibilities than
coalition. For instance, in March he offered the navy post to his old friend,
William C. Bullitt, then ambassador to France, but nothing came of this
even though as late as 9 June, Bullitt was telling FDR of his willingness to
run the navy.[16]

Coalition negotiations were resumed when the Germans attacked the
Low Countries, thereby ending the so-called phoney war and thoroughly
alarming the Western world. Knox was at the White House on 16 May,
but there is no record of the conversation. Knox's biographer observes: "it
would be surprising" if Roosevelt had not once again offered the navy job
to Knox.[17] Perhaps there is a suggestion of just that in a letter which Knox
wrote the President two days later—a letter, incidentally, in which Knox
again advanced the name of Donovan, this time to serve on a three-man
committee to coordinate industrial production. In this letter Knox hoped
that the President would have a satisfactory talk with Landon at their scheduled White House luncheon on Wednesday, 22 May, and stated that Landon
"is stopping off here [Chicago] to talk things over with me on Tuesday and I
will try to emphasize if it should seem necessary how vital a united front is
right now."[18]

The "united front" was Knox and Landon on the subject of joining
the cabinet. On 21 May Knox sent to the President, through Paul Leach
of the News staff, a brief note in which he spoke of Landon and himself
having "reached a mutual conclusion" which had been "animated solely by
our desire to promote national unity in the face of grave national peril."[19]
Actually, there was not as much united front as Landon would have liked.
Landon generally supported Roosevelt's foreign policy, but he genuinely
and firmly believed that the two-party system was seriously endangered by
Roosevelt's unwillingness to take himself out of the 1940 presidential election. Landon, therefore, pressed Knox, who was much more willing to enter
the cabinet, not to do so without a Roosevelt promise to take himself out
of the race. In this he was echoing the sentiments of the most powerful elements of the Republican party, who had been alarmed at the prospect of

Roosevelt capturing the titular leaders of the party on the eve of the national convention. On the eve of his meeting with Roosevelt, at which there was general expectation that he would be offered a cabinet post, the Kansan made provocative public statements which prompted the White House to call off the luncheon. A day later, the President, caught in the White House staff's confusion, personally telephoned Landon, renewed the invitation for lunch, and then on the twenty-second spent two hours with Landon discussing everything but the idea of a coalition. This comedy was concluded with Roosevelt accusing the press of having invented the idea of the coalition and declaring he had no intention of naming any outsiders to the cabinet.[20]

At this point, Landon was out, but Knox was still a good possibility. This probably sat well with the Chicagoan, who still wanted Donovan as his fellow Republican in the cabinet, who was more concerned with the gravity of the international situation than with suspected Rooseveltian thrusts at the two-party system, and who, moreover, was personally tired of the Landon-Knox couplet. Of Landon, Knox had said, late in 1936, that he "had played second fiddle to that second-rater for the last time."[21]

The next month was one of uncertainty for Knox. On 27 May he wrote the President telling of the meeting two days earlier of the group interested in promoting training camps for aviators, a group which was to be headed by General Malin Craig and which included among its members Colonel Donovan, General Frank R. McCoy, and Lewis Douglas.[22] On 5 June, he arrived in New York where he breakfasted at Bill Donovan's home. There he discussed the aviation project again and then left for "a lunch date with Bill at the Vanderbilt." In writing his wife on that day, he remarked, "There is nothing new to report on the Washington situation except that Bill told me Mrs. Roosevelt asked Mrs. Meloney (Missey) whether she thought Donovan would be loyal to F.D.R. if given a place in the cabinet. Of course you know what Missey would reply to such a question."[23] Then, on 11 June, Knox wrote the following to his wife in New Hampshire:

> Curiously today at lunch at the [Chicago] Club a rumor circulated that I had been appointed Secretary of the Navy. One LaSalle Street man said it was current in financial circles. I said I had no knowledge of any new developments and I found none when I returned to the office. I didn't tell anyone however that just before lunch I was informed by Professor Brownlow of the University of Chicago . . . who had a talk with the President Saturday that F.D.R. was unchanged in his determination to have me as his Secretary of the Navy and was now engaged in trying to find a satisfactory Republican or non-Democrat for war in order to meet my condition that other Republicans be included in the cabinet. Brownlow asked

me who I would recommend and I again suggested Bill. Later Brownlow called me to say he thought well of the suggestion and would convey it to the President.[24]

In Brownlow's version of the meeting, Knox raised the subject of the cabinet post by asking the professor to tell the President that he, Knox, was now ready to serve him "in any capacity that he wants me to serve and without any conditions whatsoever." He then corrected himself to say that the only condition was that he not be called prior to the Republican convention, which was to open in Philadelphia on 24 June.[25] Even so, on 15 June, Knox wrote Annie that he still "had no word of any kind from Washington and I am beginning to believe that I will not—and this produces a sense of personal relief rather than disappointment."[26]

When Brownlow reported to Knox that the President was endeavoring to find another Republican for the cabinet, he apparently did not know that that other Republican was Henry L. Stimson, as prestigious, experienced, and authentic a Republican as any on the scene, even though Brownlow was at that time, at the President's request, canvassing various press people for their comment on the suitability of Stimson as spokesman for the President on foreign affairs. The Stimson story, in shortened form, had begun "in the middle of May" when Grenville Clark, an old friend of Roosevelt's, a distinguished but quiet public servant, and then a vigorous proponent of universal military conscription, "woke up one morning . . . with the firm conviction that the only way to achieve his purpose was to obtain a Secretary of War who would 'push it through.' He needed, he decided, someone like Henry L. Stimson."[27] Here was a Republican of the first rank, a servant of four Republican presidents—notably, secretary of war under Taft and secretary of state under Hoover—and an advocate of conscription, national defense, and aid to Britain.

This project Clark discussed with Felix Frankfurter, the justice of the Supreme Court, "the Talleyrand of the times."[28] The two of them went over Stimson "and other names—especially William J. Donovan and Lewis Douglas—but they always came back to Stimson."[29] On 3 June, Frankfurter, who a month earlier had arranged Stimson's first meeting with Roosevelt in years, pushed upon the President the idea of appointing Stimson as secretary of war and Robert P. Patterson as assistant secretary. Once assured of the good health of the seventy-three-year-old Stimson, FDR was easily sold on his appointment. When Brownlow returned from Chicago with the news of Knox's availability, the President had his coalition cabinet in prospect. Both men were contacted on 19 June, Stimson at his office in New York, and Knox while lunching with friends at the Skyline Club in Chicago; and the news of their appointment was broken by Roosevelt on 20 June to the surprise of the capital and the bitterness of the Republican high command, who virtually read the two appointees out of the party on the grounds of party betrayal. Among the minority of Republicans who rallied to the support of Knox and Stimson was Donovan, who sent a telegram to the Republican Convention urging the delegates "to approve the designation" of the two as a means of strengthening the defense of the country.[30]

Publisher Becomes Secretary

There is no need to follow the two men through the successful process of Senate hearings and confirmation except to note the close collaboration of Knox and Donovan. So close was this, in fact, that upon accepting the appointment Knox told an associate, while still at the Skyline Club, that he "intended to ask Bill Donovan to become Under Secretary." Donovan, for whatever reason, was "unable to serve."[31] When Knox arrived in Washington on 1 July, he told his wife he found Donovan there waiting to meet him and help him get ready for the Senate Naval Affairs Committee. They immediately repaired to Donovan's home in Georgetown,[32] where they were joined by Senator Scott Lucas for lunch, and the three spent the afternoon preparing for the hearings, which covered much of Tuesday and Wednesday. Knox, as a matter of fact, moved in with Donovan: "Bill was most anxious to have me stay with him until I had a chance to get the details of starting on a new and difficult job under weigh [sic] . . . Bill is there alone and only part of the time but keeps three servants on duty anyway. Mrs. Donovan is in Maine right now and will be there for some time so I told Bill (fine, if he lets me pay my share). He finally agreed so I will be there for two or three weeks at least. It is ideal for me for it gives me freedom and privacy."[33]

Donovan also had his own business to pursue in Washington. On 3 July he appeared before the Senate Committee on Military Affairs in support of the selective service act and gave a three-page statement and answered questions, on the basis of extensive experience in battle and observation of recent warfare in Ethiopia and Spain, on a subject which was always dear to him, the training and leadership of men in battle. He was to do the same on 10 July when he appeared before the House Committee on Military Affairs.

Indeed, if one can accept at face value Donovan's own account of the origin of the trip, then it was on 3 July he was called to the White House and asked to go to London. This account, however, leaves so many questions unanswered that it is best left to later consideration in Chapter 3. Suffice it here to note that it probably was some time between 3 and 10 July that the trip was officially proposed and approved.

Late on the tenth, Knox was confirmed by the Senate, and he was sworn in by the President on the eleventh; he then went for the first time to the Navy Department but left soon, he wrote his wife, "for lunch with several of my friends at Bill's." On Friday, the twelfth, he had a session with the whole general board of the navy. That afternoon he held an impromptu reception for the three hundred to four hundred bureau chiefs, and "Friday night Bill had a few in to dinner." He was called to the White House the next morning at 11:45. This report to his wife on his first few days in office ends with the following account of Donovan's departure for London plus the usual note on his living arrangements:

> All offices close at noon Saturdays so when I got back from the White House Bill Donovan, John Sullivan, Jack Bergin of N.Y., Jim Forrestal of White House staff and I went aboard the Sequoia, the Secretary of the Navy's yacht, had lunch aboard and cruised down the Potomac until about 6 o'clock. Then Bill and I got into dinner clothes and went to dine with the British Ambassador Lord Lothian at 8 P.M. The only other guest was Minister Casey of Australia and the four of us talked until nearly 11 o'clock. Bill is leaving by Clipper for London today and we had much to discuss before he got away. I will tell you why he is going when I see you as I hope next week. Bill left at midnight for New York and sailed by Clipper for Lisbon at 3 P.M. today.
>
> I am moving much of my things aboard the Sequoia where I have a luxurious cabin . . . the only cost is the food. Bill insists that I keep some of my clothes at his house and stay there whenever I may want to until you come. . . . This solves the living question until you come in the fall.[34]

One can only imagine at this date what Frank told Annie, when he saw her, about the purpose of Donovan's trip. It probably did not occur to him, however, to emphasize what must be emphasized here, namely, that almost his first act as secretary of the navy, indeed, an act that was decided upon before he was actually confirmed, was to send his good friend Bill Donovan on a secret mission to Europe. How this happened, and to what extent the new chief of British intelligence in New York, William S. Stephenson, was involved, will be told in the next chapter.

All that matters here is that for the first time in the eight years of the Democratic administration of Franklin D. Roosevelt, William J. Donovan, a lifelong Republican and a foe of the New Deal, but a vigorous internationalist and a close friend of the new navy chief, had in that friendship a firm operating base in the machinery of the national government.

3

--·--·-

Stephenson, Hoover, and Donovan

WHATEVER KNOX DID TELL HIS WIFE ABOUT DONOVAN'S TRIP, NEITHER he nor anyone else has left behind a complete picture of its genesis. Both Stephenson, who claims to have initiated the trip, and Donovan, who made it, have given conflicting accounts, and independent evidence does not conclusively resolve the difference. In considering this evidence, it is well to begin with a brief look at William S. Stephenson himself and his activity in the United States in the months before the trip was conceived.[1]

"The Quiet Canadian"

At the outbreak of war, Stephenson (fig. 2), at forty-three, was a man of many accomplishments, much money, and many influential friends. His friendships reflected a personality which caused a one-time foe, Assistant Secretary of State Adolf A. Berle, to remark years later: "It was impossible not to like Bill Stephenson." His accomplishments reflected his versatility. As a pilot in the Royal Flying Corps in World War I his exploits had won him Britain's Military Cross and the Distinguished Flying Cross, and France's Legion of Honor and Croix de Guerre with palm. At the same time, he had gone in for boxing; and at Amiens, early in 1918, as corps member of the Inter-Service Boxing Teams, he won the amateur lightweight championship of the world. It was on this occasion that he met Gene Tun-

31

Fig. 2. Sir William S. Stephenson (passport photo, 1942)

ney, who also won a title then, and whose friendship was later to be the link between Stephenson and J. Edgar Hoover of the Federal Bureau of Investigation.[2]

After the war, the Canadian-born Stephenson moved to Britain where "his peculiar inventive and commercial genius transformed him into a millionaire" before he was thirty. Not only had he patented and commercially exploited a can opener he had found while a German prisoner of war,[3] but he had become the inventor, in a field dearer to his heart and talents, of a device for the faster wireless transmission of pictures, both still and moving, a device which was headlined in 1924: "Moving Pictures by Radio on Way; May Soon Be Possible to 'See-in' as Well as 'Listen-in' at One's Home."[4] By the 1930s he controlled a score of companies—in radio, films, cement, plastics, and so forth—the most important of which, from the point of view of his subsequent career in intelligence, was the Pressed Steel Company, which made 90 percent of the bodies for the major British automobile manufacturers. It was Pressed Steel which brought him into touch with German steel production, and in the years after the rise of Hitler and with the rearmament of the Reich it was his information that was fed to Winston Churchill, who used it in his public and parliamentary warnings against the danger of Nazi Germany.

Inevitably, and especially after September 1939, Stephenson was brought into contact with Britain's Secret Intelligence Service, whose chief was Colonel (later Major General Sir) Stewart Menzies—pronounced, to the dismay of many, "Mingiss"—known in the service simply as "C." With the hearty support of Churchill, then back as First Lord of the Admiralty, and the collaboration of the SIS, Stephenson undertook, but finally had to abort, a project to sabotage the German supply of Swedish ores. From Stockholm Stephenson was then sent on to Helsinki where he discussed modes of aid, by subversion or sabotage, to the Finns then under assault by the Russians.

On his return to London, he was asked by British intelligence to go to the United States in order to "establish relations on the highest possible level between the British SIS and the U.S. Federal Bureau of Investigation." Returning shortly thereafter to London, he was again asked to go to the United States, this time by Churchill, who was now prime minister, in order to render Britain a much larger list of services.[5] These are the two trips which he claims brought him into contact with Hoover and Donovan. Since both these contacts are fundamental to the story of the development of Stephenson's organization, British Security Coordination, and of Donovan's COI, their dates must be established before the details of Stephenson's activity in the spring of 1940 can be profitably spun out.

Arrival in the United States

About the second arrival in the United States there is no doubt. The record clearly shows that when the SS *Britannic* arrived in New York harbor on Friday, 21 June 1940, two of its 760 passengers were Stephenson and his wife Mary (fig. 3), who gave the Waldorf Astoria as their address and "indefinite" as the length of their intended stay. Stephenson listed himself as a civil servant with diplomatic status.[6]

Unfortunately, the earlier arrival is not so easily verified, but evidence shows that it did occur, although not exactly when. Thus, the record just cited also shows that he stated that his last previous entry into the United States occurred in "1940" when he visited "New York and Cal[ifornia]." Visa records show that he had been issued a visa sometime in the last two weeks of March, and that he was traveling to the United States as a "Government Official [and] Company Director [who was] Proceeding to the United States on an Official Mission for the Ministry of Supply."[7] Moreover, the SIS, in response to a query on this very point, has categorically affirmed: "Stephenson visited the USA in April 1940."[8]

Perhaps the most interesting item on this point turned up in a most unlikely place: a memorandum on "German Activity in Mexico," which had been sent to G-2 at the Presidio in San Francisco by the "Head Inspector, Air Plant Protection Control" for the army's western procurement district.[9] The inspector reported on 20 June 1940, the day before Stephenson's second arrival in the States, that he had been informed of "a recent visit" in California by "Mr. W. S. Stevenson [*sic*], Attaché of the British Foreign Office at London." Though the name is misspelled, a common error, it can hardly refer, as the body of the report shows, to some other person. For this reason, and because of its reference to a Stephenson-Hoover meeting, a point which needs to be documented, it is worth quoting:

> Mr. Stevenson had advised him (Mr. B. [E.] L. Cord, former airplane and automobile manufacturer) that all of the information furnished Mr. Cord had previously been furnished to Mr. J. Edgar Hoover, Director of the Federal Bureau of Investigation, with whom he had been in conference for 14 hours just prior to his visit with Mr. Cord.
>
> Mr. Stevenson advised Mr. Cord that the Russian Government had shipped 50,000 Spanish-Loyalist refugees to the Republic of Mexico during the past year and that the German Government had shipped 37,500 troops to the Republic of Mexico during the past three months. He also stated that the German troops were equipped with machine guns, hand-grenades, and small artillery sufficient to equip an army of 200,000 men.
>
> Mr. Cord stated that he was quite satisfied this information had been

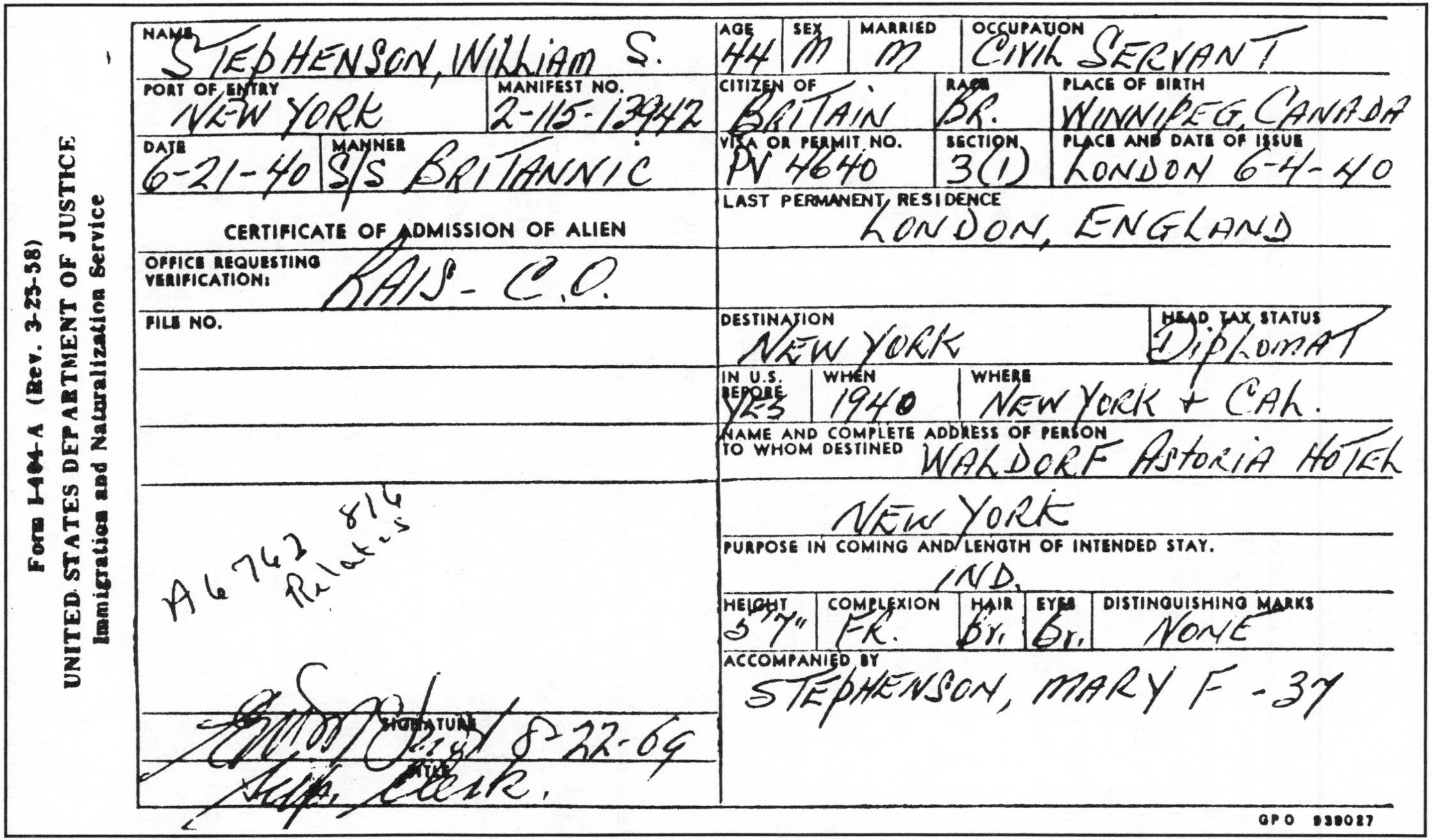

Fig. 3. Stephenson's Certificate of Admission, 21 June 1940. (Courtesy of U.S. Immigration and Naturalization Service)

furnished to the Federal Bureau of Investigation and the proper War Department authorities by Mr. Stevenson during his recent visit.

While this is not the place to evaluate the accuracy of the numbers of Spanish Loyalist refugees and German troops in Mexico, and while it takes us a little ahead of the story, it is pertinent to note that the supplying of such intelligence as this to the FBI was one of the purposes of establishing liaison between SIS and the bureau.

Stephenson, then, did arrive in the United States early in the spring, in April, but his approach to the bureau at that time was not the first approach of British intelligence to an intensification of liaison with the FBI. An approach was already being made at the time Stephenson was getting his visa for the United States; and whether there was any connection between the two is hard to say. The earlier approach, by members of the allies' purchasing commissions, is nevertheless part of the background to Stephenson's own work and hence must be considered before finally turning to the Stephenson-Hoover relationship.

British Intelligence and the FBI

On 19 March an FBI official met for three-quarters of an hour in Washington with Mr. Hamish Mitchell, special assistant to the director general of the British Purchasing Commission, and Mr. Charles T. Ballantyne, the Washington representative of the Anglo-French Purchasing Commission. Mitchell apparently did all the talking, and the gist of his message was that the British were so concerned about preventing a repetition of the unfortunate World War I experience of seeing much of their war materials sabotaged in the United States that they were suggesting "the advisability of utilizing an undercover branch of the British service to secure information with respect to possible sabotage so that the enemy's movements . . . could be anticipated and forestalled." Mitchell was also concerned about the bureau's plant protection surveys and supervision and about the role of railroad police in protecting materials in transit. He wanted the bureau's assistance in getting information about the many Americans the commission had had to hire; he offered to make available to the bureau the "considerable information" which he had acquired in the pursuit of his duties; and finally, he inquired as to whether he might make similar contacts with other bureau offices in the United States.[10]

Mitchell's approach was duly communicated by Hoover to Assistant Secretary of State Adolf A. Berle, who served more or less as the President's overseer of the Interdepartmental Intelligence Conference (IIC).[11] In a memorandum of his own, Berle referred to the proposed "undercover unit" as a "unit of British Intelligence . . . reporting" to the Purchasing Commission and noted: "The F.B.I. reacted instantly and unfavorably." He continued:

> I feel we should discourage activities of this kind. If we are to have a combined counterespionage and secret intelligence unit, it should be our own, and not foreign. But I do think that this suggests a more expeditious way of getting information from these people into the hands of our own agencies, so that if there is thought of German or Russian espionage or sabotage we can deal with it promptly. Specifically, I think an officer of either the F.B.I. or the Department ought to be detailed to receive and examine any reports or indications which the Purchasing Commission may have to offer. We should do this for any private company, or at the behest of any government, in equivalent circumstances.[12]

On 4 April Berle informed Mr. Edward A. Tamm of the bureau that "this Government could not permit an extension of the British activities in this country in the matter suggested."[13]

Meanwhile, Hamish Mitchell again approached the FBI on the same subject; this time he approached the New York office on 30 March. Again, he expressed a desire to cooperate with the bureau and indicated his office was endeavoring to keep informed on possible sabotage to British war materials. He also referred to a document, sent by the British embassy to the Department of State, describing the setup of "the German organization for developing information in this country."[14]

When informed of this second approach, Berle advised Mr. James C. Dunn, the department's advisor on political relations:

> The F.B.I. declined to entertain any suggestion of "cooperation" or the building up of any "cooperating" organization under the British Purchasing Commission. I stated that I thought they were entirely right in this regard. I am not so clear, however, that they might not maintain contact for the purpose of getting whatever information may be passed on to them, provided this is promptly and adequately reported here, so that we know what is being done.
>
> In other words, I am not clear that the Scotland Yard tie-up works very well in connection with American matters, and the British may know things that we ought to know promptly. I should be glad to have your comments.[15]

Was Mitchell representing Scotland Yard? Possibly. Did he have any connection with William Stephenson who visited the United States in April? Surely there was some coordination.[16] In any case, Dunn told Berle that "it should be made entirely clear to the F.B.I. and Justice that entire responsibility with regard to these matters within the United States lies with the Department of Justice." He went on to say: "I would not, for my own part, consider it advisable that any secret service organization of a foreign country should be permitted to carry on its operations in the United States." As for "cooperation" with a foreign organization, in matters relating to sabotage and espionage inside this country, that is the responsibility of the Justice Department.[17]

In the meantime, the minutes of the Interdepartmental Intelligence Conference show that on 9 April the FBI informed G-2 (the army's military intelligence division) and ONI (Office of Naval Intelligence) as well as State: the "British Purchasing Commission desires to set up an intelligence service in [the] U.S."[18] Strangely enough, this very same entry shows up in the minutes of the meeting of the conference on 13 May,[19] almost three weeks after Dunn had written the above message to Berle, the last message in this Mitchell-FBI episode. Then on 31 May, Mr. Hoover, when asked about the operations of foreign agents in the United States, told the conference that the bureau had "within the past few months been developing an increasing store of information upon this subject." He indicated that "the British and Canadian intelligence services in the United States appear to be particularly well organized and that these services have been furnishing considerable information to the FBI."[20]

Then on 16 July Hoover told his fellow members in the conference:

"The relations and dealings of the FBI with the British intelligence service had been extended to a considerable extent and the Bureau hoped to possess within the course of a few days a complete outline of the organization of the British intelligence service within the Western Hemisphere."

This information would, of course, be transmitted to the military and naval intelligence services.[21] Ten days later, General Sherman Miles, the army's intelligence chief, inquired at the conference as to whether any additional information had been received on some "German documents received from the British Secret Service. Mr. Hoover advised that the source of this information would call on him Saturday, July 27, 1940."[22]

It is idle, of course, to speculate on whether that "source" was Stephenson himself. It is not idle, however, to ask whether or not the obvious buildup in relations between the FBI and British intelligence reflected the hand of Stephenson at work after the relative failure of the Mitchell approach. In any case, it is time to go back to Stephenson's first arrival in 1940 in this country.

Stephenson and Hoover

Stephenson's story, in *The Quiet Canadian*, is that he was asked to go to the United States in order to effect an FBI liaison, that he was informally introduced to Hoover through his friend Gene Tunney, that Hoover insisted upon a personal liaison with him, with presidential approval and without the knowledge of the Department of State, and finally that Roosevelt's authorization was acquired through the intervention of Mr. Ernest Cuneo, an influential lawyer, newspaperman and friend of Roosevelt's. Cuneo is reported to have carried back to Stephenson FDR's statement: "There should be the closest possible marriage between the F.B.I. and British Intelligence," a statement which Roosevelt is later supposed to have made to Lord Lothian, Britain's ambassador in Washington."[23]

Gene Tunney has corroborated the account of the meeting with Hoover:

> Through English and Canadian friends of mine, I had known Sir William for several years. He wanted to make the contact with J. Edgar Hoover and wrote a confidential letter from London. I arranged to get the letter into the hands of Mr. Hoover, having known him quite well. Sir William did not want to make an official approach through well-placed English or American friends; he wanted to do so quietly and with no fanfare.
>
> J. Edgar Hoover told me on the telephone that he would be quite happy to see Sir William when he arrived in the United States, so when he did come to Washington everything was set up for him; this was sometime early in 1940. Naturally, I had to stay out of whatever business was between them, but it was my understanding that *the thing went off extremely well.*[24] (My emphasis.)

Ernest Cuneo, when asked about his part in this episode, was unclear about any such meeting so early in 1940. Asked about the statement on "the closest possible marriage," his reply was: "No. The President did not say that to me." He claimed that his role as intermediary was played later when relations between Stephenson and Hoover had dropped considerably from the level of amicability on which they had been originally established. Cuneo agreed with the suggestion that the intermediary with the White House could well have been the wealthy Vincent Astor, who was not only a close friend of both Stephenson and the President but who also played a virtually unknown role as intelligence source for the President.[25]

While this White House angle must be left unclear, liaison between Stephenson and Hoover was effected. The FBI itself has stated that the two first met in March 1942; this was described as their first "official" meeting, and it was said that they had met "once or twice."[26] There is considerable evidence that they had met long before March 1942. On 29 January 1942 Hoover and Stephenson were two of thirteen American, British, and Canadian officials who met at the FBI for a "Hemisphere Intelligence Conference."[27] In July 1941 Hoover and Stephenson discussed the many secret messages that British intelligence was sending to London weekly on the FBI radio.[28] And in a remarkably undiscovered statement, though publicly printed in 1948, and probably the first significant public statement about Stephenson's role in World War II, Robert Sherwood declared: "By the spring of 1941, six months before the United States entered the war [May?] . . . there was, by Roosevelt's order and despite State Department qualms, effectively close cooperation between J. Edgar Hoover and the F.B.I. and British security services under the direction of a quiet Canadian, William Stephenson. The purpose of this cooperation was the detection and frustration of espionage and sabotage activities in the Western Hemisphere by agents of Germany, Italy and Japan, and also of Vichy France. It produced some remarkable results."[29] On 14 March 1941 Vincent Astor, forwarding to the President some intercepted mail which he had acquired as the result of the British opening of diplomatic pouches in Bermuda and Trinidad, remarked: "It really is a good thing that you made F.B.I. the contact with British intelligence. If O.N.I. and M.I.D. [the army's Military Intelligence Division, G-2] were in it too, nothing would ever be forthcoming. At present this situation is working perfectly."[30]

When this evidence is added to the earlier testimony of Gene Tunney, to the SIS reference to Stephenson's "discussion with the head of the FBI," and to the California plant inspector's report, the very strong presumption follows that the two men met long before March 1942 and much closer to the time when Stephenson says he came here for that specific purpose. The evidence also indicates that the liaison which was then established was not set up without the knowledge of the State Department, even though there might have been some lack of clarity on the nature of the relationship, and even though the department could well have had the "qualms" of which Sherwood spoke. Certainly, Stephenson, Hoover, and Berle were later on to have their problems.

Stephenson and Donovan

What now about Stephenson and Donovan in the first half of 1940? The Stephenson story is that he was asked by Winston Churchill himself to take the assignment as passport control officer in New York, which Menzies had first offered him. The job, as Stephenson had outlined it to others even before it was offered to him, was to do everything possible "to assure sufficient aid for Britain, to counter the enemy's subversive plans throughout the Western Hemisphere, . . . and eventually to bring the United States into the War."[31] In the quiet of retirement, Stephenson related how Churchill, in the first month of his premiership, and speaking from a full awareness of the importance of American aid and support to the survival of Britain, said to him with directness and without reserve: "Help me!" Stephenson stressed that he alone, unlike other prominent Canadians and Britons who served in this country—Arthur Purvis in purchasing, Arthur Salter in shipping, and the Treasury expert Sir Frederick Philips—was "the personal representative" of the prime minister. Indeed, Stephenson revealed considerable contempt for Menzies and the SIS as he found it in 1940, and insisted that he sent many of his communications direct to Churchill rather than to Menzies, who was at least his nominal superior.[32] For his part, Menzies "was indeed always at pains to describe Stephenson as 'my representative' and inclined to be jealous of occasional communications not sent by or through SIS."[33]

Having returned to the United States on 21 June, Stephenson allegedly immediately renewed an acquaintance with Donovan whom he had "first met during a visit [by Donovan] to England" and "instinctively" concentrated on him as the individual above all others who could help in the procurement of badly needed war materials.[34] Queried later as to when he and Donovan had first met, Stephenson was unclear; he did recall that their friendship was given an initial impetus when it was discovered that both, unbeknownst to one another, had been in the same French town at the same time in World War I, Donovan on duty with his troops and Stephenson an accidentally downed fighter pilot. They were to meet occasionally throughout the thirties in London, he went on, whenever "Bill was in town."[35]

When Stephenson did arrive in New York, he stayed not at the Waldorf Astoria but at the St. Regis at the insistence of his friend Vincent Astor, who referred to the hotel as "his broken-down boarding house."[36] On calling Donovan, Stephenson was told to "stay where you are," and in twenty minutes Donovan and Stephenson were face to face again.[37] Shortly thereafter, according to a British intelligence document, which was written in 1945, and which Stephenson "commissioned and read," Stephenson "suggested to Donovan that he should pay a visit to Britain with the object of investigating conditions at first hand . . . [and] Donovan referred the proposal to the President."[38]

Additional details were added about 1960 in a memorandum which Stephenson dictated for an OSS historian, and the same account then appeared in 1962, in *The Quiet Canadian:*

In June of 1940, very shortly after I arrived in the U.S., he [Donovan] arranged for me to attend a meeting with Knox and Stimson where the main subject of discussion was Britain's lack of destroyers and the way was explored towards finding a formula for the transfer, without legal breach of U.S. neutrality and without affront to American public opinion, of 50 over-age American destroyers to the Royal Navy. It was then I suggested that he should pay a visit to Britain with the object of investigating conditions at first hand and assessing for himself the British war effort, its most urgent requirements, and its potential chances of success. He referred to Knox and they jointly referred to the President.[39]

In 1968 Sir William additionally claimed: "General Donovan and I left for London by air July 14th. . . . We flew back to Washington early in August."[40]

The first and by far the chief difficulty with this account of the origin of the trip is that its major premise, the renewal of a preexisting Stephenson-Donovan friendship, has been denied by Donovan himself. In November 1944 Donovan received for comment a British paper entitled "British Relations with OSS." This was a British submission to an early but abortive OSS history; and since it deals almost solely with Stephenson's relations with Donovan, it must have been read by Stephenson, and it may well have been the basis of the 1945 history mentioned above. In any case, a passage that drew Donovan's attention reads: "When Mr. Stephenson was first posted to the United States in June, 1940, one of the first people he got into contact with was General, or as he then was, Colonel Donovan. As a result of their discussions, the President sent Colonel Donovan over to London in July, 1940, ostensibly to discuss with the competent authorities, British methods of dealing with all forms of German propaganda; in fact his mission from the President was to ascertain the true extent of the German menace and to report on the methods as to how it could be stopped."[41] In reading this Donovan circled the words "As a result of their discussions" (fig. 4) and pencilled in the margin: "Did not know S[tephenson] then. I met him only after return." This, of course, is impressive testimony which pits Donovan's memory against Stephenson's but which is so specifically focused on a cardinal point as to seem controlling in the matter; and therefore its authenticity must be established. The covering memoranda show conclusively that this British draft had been submitted to General Donovan "for any comments that you think are called for," that "the General's corrections on the attached document" were noted, and that a subordinate was reminded to "please note the comments which the General has made on the attached manuscript which you forwarded to him."[42]

Secondly, there is textual evidence that undercuts Stephenson's claim to having inspired the trip and his claimed travel with Donovan to Lon-

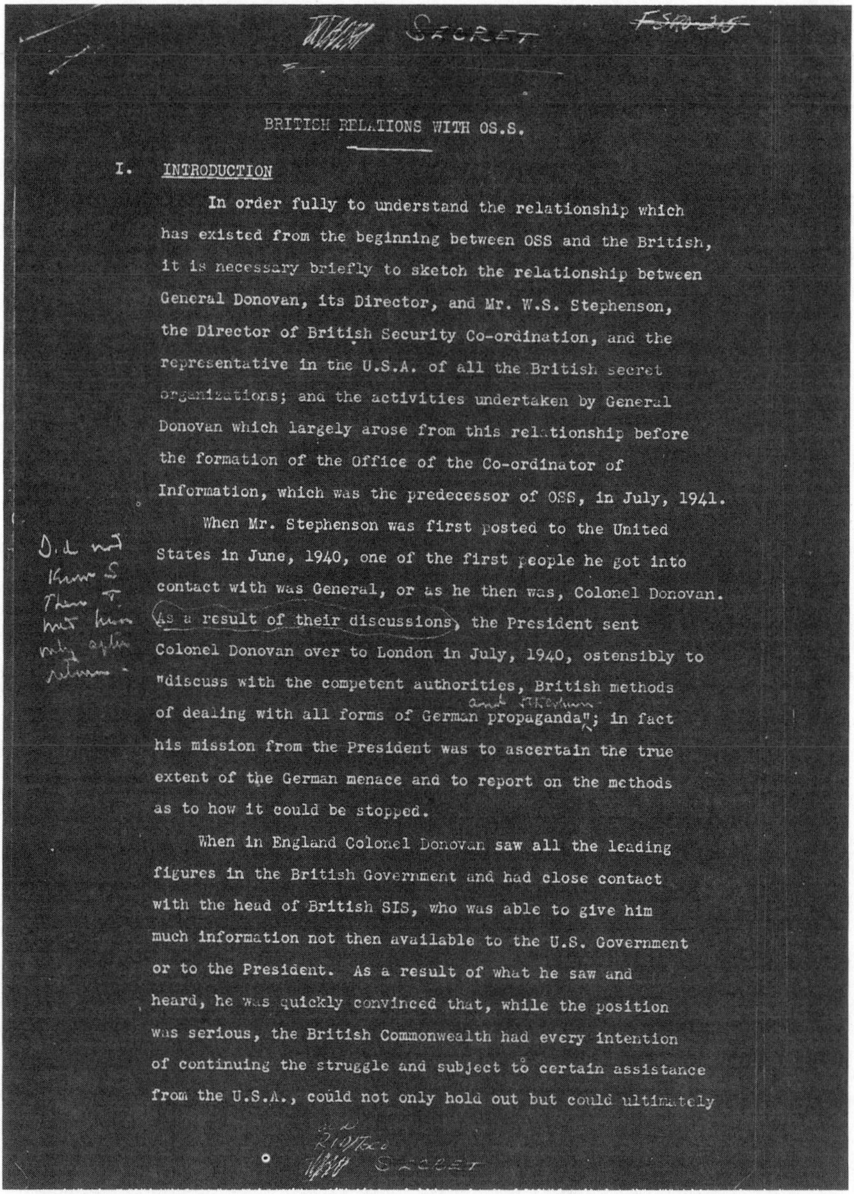

SECRET

BRITISH RELATIONS WITH OS.S.

I. INTRODUCTION

In order fully to understand the relationship which has existed from the beginning between OSS and the British, it is necessary briefly to sketch the relationship between General Donovan, its Director, and Mr. W.S. Stephenson, the Director of British Security Co-ordination, and the representative in the U.S.A. of all the British secret organizations; and the activities undertaken by General Donovan which largely arose from this relationship before the formation of the Office of the Co-ordinator of Information, which was the predecessor of OSS, in July, 1941.

When Mr. Stephenson was first posted to the United States in June, 1940, one of the first people he got into contact with was General, or as he then was, Colonel Donovan. As a result of their discussions, the President sent Colonel Donovan over to London in July, 1940, ostensibly to "discuss with the competent authorities, British methods of dealing with all forms of German and Italian propaganda"; in fact his mission from the President was to ascertain the true extent of the German menace and to report on the methods as to how it could be stopped.

Did not know S. Then I met him only after return.

When in England Colonel Donovan saw all the leading figures in the British Government and had close contact with the head of British SIS, who was able to give him much information not then available to the U.S. Government or to the President. As a result of what he saw and heard, he was quickly convinced that, while the position was serious, the British Commonwealth had every intention of continuing the struggle and subject to certain assistance from the U.S.A., could not only hold out but could ultimately

SECRET

Fig. 4. Donovan says he met Stephenson *after* July 1940. (Courtesy of National Archives and Records Administration, Washington, D.C.)

don. It makes clear that Stephenson had advance knowledge of the trip and that Menzies acted as Donovan's mentor in London. It is also clear that Stephenson knew Menzies and Donovan were in frequent contact.[43]

Stephenson could easily have had "advance knowledge" of the trip from Lord Lothian with whom he was undoubtedly in touch, but the text leaves one with the implication that that was all he had. That Menzies was writing to him, presumably in New York, and that Menzies was Donovan's "mentor" in London does not help the travel claim. That Menzies told Stephenson he was intent upon Donovan seeing the most important people certainly does jibe with Stephenson's own capabilities and his claim that he "arranged that he [Donovan] should be afforded every opportunity to conduct his inquiries."[44] This claim Donovan himself seems to have supported, for when he read the sentence "Lord Lothian . . . arranged for Donovan to see Churchill," he struck out "Lord Lothian" and in the margin wrote "Bill Stephenson."[45]

Thirdly, there is not the slightest indication anywhere of a meeting of Stephenson, Donovan, Knox, and Stimson. Nothing shows up either in the letters of Knox to his wife or in the Stimson diary, and both cover this period quite well. Moreover, the known chronology of the destroyers-bases agreement makes it unlikely that these four men were meeting at that time to discuss the *legal* aspects of the deal.[46] Such a meeting was much more likely to have taken place in August, after Donovan's return, when the legal problems were really being faced, when Knox and Stimson, and especially Knox as secretary of the navy, were officially seized of the problem, and when Donovan himself, fresh from importunate conversations on the subject, was resolved to do something about it.

Finally, one wonders why, if Stephenson had suggested the trip and had traveled to London with Donovan, he was not present at the British Embassy when Knox, Donovan, and Casey of Australia had dinner with Lord Lothian and had, as Knox wrote his wife, so "much to discuss before [Bill] got away."

In this conflict of memories, the Stephenson story, first put to paper in 1944, and repeated thereafter, has only that tradition to support it; what evidence there is casts doubt on it or contradicts it. The likelihood is that Stephenson has read history backwards. He was to develop such a close and mutually fruitful collaboration with Donovan, was to make so many Atlantic crossings with him, was to play such a creative role in the establishment of COI, and was to be in such weekly, almost daily, contact with Donovan for the rest of the war, that it is quite probable he has unconsciously pushed the line of collaboration back to the beginning of the trip, transforming, in the process, "advance knowledge" into the conception of it.

Donovan's Trip to London

As has been mentioned, Donovan has left an account of how he happened to go to London. Like Stephenson's account, this also has given rise to a tradition, but it too leaves many questions unanswered. In an off-the-record address in 1941 before the prestigious Union League of Philadelphia he recounted:

> Last July I was in Washington, appearing before the Military Affairs Committee of the Senate on the Conscription Bill and I was called to the White House. Being what I am [a strong anti–New Deal Republican], that was a very surprising invitation to me. I saw there the Secretaries of State and of War and of the Navy, and the Secretary of State was very disturbed about conditions in South America. I was asked if I would go abroad, go to England, and see if I could learn something of what had been the activities of the Fifth Columnists in the various sections of the Continent that had then been taken over by Germany, and also if I could learn something how [sic] England was dealing with that problem. I said I would do it, and then other departments of the Government asked me to get certain information.[47]

On the face of it then, the trip was conceived at the White House, sprung on Donovan without any prior notice, and proposed—though the text is vague—by Secretary of State Cordell Hull. But other evidence must be considered before these conclusions are reached. On 10 July, Lord Lothian cabled London that Knox:

> said to me *last night* that he was most anxious to make survey of the Fifth Column methods, as they have been disclosed in Norway, the Low Countries, France, etc. in order to warn the American public. He has appointed Edgar Mowrer, press correspondent now in England and Colonel 'Bill' Donovan who had a very fine war record in the American Expeditionary Force, was Assistant Attorney-General and may now become influential adviser of Colonel Knox to make investigations in England from official sources, refugees, etc. Donovan is leaving by boat or clipper end of this week. Colonel Knox has asked me to secure for them all reasonable facilities for getting information which can be [useful] to the American public but particularly privately for himself. I have assured him that you would see that both Mowrer and Donovan were given every facility. Could you send a telegram that you could do this which I could show him eventually?[48] (My emphasis.)

A few hours earlier on 10 July, Hull cabled Ambassador Kennedy: "Edgar Mowrer of *Chicago Daily News* at the request of Secretary-designate Knox is now in England seeking data on fifth column activities there which might prove of value here. In view of the interest Mr. *Knox expressed to me* in this subject, will you in your discretion afford to Mowrer such assistance as you may find to be appropriate and advisable."[49] (My emphasis.)

Approximately thirty hours later, Hull sent Kennedy the following about Donovan: "*Colonel Knox desires to send* Colonel William J. Donovan to England for a brief survey and report on certain aspects of the British defense situation. The President has approved of this trip, and Colonel Donovan plans to leave New York on the clipper July 14, and will report to you on his arrival. We would appreciate any arrangements and preparations which would facilitate Colonel Donovan's mission. Colonel Donovan asks that reservations be made for him at Claridge's."[50] (My emphasis.)

It becomes clear that the initiative in this trip was being taken not by the secretary of state, who, as a matter of fact, never had any particularly close relation with Donovan, but by the secretary of the navy. This is particularly clear when one appreciates the role of Edgar Ansel Mowrer, who gets prior billing in Lothian's cable and is mentioned by Hull thirty hours before Donovan. It almost leads to the conclusion, which the British were to make, that Knox was acting not as the secretary but as the proprietor of the *Chicago Daily News*.

It also becomes clear that the White House meeting to which Donovan was summoned must have taken place on the ninth, the day on which Knox informed Lothian of his plan to send Mowrer and Donovan to London. Between the first and the evening of the eighth, Stimson was not in town, and at 5:15 on the ninth, Knox and Stimson were at the White House with the President; an hour earlier Knox had met with Hull at the State Department. While there is no documentation that Hull was at the White House on that date, he could easily have walked across the lane with or shortly after Knox.[51]

Knox's role shows up strongly in the letters of introduction, which were written for Donovan, and practically all of which were written on the eleventh. Knox himself, in writing to Lord Beaverbrook, then minister of aircraft production, stated that Donovan was abroad "on an official mission for me, with the full approval of the President." He hoped that Beaverbrook would be "as frank in talking to him as you might be in talking to me if I were able to go over myself."[52]

That last clause may contain the gist of the original idea; one of the letters of introduction written at Knox's request reads: "Colonel Knox had hoped to make this trip to England himself to investigate first hand the question and methods of modern defense, both from a physical and a morale standpoint, but finding it impossible to do so at this time has prevailed on Colonel Donovan, who is eminently qualified, to do this job for him."[53] By itself, the preceding sentence may be factual or conventional dressing, but the former seems more likely when it is realized that such an idea was hardly less than instinctive with a man who was a newspaper publisher, a national political campaigner, and a newly appointed cabinet officer. Evidence of how his mind worked in December 1941 may shed some light on how it *could* have worked in July 1940. He gave the following account to Paul Scott Mowrer of how he came to travel to Pearl Harbor shortly after 7 December: "That trip of mine to Hawaii was an inspiration that came to me just as I heard the President read his message. Immediately, the air was filled with rumors. There was a prospect ahead of a nasty congressional investigation, and I made up my mind in a flash to go out there and get the actual facts, and if the facts warranted it, to initiate the investigation myself."[54]

Did something like this happen to the new secretary of the navy as he contemplated the collapse of France, the imminence of a Nazi assault on Britain, and the insidious threat of political termites, a Fifth Column that threatened not only Europe but the entire Western Hemisphere? If it did, and inasmuch as his new responsibilities kept him closer to Washington, then who was a better substitute than his friend Bill Donovan, who needed nobody to suggest a place to visit, who had been to Ethiopia in 1936, to Spain in 1938, who had toured Germany in 1939, and who, like Stephenson, was to make many Atlantic crossings throughout the war?

In the absence of contradictory evidence, it seems reasonable to conclude that at the meeting of the secretaries with the President either Knox proposed the trip and, realizing that he himself could not go, suggested Donovan go in his stead, or someone else proposed the trip and Knox quickly suggested the name of his good and much travelled friend.

"Bill left [Washington] at midnight for New York." Some time on the fourteenth he telephoned his wife that he was going abroad on "a secret mission."[55] His flight, which was scheduled to leave at 3 P.M., did not depart until 4:05. He left "on what he said was private business," but he was "in possession of what customs men said was a special passport from Washington. He declined to discuss the nature of the 'private business.'" Among the six other passengers were Jean Bodard and Edward B. Amouroux of the French Purchasing Commission, and Charles C. Goetz of a Portuguese arms mission.[56]

As he left New York, he probably had no idea how much confusion the trip had already generated in London.

4

·-·-·-

Donovan:
To and from
London

HOWEVER THE TRIP ORIGINATED, IT TOOK SHAPE SO QUICKLY THAT THE visitors, Mowrer and Donvan, were either on the scene or on the way before their hosts, Ambassador Kennedy and the British government, really knew what was going on. Mowrer, who was in Spain and Portugal at the time, was ordered by Knox to fly to London and put himself at Donovan's disposal,[1] and was thus the first to arrive, to the anger of Kennedy and the confusion of the British. It was from Mowrer, apparently, that Kennedy first learned of Donovan's imminent arrival, and from the British Kennedy was soon receiving calls asking for clarification of the status of the correspondent whom the new secretary of the navy was sending to them.[2]

An Angry U.S. Ambassador

Kennedy, who had been notified of Mowrer's arrival by Hull's cable of the tenth and of Donovan's coming by a separate cable of the eleventh, thirty hours later, exploded on the twelfth. For his part, Mowrer was a newspaper man butting in on the normal working of both governments, and it was "utter nonsense" that various officials of the British government should have to query him on Mowrer's status.[3] As for Donovan, he would be happy to make any arrangements or preparations if he only knew "the nature of his mission." As indicated, Hull had only told him that Colonel Knox de-

48

sired to send Donovan to England "for a brief survey and report on certain aspects of the British defense situation." In any case, the British preferred to deal with "permanent attachés" and have "frequently declined to furnish information to anyone else." Kennedy further considered that his staff was doing its job perfectly well, and "to send a new man in here at this time, with all due respect to Colonel Knox, is to me the height of nonsense and a definite blow to good organization."[4]

Kennedy's explosion was as much the latest in a series of frustrations and humiliations, as he saw them, at the hands of the President, as of annoyance and anger at not being consulted prior to the sending of Mowrer and Donovan. For instance, at the outbreak of war, he had been "furious" because he had not learned earlier than he did of the projected but subsequently abandoned purchase by the United States of both the *Normandie* and the *Queen Mary*.[5] So later, on the twelfth, in replying to Hull's second cable, the ambassador denounced the Mowrer mission as "utter nonsense," and anyhow: "We are making an investigation here on this subject [the Fifth Column] and [Harvey] Klemmer of my office is handling it." Unless ordered otherwise, he intended to tell the British that Mowrer was just a newspaper man who was not "entitled to confidential files and discussions with Government officials." As a final blast he warned: "If Colonel Knox does not stop sending Mowrers and Colonel Donovans over here this organization is not going to function effectively."[6]

Still on the twelfth, he called the State Department on the transAtlantic phone, not exactly an unusual thing for him to do, and asked Under Secretary Sumner Welles to lay before the President the cables he had received from Hull along with his own strong protest against the whole procedure. FDR forwarded the papers to Secretary Knox with the note: "Please take this up with Secretary Hull and try to straighten it out. Somebody's nose seems to be out of joint!"[7]

The next day Kennedy cabled a strong request to Washington that Mowrer's assignment be called off. "I am definitely sure that this whole picture," he wrote, "is full of dynamite." He complained that the British thought Mowrer had an official capacity, that the embassy was put in the position of backing one paper against others, that Mowrer was not needed, and finally: "It is most embarrassing to me."[8]

Meanwhile, State endeavored to clarify Mowrer's role and mollify its ambassador. Hull reported that he had been advised by the secretary of the navy that the latter was taking "these steps in his official capacity" and that he was intent on gathering "comprehensive material as to the methods of subversive activities and propaganda the Germans are now using . . . for general distribution . . . to all the press." Mr. Kennedy was assured that

Colonel Knox appreciated "the excellent reporting of the Embassy" and did not desire to interfere in any way with either the embassy or the service attachés. With this cable State had the last word.[9]

Was Kennedy the victim of a "calculated snub" by the President? This statement has often been made, and certainly Kennedy would have affirmed it, and there probably was enough coolness between Kennedy and Roosevelt to give rise to it.[10] But the speed of events suggests there was less "calculation" than thoughtlessness or indifference. The navy, for instance, did not notify its naval attaché in London, Captain Alan G. Kirk, that he soon would be responsible for the care and custody of Colonel Donovan, a high-level visitor from the secretary of the navy himself, until Kirk had advised his superior to read the Kennedy-Hull cable traffic of 12 July.[11] Like Kennedy himself, and the British, Kirk also had to catch up with events.

Confused Britons

While the Americans were regularizing the situation, the British were engaged in the same business. At the same time that Lothian was informing London of the approach of the two visitors, Mowrer was knocking on various Whitehall doors, especially on the door of Lord Swinton, who ran the Home Defense (Security) Executive, an enlarged MI-5 operation. Swinton had no trouble as long as he and Mowrer discussed general questions and the Fifth Column on the continent, but the Britisher wanted to know what he was to do with this inquiring newsman who "finds us interesting and helpful and will be a frequent visitor."[12]

Other officials were no less perplexed. One opined that in sending Mowrer, "Colonel Knox was speaking as proprietor of the *Chicago Daily News* rather than as Secretary of the Navy. Otherwise the request should have been put forward by the State Department." He also asked: "To what quarters are the appointees of Colonel Knox [to] be told to address themselves? (One of them is here already)."[13] The Foreign Office cabled Lothian as late as the sixteenth: "Please telegraph urgently whether status of Donovan and Mowrer as regards this investigation is official or journalistic, in order that we may know how to treat their further requests for information."[14]

Even Mowrer was not certain of his status, for in the cable of 16 July the Foreign Office declared that "Mowrer believes that investigation is being carried out for official purposes." This merely echoed an earlier marginal note that Mowrer did not think he was acting "on behalf of the *Chicago Daily News*," and, anyhow, the writer thought Mowrer should get together with Donovan as soon as he arrived in order "to avoid reduplication."[15]

The British got no enlightenment from the U.S. Embassy, which was not only uncertain about Mowrer's status but whose ambassador also looked upon Mowrer "with disfavor as a newspaperman employed by Colonel Knox apparently for his own paper."[16] In time the Foreign Office and the embassy had representatives get together to clarify the matter. These gentlemen fell back on a "two hats" theory and concluded, whether with or without a straight face is hard to say, that Mowrer was both an official representative and a newspaper correspondent, that he had "two wholly separate positions," and that it would be necessary, therefore, in each case to determine whether he was acting as a correspondent of the *News* or a representative of the secretary of the navy.[17]

Meanwhile, Lord Lothian was sending a series of cables to London explaining Mowrer's mission and stressing the importance of Donovan as a potentially valuable friend because he was a close advisor of the secretary. On Mowrer, Lothian told London on 18 July that "Knox does not want information for the *Chicago Daily News*. He wants part of it [for the] F.B.I. here and the balance for dissemination through the press so as to explain to and warn the public about characteristic 5th column activities against which they should be on their guard."[18]

On Donovan, Lothian was emphatic. On 10 July, when he sent his first cable on the subject, he said he had assured Colonel Knox that London would provide Mowrer and Donovan with every facility. The next day he said: "I think it would be very well worthwhile for the Prime Minister to see him [Donovan] when in London. On the thirteenth he cabled Alfred Duff Cooper, the minister of information: "I told Colonel Donovan to go and see you as soon as he arrives. . . . He will tell you what he wants. Please arrange with him to [meet] the people he wants to see. He may exercise considerable influence here on his return owing to his close association with Mr. Knox." Again, on the fifteenth Lothian cabled: "Have had letter from Frank Knox saying Donovan is going to England as he is [sic] representative on a very important mission which has full approval of both the President and the Secretary of State. Knox is most anxious that Donovan should have the opportunity of meeting the Prime Minister and I hope very much that this can be arranged and that Donovan can also be put in touch with other leading personalities at home."[19]

By this time, London had a firmer handle on the situation. When Donovan arrived on the nineteenth, he was met by Captain Kirk's duty officer and ensconced in Claridge's, as he had asked, and the following day began a round of visits and calls that indicated the British were happy to see him even if Kennedy was not.

The Red Carpet

With Kirk taking the initiative, and other Britishers and Americans joining in, Donovan saw in two weeks as many important people, visited as many different civil and military establishments, and discussed as wide a variety of subjects as was humanly possible and as only a very high-level visitor could have had the opportunity.

He saw the king and queen; and, reconstructing the event, this probably occurred at the home of Lady Astor at 4 St. James Square on Tuesday, 30 July, in the middle of a two-day tour of various coastal command installations.[20]

Just how the meeting with the prime minister was arranged cannot be determined, but many people were quite clearly endeavoring to arrange it. Knox had requested it; Lothian had urged it; undoubtedly, Stephenson had lent his weight in that direction. The chief diplomatic advisor to the foreign secretary, Robert Vansittart, writing as though no one had informed the prime minister of Donovan's presence in the country, and looking for the proper occasion for Churchill to send another message to Roosevelt regarding the need for destroyers, sent the following note to the prime minister:

> And in this connection I would like also to make another suggestion: — There is at the present moment over here a Colonel William Donovan (he is staying at Claridge's), who is one of the best soldiers produced by America in the last war. He afterwards became one of the most successful lawyers in the country. He was for a time Assistant Attorney-General under Hoover [Coolidge] and has an enormous practice of his own. He is a Republican, but he is a friend of Roosevelt and has been sent over here on a mission by consent of the two political parties in the United States, his real object being to collect as much information as would be useful in the event of America coming into the war. He is returning to America almost at once. Would it not be possible for you to reinforce any cabled message you may have sent or be sending to Roosevelt by a personal message sent through Donovan? It would be very easy to introduce the subject in the course of a ten minute conversation with him; if you could spare the time I think that in any event you should see him for a short while. He is an important person, and will be still more important to us in the future. And it would probably pay to give him this pleasure.

This was written on 23 July; and Churchill penned on it, on the twenty-fifth: "I am meditating a message (today or tomorrow)" and at the top of the page was written: "Colonel Donovan has been asked to call to see the P.M. at 5:30 P.M. on Thursday, July 25th."[21]

In the meantime, other arrangements were also being made to bring the prime minister and Donovan together. Lady Diana Cooper invited the Colonel to dinner on Sunday, 28 July, in order to meet the prime minister. Ironically enough, this coincided with another invitation for dinner on the same day, this time with Ambassador Kennedy at his residence. Since *The Quiet Canadian* makes the point of stating "one person Donovan did not see in London was the defeatist Ambassador Joseph Kennedy," and since this has been repeated in many accounts of Donovan's visit to London, it is well here, and fair to both men, to set the record straight.

Donovan did see and did dine with Kennedy. Whether or not he needed the urging of Captain Kirk to do so is not demonstrable, but Kirk did exert himself to bring about the meeting. On 25 July Kirk informed Donovan of the ambassador's dinner invitation and asked him to "confirm these arrangements as Mr. Kennedy is rather particular about knowing whether you are coming Sunday night or not." Again, on the twenty-seventh, he wrote: "Having learned of the possible complications for Sunday evening, I offer you, in the most friendly way, my personal suggestion:—to wit: Come to the Ambassador's dinner." After arranging to meet him that evening, Kirk concluded: "I think it would be a mistake indeed if you are diverted to another party that night—and the details have been given to me, so I realize all the ramifications."

The best, and surely conclusive, evidence that Donovan did pass up Lady Cooper's party in order to be wth the ambassador at St. Leonard's just outside Windsor is the following charming message from the Lady herself to "Dear wild Colonel":

> Thank you so much for the yellow roses. They comforted me a little for your absence. I was so disappointed that the interest of our two countries came between us.
>
> I am happy to tell you that Winston was in his most engaging and invigorating form and I am sure you would have enjoyed it enormously. I had too, for your delight, the beautiful Eve Curie and my prettiest niece. I hope you had a hideous evening with Joe and I hope too that you will lunch or dine another day.

And just to complete this side story, the following telephone message to Donovan indicates that the latter had endeavored to return the dinner favor: "His Excellency the American Ambassador telephoned Colonel Donovan to say that he regrets that he will be unable to lunch with him on Friday next, but he is attending a Red Cross luncheon at Claridge's the same day."[22]

The head of the British secret service, Colonel Menzies, has already been described by the sis as having acted as Donovan's "mentor" while in

Britain. Menzies' name shows up on two scraps of paper found in Donovan's files—as do numerous other names on other scraps; one notation is followed by "Sunday—11:30, 54 Broadway," the SIS headquarters. Donovan did write to Menzies after he returned to the States in August and indicated that he was "in touch with many of your representatives here" and have "checked with them"; but the context is clearly related to the "harder blasting" which the British were then taking from the Luftwaffe and the continuing belief of Donovan that the British would survive. Perhaps the most meaningful comment made by Donovan was his acknowledgment: "I know that it was due to your thoughtfulness in opening so many doors that I was able to tell our people in authority the reasons for my conclusions that gave them confidence in my report." For what it is worth, Donovan made no such acknowledgment to any of his other English correspondents; and "opening doors" had been Menzies' "main objective" in assisting Donovan.[23]

An intelligence official with whom Donovan seems to have developed a more personal rapport was the director of naval intelligence, Admiral John H. Godfrey. This contact had been initiated by a conventional letter of introduction from Godfrey's American counterpart, Admiral Walter S. Anderson to Captain Kirk, and then given more substance by Kirk, who had recently developed close relations with Godfrey. The latter met with Donovan during a two-day program that Kirk had laid on for him in the Admiralty, and Godfrey was to have a hand in making "detailed arrangements" for Donovan "to consult people conversant with your special line"—presumably the Fifth Column. The two men met at Godfrey's home for a lengthy discussion the night before Donovan left for home;[24] and Donovan told Godfrey what he was going to do when he returned: his intentions were embodied in a "precis," which Godfrey immediately sent up the line to the first sea lord, the first lord, and the prime minister. According to this, "Donovan urged the appointment of a 'sensible ambassador,' who would go back and forth across the Atlantic and keep the two countries in touch. . . . Donovan took back the suggestion of full collaboration in intelligence and access for the British to US consular officers' reports, especially from the French ports and North Africa. He recommended direct liaison between Godfrey and the American DNI, as well as the starting of direct and secret communications through special signal systems."[25]

This is a plausible account of things the two men might have discussed, but there is no echo of it in any documents.[26] A hint of it may be found in the letter Donovan wrote Godfrey on 27 August when he reported to the DNI on what he had done for him in regard to destroyers, the bombsight, and "various items." He wrote: "The other items in our little agenda I am sure are being cared for." What "items" in what "little agenda"? Queried in

1968 as to whether "our little agenda" and the "precis" are the same document, Godfrey could only write: "Alas, I have no copy, but the destroyers and the bombsights were the most important."[27]

In dwelling at some length on these meetings with Menzies and Godfrey, one runs the risk of distorting their place in the context of Donovan's journey. Similar paragraphs of fact, evaluation, and speculation could be written on Donovan's encounters with Air Commodore J. C. Slessor, Brendan Bracken, Valentine Williams, Robert Vansittart, Sir Cyril Newall, General Malden, Geoffrey Cunliffe, Lord Gort, and almost countless others. Indeed, it would be tedious just to list and title them all.

He met everybody, and while he visited many military installations, especially air facilities and training establishments, his conversations and meetings ranged encyclopedically over the full gamut of military, political, economic, and social factors and problems relevant to the waging of war, in particular, to the defense of England against the Nazis. He went to make "a brief survey," but he covered the waterfront in such catholic fashion that Vansittart seems not far wrong when he informed the prime minister that Donovan's "real object" was to collect as much information as would be useful in the event of America coming into the war.

One name more, however, must be mentioned; in view of the British confusion and Kennedy's anger at the outset of this trip, something must be said of Edgar Ansel Mowrer. At the outset he too had problems; by a combination of "intrigue, influence, and bluster" he and his wife finally obtained airplane seats for the flight to England. After he had put himself at the disposal of Donovan, he proceeded "as a newsman . . . to poke my nose into everything and ask indiscreet questions." He and his wife "visited several defense centers and shuddered at the lack of military preparations;" they too talked to everybody and dined with the Churchills at No. 10 Downing Street. Before they left London, Donovan and Mowrer agreed they would report to Roosevelt that "Britain under Churchill would not surrender either to ruthless air raids or to an invasion."[28]

Donovan left England at 2:00 P.M. on 3 August in a four-motored British flying boat, the *Clare*, which was camouflaged with green and blue patches. The *Clare*'s flight marked the resumption of trans-Atlantic passenger service, the first such run since the interruption of service in October 1939. The trip had been arranged by the chief of the air staff, who also threw in some champagne. Brendan Bracken added some books "to mitigate the tedium of the journey." Even so, Donovan told Colonel Raymond E. Lee, the U.S. military attaché, that the trip home "was as boring as the Clipper" on the outward flight. Perhaps the only significant thing about the boring trip is the passenger list, which showed only two other persons beside Donovan, Mr. C. R. Fairey, an English airplane manufacturer, and Geoffrey Cunliffe, traveling as an official of the British Air Ministry. Both the travel arrangements made by the British and the *New York Times* account agree on this matter, and thus they undercut Stephenson's claim to having returned with Donovan.[29]

Reporting to Washington

Donovan returned to a round of meetings with top American officials. He arrived in New York at 7:00 P.M. on Sunday evening, 4 August, and the next morning he spent an hour with Secretary Knox in Washington.[30] That evening the secretary had as dinner guests Donovan and Mowrer, as well as Admirals Stark and Anderson, Assistant Secretary of War Patterson, General Sherman Miles, James Forrestal, the new undersecretary of the navy, and John O'Keefe, Knox's secretary and friend of *News* days. Both Donovan and Mowrer, Knox wrote his wife, "were extraordinarily interesting and we had a long evening of talk—very informative. Both men brought home a great fund of useful information." The two were "inclined to think the British can defeat an attempted invasion. They agree morale is high, but say British equipment is deficient."[31] This emphasis on morale and the need to replace the vast quantities of equipment lost in the Battle of France were among the major points Donovan was to make in this and other meetings with American officials.

On the evening of 6 August Donovan, along with Assistant Secretary of War Patterson and his wife, were dinner guests of Secretary and Mrs. Stimson. In his diary, Stimson noted that Donovan's trip had been "taken on the instance and at the expense of Frank Knox"; the latter phrase must refer to Knox in his official capacity. Again, Donovan told "a very interesting story," because, as Stimson noted, "he had come into contact with all the Chiefs of the British Army; had been taken all over their countries [sic] and had gone up and down the Islands, so that he knew everything an outsider could learn." While stressing British morale, Donovan did see as "the greatest danger in the future" a "letdown" in morale which could develop if the expected invasion did not materialize and when "the long boring days of winter set in." He "laid special emphasis" on the home defense units, the role of women and older men in these units, and their need for 250,000 Enfield rifles. On a larger scale, the need for destroyers, a subject then greatly occupying the minds of British and American officials, was pressing.[32]

In these and the next few days Donovan met with members of both houses of Congress and most of the cabinet, but, with one exception, no record of these encounters seems to have been made. He did stress with some congressional groups concerned with the passage of the controversial conscription bill "the importance of having training before war is upon them."[33] Otherwise, he would undoubtedly have only repeated what he had told the Knox and Stimson parties.

The President, at a White House press conference on the sixth, had refused to discuss Donovan's mission, and this had certainly been standard policy for everyone from the moment the trip was planned. Three days later, at another press conference on the eve of an inspection trip to New England, the President stated, in answer to a question about Donovan: "Oh, I will tell you who is coming up with [Secretary Knox] and going to be on the train and going down on the Potomac: Bill Donovan, so he can tell me what he found on the other side when he went over." When pressed for "any indication of the nature of Donovan's mission abroad," he replied: "I cannot, and he won't tell you."[34]

What Donovan told the President, after joining him at the Hyde Park railroad station on 9 August and in the course of the next two days, must be pieced together from letters he wrote later in the month to friends in England and from what he was to tell, a few days hence, a group of army and navy officers at a luncheon for him hosted by General Miles:[35] that Britain would withstand a German invasion, that British morale was excellent, and that the military needs of the country were both great and urgent.

For his listeners, Donovan, who had studied the British defenses and had discussed them not only with Britishers who tended to give him an encouraging view but also with more dispassionate American observers like Kirk, Lee, and Colonel Carl T. Spaatz, ticked off the factors that would give the British the edge: the excellent organization of the coastal air command, the dispersal of British airfields, the camouflage of these fields and the shelters provided for the planes, the barbed wire and machine guns on the coast, and the various defense zones well organized behind the coastal defenses. Donovan was reported so sure the Germans would be frustrated, assuming that they would dare to attack—which he doubted—"that he was already considering if they could take the offensive next spring."

These "conclusion" Donovan communicated to the President and all others with considerable vigor and conviction. In his letters to friends in London, he repeatedly referred to "the healthy" effect which his report had on the mood of his listeners. In December, when back in England, for a second visit, he was quoted on his meeting with the President: "On his return to Washington . . . he had found the Administration in a mood of extreme depression to which, he remarked sourly, Mr. Kennedy had himself largely contributed. Without any self-conceit he took credit to himself for having been instrumental in giving impetus to the Destroyers-Bases Agreement, saying that he had been at great pains in an interview with the President, who had at first tended to make the interview a monologue, to dwell upon our excellent prospects of pulling through.[36]

Donovan had come back not only to report and evaluate the British prospects, and not only to bolster morale, but also to press at the highest level for the supplying to the British of the supplies they so badly needed from the United States. Destroyers topped the list; behind them came the Sperry bomb sight, flying boats, Flying Fortresses, and many aspects of the critical need of the British for pilots, air instructors, training aircraft, training facilities, and especially U.S. government cooperation in solving the nice political and diplomatic problems involved in extending such aid to a belligerent. On these Royal Air Force necessities Donovan was to spend much time throughout the autumn.

The destroyers, however, drew most of his attention, for on his return he found the President, Knox, Stimson, Hull, and numerous other official and unofficial advisors wrestling agonizingly with the legal, legislative, and political complexities of the deal. There is no question but what Donovan conveyed to all these men the British sense of urgency. When he said he had been "instrumental in giving impetus" to the agreement, he was making a modest claim. Lord Lothian cabled London that "Donovan helped a lot."[37]

There also seems no question but that he was in touch with Stephenson on this matter at this time. For the Canadian it was a matter of the highest priority ever since the request for destroyers had first been communicated to the United States by Churchill on 15 May. On 8 August, Stephenson cabled London that Donovan was strongly urging the British case; Lothian sent his appreciation a week later; on 21 August, Stephenson advised London: "Donovan believes you will have within a few days very favourable news;" on the twenty-second Stephenson announced that "the figure of fifty destroyers had been agreed by the President and that forty-four were in commission for delivery." That Stephenson and Donovan were now in close touch seems evident from the telegram Donovan himself sent to London apparently just hours after Stephenson sent his: "Informed that 50 destroyers were agreed last night. 44 are in commission available for delivery. Present intention all to be delivered to Halifax beginning so soon as British crews are available. Impression in Navy Department that British crews have not yet sailed.

"Knox remarked that there will be a hell of a row in Congress tonight but [the] die is already cast."[38]

Did Donovan provide more than an "impetus" to the agreement, which still had hurdles to leap? Stephenson has said that Donovan also played a role as a lawyer in this matter which was half constitutional law and half domestic politics. Lord Louis Mountbatten, speaking many years later, stated: "The great contribution that General Donovan made as a lawyer was to find a way by which [the agreement] could be done without having to go to Congress."[39] Members of Donovan's law firm, then known as Donovan, Leisure, Newton and Lumbard, reportedly recalled writing briefs on the subject.[40] None of the literature mentions a Donovan role here. This firm, however, of which Donovan was the senior partner and cofounder, and which was then located at Two Wall Street in New York, was and is one of the city's large and respected firms.[41] It is therefore not hard to imagine, elusive though proof may be, that Donovan, so deeply seized with the needs of Britain in the summer of 1940, should commission his subordinates to address themselves to the legal problems which so largely delayed consummation of the deal.

There was at least one other item of business that Donovan took up with the President and others: the Fifth Column, the threat on the horizon that played so prominent a role in the inception of the trip, a new military-political phenomenon that was agitating many Americans—and not just the easily frightened. Donovan told Bracken, Churchill's secretary, that the "Administration was very anxious that something should be said about fifth columnists and hence the articles" which he and Mowrer wrote jointly and which Knox, who wrote a preface for them, had disseminated to the press. Donovan told Menzies: "You may have noticed that I identified my name with certain articles that were appearing. This was done at the instance of the President."[42] The articles drew more praise from that inveterate letter writer, Felix Frankfurter, than from either the State Department or the British ambassador. Justice Frankfurter sent Knox a note of praise of Donovan, Mowrer, and Knox himself for the public service they had rendered.[43] State, treasuring its own report on the Fifth Column, which had been prepared by Klemmer at the ambassador's direction, described the articles as "very general in character" and as containing little not already known; moreover, in view of the fine relations between the embassy and Whitehall, it did "seem ironical that a newspaper correspondent would be commissioned to undertake such work."[44] Lord Lothian cabled: "With the exception of the fourth, these articles are rather slight and I cannot say that they have caused any stir. They certainly hardly justify Colonel Knox's prefatory claim that they contain the results of Messrs. Donovan and Mowrer's 'careful study, made with every official source available.'"

The appropriate rejoinder to this depreciation was made at the foreign office by J. V. Perowne, who noted on Lothian's cable: "The importance to us of Colonel Donovan's visit to London is not to be measured by the 'weight' of these articles or even of the attention they may attract in the U.S.

or elsewhere."[45] He did not go on to specify that "importance," and there is probably no reason to think Lothian really had to be enlightened. Several days earlier, for instance, a measure of that "importance" was brought to the attention of London, when Arthur Purvis of the British Purchasing Commission cabled London that as a result of the welcome accorded Donovan and because of the extent to which secret information had been disclosed to him, "Colonel Donovan was working with great energy in our interest. We now had a firm friend in the Republican camp [with the presidential election in process] and this was proving of immense value."[46]

Donovan has already been quoted as saying that after he had been asked to go to London "other departments of the Government asked me to get certain information." These and many other requests of his own he had levied on the British when in London. The replies had begun to come in even before he had departed for home, but the majority had necessitated special research and preparation and hence it was late August and September before they arrived. In the meantime, Donovan, as a middleman, was in touch with the "producers" in London and the "consumers" in Washington; and he was to spend much time "disseminating" the finished product: a report on economic controls to Edward Stettinius of the Advisory Commission to the Council of National Defense; answers to questions on armaments sent to Admiral Emory S. Land of the U.S. Maritime Commission; a report on aluminum control to Stettinius; a report from the Ministry of Economic Warfare to James Forrestal at the White House; and to General Miles and Admiral Anderson, the service intelligence chiefs, went several studies or documents on the British army, propaganda, military actions, and economic problems.[47] In an embryonic way, the soldier-lawyer was already a "coordinator of information."

Had such an idea occurred to Donovan during and after his trip to London? To say "Yes" would amount to reading too much into too little. He was to say in 1949 that he "had two main objectives when I visited Britain: (1) to find out about the 5th column there, (2) to learn whether the British were 'falling on their faces' as everybody said."[48] The latter objective caused him to view the situation as a totality. He sought to learn what the British were doing, what they could do, and what they needed if they and the West were to survive. As a strategist he studied the terrain, the people, the military forces, the economy, the organization of the government, anything related to defense and offense; and these he then interpreted as capabilities and requirements and fused them for both the British and the American governments as an order of priorities. He had come home with the facts; he gave a lift to morale; and he pushed for badly needed supplies.

From the British point of view they had gotten an excellent and encouraging view of a personable, vigorous, experienced, and influential advisor of the secretary of the navy, and friend of the President—and a Republican, if that party happened to win in the fall! Their satisfaction with Donovan was to be made amply evident when they learned of his second trip in December. But just before that happened, they put the stamp of approval on him when Lord Lothian was authorized on 28 November "to drop a hint to U.S. authorities that, if Mr. Kennedy is not returning [from the United States as ambassador], it is to be assumed that appointment of Colonel Donovan would be welcome."[49]

Donovan had not yet carved out a role for himself in the war that was shaping up for the United States. When he dined with the Stimsons on 6 August, the secretary asked him to head one of the training camps then being revived by the army. "He said he would not say no." Stimson then observed: "He was determined to get into the war some way or other and was the same old Bill Donovan that we have all known and been so fond of."[50]

Donovan soon flew out to Wyoming to handle a lawsuit and then went to San Francisco and Pearl Harbor on an inspection trip with Secretary Knox. On returning, he reminded General George C. Marshall, army chief of staff, of the general's earlier suggestion that he visit some of the army camps and mobilization centers. He then spent the first ten days of October at Forts Benning, Sam Houston, Sill, and Knox. He had already written Vansittart that he had "refused the nomination of Senator from this state, also to take any place with the government. I intend to go with troops, and as it looks now I shall probably spend the winter in Alabama training a division."[51]

Such was not to be the case, and the explanation is not at hand. Another six to nine months were to pass before the war and his plans were to fuse in a task and a position.

In the meantime, Stephenson was busily tackling the functional, organizational, and geographic aspects of the establishment and operation of his own British Security Coordination. These considerations kept him in contact with the FBI. Since, however, they required from his point of view a new kind of American organization as a counterpart, they gave him cause to cultivate Donovan. Hence activity in the last half of 1940 and early 1941 must now be studied if its impact on Donovan is to be appreciated.

5

·—·—·—·

Stephenson's British Security Coordination

WHEN CHURCHILL RETURNED TO THE BRITISH GOVERNMENT IN SEPTEM-
ber 1939, as the first lord of the Admiralty, the fleet was informed of the
event by the electrifying message: "Winston is back." After he replaced
Neville Chamberlain as prime minister on 10 May and reorganized the government on the next day, the world soon became familiar with the "V for
Victory" as the sign that Churchill was, as Stephenson described him years
later, "no mere bold facade but the very heart of Britain, which was still
beating very strongly."[1]

What Churchill brought to the scene was a fierce determination to
meet and fight the enemy on any and all fields of battle so that the British
would survive as a free people. The issue was simple but the resultant encounters—defense of the homeland, withdrawal from Dunkirk, a decision
on Greece, protection of the Suez Canal, see-sawing in the Libyan Desert,
hide-and-seek in the world's shipping lanes, and enough more to fill up six
volumes, 226 chapters, and 4,986 pages of Churchill's *The Second World
War*—were kaleidoscopic in the character of their challenges, requirements,
resources, and responses.

When Churchill looked out beyond Dover and Dunkirk, few areas appeared as important, or offered as much hope and promise, and yet provided
as many frustrations and challenges as the United States and the Western
Hemisphere. Here again, the objective was clear, and perhaps nowhere did

Churchill express it so emphatically as when, in a burst of annoyance with one of his admirals then engaged in Anglo-American staff talks, he wrote: "Our objective is to get the Americans into the war. . . . The first thing is to get the United States into the war. We can then best settle how to fight it afterwards. Admiral Bellairs is making such heavy weather over all this that he may easily turn the United States into a hindrance and not a help to the main object, namely, the entry of the United States.[2]

In the meantime, the United States was both a promise and a pain—a promise because it was the arsenal, the workshop, the bank, the friend, but a pain because it had to be cajoled, mollified, and suffered while its mood ripened, its organization took shape, and its contributions were impatiently awaited. The United States was neutral; its mood was sympathetic but "keep it over there" referred to fighting in Europe; its sensitivies—political, economic, religious, ethnic—were tuned to British as well as Nazi-Fascist actions. This friendly but touchy hope of salvation was also the kingpin in a wider hemispheric world of friends and foes, supplies and resources, strategic locations, channels of communications. If Britain found in this Western Hemisphere so much that was vital, so also did the Nazis, and hence it was that in 1940-41 the New World was a battleground on which political and economic warfare was waged.

Churchill had come to power with a willingness to confront new problems and challenges with appropriately new and invigorating men, ideas, organizations, and activities. When the Germans took over much of Western Europe early in 1940, he had brought into being the Special Operations Executive (SOE) in order to wage war against the enemy overseas by way of subversion and sabotage, or, "to set Europe ablaze."[3] He had no intention of setting America ablaze, at least in the same sense, but he intended to use every workable means in the book to line it up behind Britain. He had his diplomats, treasury experts, shipping and purchasing chiefs. Surely he needed an intelligence chief; in terms of the challenge, there was no adequate British intelligence and security system in the Western Hemisphere. For this job he picked Stephenson.

The New Passport Control Officer

Stephenson's first job, after he and his wife Mary—Mary French Simmons, the daughter of a Tennessee tobacco exporter—had moved into Vincent Astor's "broken-down boarding house," was to set up shop as His Majesty's passport control officer (PCO) in New York. His predecessor, Commander Sir James Francis Paget, R.N., had his office in the Cunard Building in lower Manhattan's Exchange Place, in what Stephenson considered "cramped and depressing offices," and so he immediately moved the shop uptown, in new and more spacious quarters on the thirty-sixth floor of Rockefeller Center.[4] This move foreshadowed the imminent transformation of Britain's intelligence operations in the United States.

Before that transformation could be accomplished, however, the new PCO also had equally important things to do, all at the same time: conduct high-level diplomacy, intensify liaison with the FBI, and mount selected "special operations" against the Nazi-Fascist foe. On the first of these items, Stephenson may be wrong in the matter of "renewing" an acquaintanceship with Donovan, but there can be little doubt but that he quickly established and reestablished contact with such influential persons as Tunney, Hoover, Astor, Ernest Cuneo—whose chain "controlled" Drew Pearson and Walter Winchell—Edward G. Budd, the steel and rail enterpreneur, Harry B. Lake of the international banking firm of Ladenburg, Thalmann and Company, as well as Donovan. Stephenson claims to have had many private meetings with FDR, the first of which was arranged by Astor. On other occasions he made use of Cuneo, Sherwood, and Ambassador Winant as intermediaries with the President.[5]

That Stephenson established contact with J. Edgar Hoover must not obscure the fact that there had already been some liaison between the bureau and various British intelligence and security officers. This liaison also antedated the approaches made by Hamish Mitchell in March. Hoover on 31 May 1940—before Stephenson had really gotten to work—told the Interdepartmental Intelligence Conference that some of the British agents with whom the bureau was in contact had "been residing in their present quarters for as long as twelve years, indicative of the fact that they have been stationed at their post of duty for a long time." At the same time he noted that both the Canadian and British services seemed to be "particularly well organized" and that they were furnishing "considerable information to the FBI." Mitchell had referred, in his second approach to the bureau, to a description of "the setup of the German organization for developing information in the United States" which had been sent to the Department of State by the British Embassy.

Shortly after the two approaches of Mitchell, Vincent Astor was telling the President about his own dealings with Sir James Paget and the difficulty the State Department was causing. The report is worth quoting at some length:

British Intelligence in this area is in charge of Sir James Paget, assisted by a Mr. Walter Bell, who conduct the so-called British Passport Control Office, although the control of passports occupies but little, if any, of their time.

Shortly after the "club" 's [sic] formation, it occurred to me that Paget and Bell might from time to time obtain leads useful to us. I therefore arranged a meeting with Paget, at which I asked for unofficial British cooperation, but made it clear that we, for obvious reasons, could not return the compliment in the sense of turning over to them any of our confidential information. This somewhat one-sided arrangement was gladly accepted. This was natural, inasmuch as any success that we might have in discouraging sabotage, etc., would be to his advantage.

On February 16th, Bell reported to F.B.I. that State Department officials in Washington had registered a complaint because he and his superior had furnished information to U.S. intelligence units. I was away at the time, but it appears that Bell continued to give direct information, feeling that by so doing valuable time would be saved. A week later, however, Paget was instructed by his government to confine all the contacts of his office with U.S. officials to representatives of the State Department. This time both Paget and Bell stated that, though they greatly regretted this situation, there was no course left to them but to follow instructions. Mr. Hoover thereupon went to the State Department, and was there informed that the action had been taken at the request of Mr. Messersmith, now in his post as Ambassador to Cuba, and that immediate steps would be taken, through our embassy in London, to the end that Sir James Paget's orders should be rescinded. This was in early March and since then there have been no developments. In consequence, opportunities to obtain useful information are now probably being lost.

Would it be possible to expedite action by the State Department, provided such action is approved of?

Two days later, Astor was again writing the President: "Apropos of delays in the transmission of news originating in the British Passport Control Office, and transmitted via the State Department . . . an unfortunate example came to my attention yesterday. Sir James Paget made a report, via the State Department, dated March 6th, which was forwarded to us on April 17th. It is certainly a bit difficult to conduct an effective blitzkrieg of our own against malefactors when information becomes stymied in department files for six weeks."[6]

Apparently, the complaint brought some action, for by July, many weeks subsequent to these letters, the FBI seemed satisfied with its liaison with the British. Hoover was telling the Interdepartmental Conference that the source of the "German documents" about which Miles had queried him would be calling on him shortly. Again, he told the conference, twenty-five days after Stephenson landed in New York, that "dealings" with the British "had been extended to a considerable extent and that the bureau hoped to possess within the course of a few days a complete outline of the organization of the British intelligence service within the Western Hemisphere." Then, there is that period of fourteen hours which "Mr. W. S. Stevenson, Attaché of the British Foreign Office at London" allegedly spent with the director of the FBI some time in the spring.

While Stephenson was intent upon nourishing the SIS-FBI relationship through a steady flow of intelligence to the bureau, the basic objective was to gather and disseminate intelligence information in order to conduct offensive, as well as defensive, operations against the enemy. At forty-three, Stephenson had had only a short career in that field, but the United States offered him many opportunities. One of these offered itself while he was still on board the *Britannic:* he recruited an Italian who rose to the rank of lieutenant-colonel in the British Army, received the Distinguished Service Order and the Military Cross and in the meantime distinguished himself in special operations in Sicily and Italy. At the same time, there appeared in New York a German agent named Dr. Gerhard Alois Westrick who—operating as a commercial counselor with the German Embassy—began propagandizing American industrialists, selling them on a German victory already won, and luring them with commercial privileges in an Axis-dominated Europe. Stephenson, who may have gotten some lead on Westrick from Vincent Astor, fed the facts on Westrick to the *New York Herald-Tribune;* the resultant publicity caused the public to hound Westrick, and in August 1940, he left the country at the request of the Department of State.[7]

About the time Westrick was leaving, Stephenson was informing London of the possibility of organizing an anti-Vichy coup on the island of Martinique, off the coast of Venezuela, where the Vichy gold reserve of an estimated $245,000,000 and several warships had been sent for safekeeping. The event was set for 23 September, but the local forces lost heart and support when the Anglo–Free French assault on Dakar on that day was beaten off. A more successful operation came off late in the fall when four German ships attempted to run the British blockade in the Gulf of Mexico. One of Stephenson's men in Mexico City had passed word of the planned breakout; Stephenson passed it through the FBI to the navy; and State agreed to the dispatch to the Gulf of four destroyers. In the dark of night, 15 November 1940, the ships made their break, but the destroyers approached, trained their searchlights on them, and panic took over. One ship sank, two were captured, and the fourth was interned until April 1941, as were twelve Italian ships which had stayed in port.[8]

Building a British Security Coordination Office

Earlier in this work, great stress was placed on a marginal note made by General Donovan; here, equally great stress will be placed on the absence of any such note in another passage of that same work: "Colonel Donovan and Mr. Stephenson kept in close contact through the autumn of 1940. During this period Mr. *Stephenson continually pressed his view* that some extension of American intelligence organization was going to be required if the United States Government were to be adequately informed, whether under peacetime, non-belligerent, or wartime conditions." (My emphasis.)

This passage went unmarked by the general; the assumption that he read it and found no fault with it follows from the twofold fact that it was the preceding page on which he mentioned not knowing Stephenson until his return and just fourteen lines after the above passage that he dashed a large marginal "no," underlined twice, opposite a controversial point on his Balkan trip.

A year before the above passage was written, Donovan had signed a memorandum recommending Stephenson for the Distinguished Service Medal, and there Donovan spoke of Stephenson as "the earliest collaborator with and the chief supporter of the early movement" which led to COI, and as a man "whose early discussions with the Coordinator were largely instrumental in bringing about a clearer conception of the need for a properly coordinated American intelligence service."[9]

Stephenson's own account of these "early discussions" is, except for the date, in line with all this: "From the beginning, that is June 1940, I had discussed and argued with him [Donovan] the necessity for USG to establish an agency for conducting the secret activities throughout the world—an agency with which I could collaborate fully by virtue of being patterned in the matter of coordinated functions after my own organization. Early he agreed in principle."[10]

The significance of Stephenson's "pressing his view" and "argu[ing] the necessity" of an American organization "patterned" after "my own organization" can best be appreciated by first returning to the transformation of the PCO job. The latter had been accepted by Stephenson only because he saw in it the possibility of a much larger challenge and contribution to the war effort.

Stephenson gave up the Cunard office, was to change the title of his office to British Security Coordination, and proceeded, in effect, to write a new job description for himself. He did, however, keep his office in New York, not perhaps because he preferred the city to Washington, but because

New York was the chief port of the country, and the security of supplies was a major concern. New York was also the headquarters of the British Purchasing Commission, which, under the able leadership of another Canadian, Arthur Purvis, was engaged in the very difficult business of getting British war supplies, so badly depleted by Dunkirk, ordered, produced, shipped, and financed. New York was also the location of the British Information Center, whose activities related to Stephenson's own interest in Nazi efforts to exploit the non-involvement and isolationist mood of the country. New York was the center of many political activities, politically important ethnic and racial groups, and of the commercial and financial circles in which Stephenson moved easily and in which his new responsibilities brought him many new ties and opportunities.

While it is not possible to reconstruct with any accuracy the chronology of transformation, or the order in which certain basic tasks were undertaken and organizational structures and links formed,[11] it is clear that one of the basic building blocks was his takeover from the British Purchasing Commission of its responsibility for the physical security of British purchases in the United States. This job was being done only inadequately at the time because of the smallness of the staff, the rudimentary coordination with other investigative and law enforcement agencies, the diffuse character of the plants, railroads, storage areas, and ports in need of tightened security, and the only partially known dimensions of the enemy threat to American facilities and British supplies.

The takeover consisted of absorbing the commission's security officer, Hamish Mitchell, its credit investigation section, and a shipping security section. These sections formed the core of Stephenson's new Industrial Security Division, under the direction of Sir Connop Guthrie, an English businessman with a good deal of shipping experience. New personnel were brought in from England and Canada, as well as the United States.[12] To Stephenson one of the most important of these was Colonel Charles H. Ellis, whose services Stephenson demanded from SIS as a sine qua non for his own acceptance of the PCO post. Ellis arrived in New York on 7 July 1940 and as a professional intelligence officer was to serve Stephenson throughout the war as his deputy.[13]

Another basic step in construction was the development of close liaison with the Royal Canadian Mounted Police and the Canadian intelligence and immigration services. Stephenson, of course, was a Canadian— born and schooled there, active in business there before and after the war, and always loyal to it; but Canada was vital to Stephenson for other reasons. For staff, Canadians, who presumably knew better how to deal with Americans, were preferred to Englishmen. Canada's port of Halifax was a major starting point of convoys heading across the Atlantic. Canadian intelligence on the identification and movement of known or suspected spies, saboteurs, and couriers, and disaffected workers, sailors, cargo handlers, and others was essential to the establishment of a pool of intelligence without which the security job could not be done. Late in 1941 Canada made it possible for Stephenson to establish near Toronto a training establishment which was utilized by coi and oss as well as by Stephenson's organization.[14]

Almost equally as important as Canada was Bermuda, which was an air and water link between Europe and the Western Hemisphere (fig. 5). Its importance zoomed in the summer when the trans-Atlantic Pan American Clippers once more began stopping there.[15] These flights enabled British security to exercise a greater control over the movement of persons, mail, currency, and other smuggled goods between Europe and the Western Hemisphere. Bermuda was thus a strategic location for spotting, frustrating, and exploiting Axis movements in the region.

Here again there took place a significant buildup in the British capability. A censorship security officer was sent to the island in August, and then followed additional personnel to carry out passenger interrogations and the examination of documents. Because the languages spoken by the trans-Atlantic passengers and crews reflected the diversity of Europe, South America, Canada, and the United States, a small staff of linguists was set up. Thus was formed a travelers censorship unit. Examination of the mails formed a major part of the work done in Bermuda, and for this purpose Stephenson had "hundreds" of "censorettes" brought in from England. Bermuda was so central to bsc that Stephenson commuted regularly to and from New York.[16]

The necessities of running an intercontinental intelligence network, to say nothing of Stephenson's background in radio, electronics, and the films, made communications one of the first technical capabilities developed by bsc. This was required as much by the need to track down the Nazis' secret radios in the Western Hemisphere as by bsc's conduct of its own business. At the height of its operation, according to Stephenson, the communications division was "by far the largest of its type in operation—over a million groups a day." Similar capabilities were developed in the successful exploitation of Bermuda's mail censorship. Stephenson claims that it was his organization that first discovered the Germans' use of the microdot.[17]

The extension of activity from New York to Canada and then to Bermuda did not stop at that island. There were important posts in the Caribbean, such as Jamaica and Trinidad, and in South America, which had political regimes, ethnic minorities, valuable minerals, financial resources, and lines of communication which lay open to Nazi exploitation. Shortly

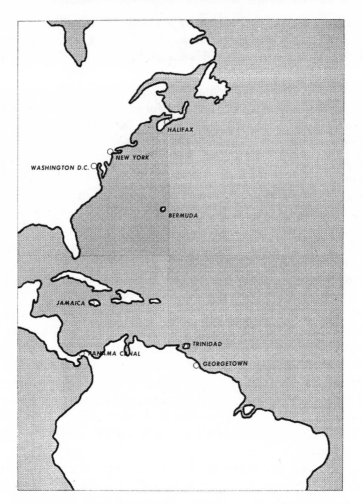

Fig. 5. The scene of Stephenson's operations

after the buildup in Bermuda, intelligence and security officers were sent from London to both Jamaica and Trinidad, and on those islands local committees were established to make certain that imperial interests and necessities were sufficiently harmonized with local and regional officials, systems, and interests to make all reasonably happy.[18]

Late in 1940 Stephenson took over the SOE responsibilities in Latin America. SOE in Europe concentrated on tactics to disrupt the German war machine in occupied Europe and behind the enemy's line: sabotage of industrial facilities, transportation networks, and lines of communication, as well as deception and propaganda. In the Western Hemisphere, where the United States was very sensitive to what the British did in the volatile areas to the south, SOE was restricted to studying and reporting on Nazi movements among the various European émigré groups and to the cultivation of contacts with leaders among them. By February and March of 1941 there was a network of agents in Venezuela, Brazil, Cuba, Columbia, and Peru.[19]

All the while, liaison with the FBI was growing. The connection with Stephenson was serving the bureau's interest because of its growing concern with the threat of sabotage and subversion. In October, the bureau requested the opinion of the Department of State on a proposal to send an official of the FBI to London "to study police problems in the time of war."[20] One of Hoover's assistant directors, Hugh P. Clegg, did go to London about that time. In March the director of postal and telegraph censorship told Donovan that he had "explained to Hoover and Clegg how we run our organization, and Clegg and Hince have been all over it here [London]; they have all our confidential documents."[21] Stephenson's activities in the Caribbean and in Latin America brought him in touch with Hoover as a result of the latter's new responsibility for investigating and reporting on activities in South America, which threatened the security of the United States. Hoover's Special Intelligence Service, which had the President's personal approval, had access to British intelligence officers as consultants on technical and operational problems before the end of 1940.[22]

The FBI may or may not have wanted to be the only American link with Stephenson's organization, but as a matter of fact it was not. Details are lacking, but on 9 October 1940 the assistant chief of staff for intelligence, General Miles, sent to his representative in New York, Major Frederick D. Sharp. a memorandum about "W. S. Stephenson" in which he advised the Major: "The subject, who is an Englishman, and whose telephone number is Circle 6-8580, will call you up in the near future. He will tell you who he is, and you will find the contact of interest and value."[23] Stephenson had apparently met the general at a meeting of "a dozen top steel men," which had been called at Stephenson's suggestion by Edward G. Budd.[24]

The army and the navy, as well as other American establishments, had long since been alerted to the possibilities of sabotage to American military installations and subversion of American personnel. With the agreement on the destroyers and bases there went a natural concern on the part of the military for the intelligence and security aspects of the new installations that were to be built on Canadian, Bermudian, Caribbean, and South American sites. Also, as the United States moved towards the convoying of supplies, the military became more concerned with intelligence relating to the Western Hemisphere and less and less inclined to rely on the FBI as the "sole channel" for the exchange of military information. Again, Donovan learned in March from the postal and telegraph censor: "The F.B.I., Navy and Army Departments and the Attorney General Department [sic] are receiving the products of our Western Stations through appropriate contacts." Army and navy officers had also been to Bermuda to study the British system of censorship.[25]

In December 1940, when Stephenson travelled to London with Donovan, Stephenson had his own problems to take up with authorities there, and among these was the best way to tie together all the geographical extremities of the Western Hemisphere's intelligence and security centers. Again, details are lacking, but apparently it was during this visit to London that Stephenson was made responsible for Bermuda and the Caribbean, and by the beginning of 1941, "arrangements had been made, at Stephenson's suggestion, to link the British intelligence network in Latin America with B.S.C. in New York."[26]

Before considering the buildup of BSC in the United States, it is well to stop to take a look at the dimensions of what was taking shape under Stephenson's direction. Philosophically, the organization was oriented to offensive, as well as defensive, operations; and there was not always a nice regard for legality. As Cuneo remarked, "for the British it was a life and death struggle," and he and others doubted not that the British were often operating illegally in this country before Pearl Harbor.[27] The territory covered by BSC extended far beyond the confines of the United States from Canada to South America and included all the intervening cities and ports—especially Halifax, New York, Bermuda, Jamaica, Trinidad— which figured in the international movement of persons, currency, goods, and ideas. This geographical coverage meant that BSC dealt with all sorts of political entities and systems: the independent and neutral United States, the Dominion of Canada, British colonies in Bermuda and the West Indies, and the South American republics. From this fact it followed that BSC also had to deal with a bewildering number of intelligence and law enforcement agencies: in the United States, the FBI, army and navy intelligence, the New York City Police, the Coast Guard, and Customs; in Canada the RCMP and other law enforcement agencies; and elsewhere in the Caribbean and Latin America similar organizations. One can only allude here to what must have been a large congeries of services awakening slowly, jealously, suspiciously, and haphazardly to the security requirements of the emergent hemispheric situation. Finally, this regional concentration on the movement of persons, goods, and ideas meant that BSC—intercepting mail, decoding messages, interrogating passengers, "vetting" crews and business firms, checking port security, tracking down enemy radio stations, sending its own traffic—was performing a full range of intelligence and security functions which had previously been done, when done at all, by different and specialized agencies.

Rather proudly, Stephenson himself described what happened to his basic position as a regional representative of the sis. "My original charter," he said, "went beyond that and indeed was soon expanded to include representation of all the numerous and generally covert [British] organizations—nine of them—also Security and Communications." Because of this last element, he said, bsc became "the only all-encompassing integrated secret security organization which had ever existed anywhere, and myself the repository of secret information at all levels beyond that of any other single individual then involved."[28]

BSC Worries the State Department

Certainly bsc had grown sufficiently in the United States by the beginning of 1941 to come to the attention of the Department of State, which had already seen fit to keep Sir James Paget in place, had frowned on the approaches of Hamish Mitchell, and in the last half of 1940 was disposing of a British effort to organize, the United States being willing, the internal security of the country.[29]

In January the department was informed by the British Embassy of the official existence of a "Director of British Security Coordination in the United States." Whether this initiative was taken on its own or whether it had been promoted by some query from State is not known. On 28 January, nevertheless, an aide-mémoire giving Stephenson's name was handed to R. B. Stewart of the Division of European Affairs. Stewart did not find the title "particularly revealing" and asked for clarification. He was told that Stephenson's work was in connection with "anti-sabotage protection at ports and also the protection of British shipments from American factories to the docks." He had already been engaged in this work "for some time" as passport control officer. The new title, Stewart was told, "had come from 'your own people' in order to make his relations with them at ports easier, since his work was obviously broader than that of a passport control officer." Apparently "your own people" was a reference to Hoover himself. While Stewart "believed there is no objection to Mr. Stephenson's activities," he did think State ought to get a detailed report on what he was doing and the names of the various Americans with whom he was in contact.[30]

Within a week, State had gotten a report from its special agent in charge in New York City, which indicated that "the quiet Canadian" was also the unobtrusive Canadian. His telephone number, Circle 6-8580, was known, but he had so far refused to make known the whereabouts of his office, and "the utmost secrecy" cloaked the whole affair. Mr. Stephenson was not known to "any of the Federal officials or agencies in New York that deal with antisabotage protection" although Americans had much to do with other British officers on such matters. It was ascertained, however, that Stephenson would now take over this entire operation and was gathering a "staff of liaison officers" who would cooperate with federal officials throughout the country. Calls were to be made upon the staff, however, not on Stephenson personally, because he "will direct the national efforts of the organization." [31]

On 25 February, Hoover informed Berle, "as of possible interest" to him, that "the British government's Director of Security Coordination in the United States has appointed officers in New York, Baltimore, Seattle, San Francisco, Los Angeles, and Houston." [32] Some time in March the Department of Justice wanted to know the position of the State Department "in connection with the very large increase of the British intelligence service which has recently taken place." [33]

In a memorandum on the subject, Berle wrote a full-dress review of the situation and its dangers and the need for action. He described the service as "functioning under the headship of a chief attached to the Embassy," a reference, perhaps, to the British minister, Sir Ronald Campbell; "but the head of their field service appears to be a Mr. William S. Stephenson, who is thought to be registered at the State Department as 'Security Coordinator'." Nominally concerned with protection of supplies, Stephenson, wrote Berle, was rapidly developing "a full size secret police and intelligence service," which had a full string of "regularly employed secret agents and a much larger number of informers, etc." Information collected was by no means restricted to ships and munitions, informal contacts were being established at all echelons of national and local government, and, said Berle: "I have reason to believe that a good many of the things done are probably a violation of the espionage acts."

Berle admitted that "granting free rein" to the British might not have serious significance, but on the other hand, who knew but what the information collected might fall into the hands of the Germans, that the data might indeed fall into the hands of a new and hostile British government—in the event of a British defeat, and that perhaps, just perhaps, the British government might use the information for extracurricular meddling in purely American affairs. "My feeling," wrote Berle, "is that the time has come when we should make a square issue with the British Government." Let the British tell us what ought to be done that is not being done, and we will take care of it; and if their activity is duplicating that of the FBI, then it ought to be stopped for that reason. In any case, legally they are on "almost impossible ground; they are in fact spies." Berle thought the entire question should be taken up with the President and that the British activity should be restricted to protection of ships and munitions and then only after authorization from and in conjunction with the FBI.

The final point made by Berle was the usual concern for the embarrassing consequences should anything go wrong. State would be called upon to explain why it had tolerated "violations of American laws," and "we should be on very dubious grounds if we have not taken appropriate steps."[34]

At the time he was writing this memorandum, Berle was also learning that none of the persons engaged in the security coordination work had been registered with the department as agents of foreign principals. He was informed that "in view of all the factors involved, including our desire to be as helpful as possible to the British in this connection," they had come under the exception which covered foreigners engaged in "the bona fide trade or commerce of a foreign principal."[35]

Berle then took up this matter in a letter to Hoover, who was told that the secretary of state thought he should be guided by the attorney general: would you submit the question to him? Perhaps he "might want to develop the question with the President, or in Cabinet." In reply, Hoover returned the ball to State's court: he had already taken it up with the attorney general, and there was, therefore, no further action he could take. He did think that Berle could take it up with Mr. Hull, and then the secretary could discuss it with the attorney general. "In this manner it may be possible to reach some decision as to the future policy to be followed."[36]

There is no need to follow this matter any further. Suffice it to say that the problem of harmonizing not just the matter of registration but also all the activities of the BSC with the requirements of American law, politics, and the bureaucracy was to become more acute when COI was established and when the entry of the United States into the war called for radical changes in many spheres of organization and activity. The problem was to become the subject of a touchy confrontation in March, 1942, between the British ambassador, then Lord Halifax, and Sir Ronald Campbell on one hand, and Berle, Hoover, and the attorney general on the other. Berle thought perhaps the British "needed a different type of man to head" BSC. A few days later at another such conference involving Halifax, Campbell, Berle, and Biddle, the ambassador asked the attorney general to get Hoover and Stephenson together so that the "two men might understand each other." By this time, and at this conference, the relationship between Stephenson and Donovan, hitherto an unspoken relevancy, was brought out.[37]

This chronicling of BSC's growth in the Western Hemisphere, especially in the United States, and of its relationship with the government has taken us well beyond the return of Donovan from London in August 1940 and those "early discussions" with Stephenson which led to COI. It has been important, however, in showing (1) the kind of problem that Stephenson must have delineated for himself when he first looked over the passport control post, (2) the kind of situation—philosophical, geographical, political, jurisdictional, and functional—with which he had to grapple, and (3) the kind of American organization he needed as a counterpart in the hemispheric conduct of clandestine, subversive, and offensive operations.

Allen Dulles has said that Donovan, in the years before the outbreak of World War II, had already been at work "planning the type of intelligence organization America would need as soon as we became a belligerent."[38] No evidence was advanced for this proposition, and it is possibly, but not probably, true. It certainly is inconsistent with Donovan's acceptance of the British statement that Stephenson "continually pressed his view that some extension of American intelligence organization was going to be required."

As far as evidence is concerned, Stephenson, operating on the basis of his own concrete necessities, communicated to Donovan—and not without difficulty—"une idée directrice" or "the idea of an undertaking or enterprise" to be realized. When taken up by Donovan, this "directive idea" was passed through the prism of his own experiences as a lawyer, soldier, military strategist, and public servant, and while differently refracted, was neither dissipated nor dissolved, and remained basically what Stephenson had in mind.[39]

Some understanding of the fact of different refraction will be gained when it is realized that Donovan, in 1940–41, clearly considered Britain as a "laboratory"[40] in which the United States could study responses to modern warfare which it more than likely would soon have to adopt and adapt to its own peculiarities. He had already gotten a "feel" for the Fifth Column phenomenon on his trip to London; he was to see more and learn more on his next trip—three months in Britain, the Mediterranean, the Middle East, and the Balkans.

6

·—·—·—

Donovan: In London and the Mediterranean

THERE IS AS MUCH UNCERTAINTY ABOUT THE ORIGIN OF DONOVAN'S second trip to London and his subsequent journey to the Mediterranean, the Balkans, and the Middle East as there is about his first trip. There is, however, less uncertainty about Stephenson's role, and the subject of intelligence and special operations can be tied down more definitely at both the beginning and the end of the trip.

"The Two Bills" Off for London

Who proposed what? And why? Stephenson, who had had "discussions" with Donovan about the need for a new American intelligence organization, also had "many discussions on what further needed doing in Europe." Donovan had been much "impressed with the necessity for the protection of U.S. supplies, which were then beginning to flow to Europe, and hence for the desirability of the convoying of such supplies by the U.S. Navy in view of the already extended commitments of the British Navy." So that Donovan could "collect further evidence to support his proposals" for convoying, Stephenson "arranged for [him] to visit Europe again."[1] Stephenson did make arrangements for the trip, as will be seen, but it was Donovan who "*proposed* that he should pay another visit to London and go on to the Mediterranean."[2] (My emphasis.)

An early story of the trip says that "on the first of December Donovan was called to Washington. By his own account, the President 'asked me if I would go and make a strategic appreciation from an economic, political, and military standpoint of the Mediterranean area.'"[3] In a later account, Donovan indicated that he went officially as the representative of his friend, Secretary Knox, but in reality as the agent of the President: "His mission was to journey to the Middle East, to collect information on conditions and prospects and, more importantly, to impress on everyone the resolution of the American Government and people to see the British through and provide all possible assistance to countries which undertook to resist Nazi aggression."[4]

When asked by the President, "he accepted with alacrity." His directive was apparently "so broad that it did not indicate with any precision where he was to go."[5] The Mediterranean was the area, for it was here that Britain's position was most critical; the Italians had opened hostilities in Libya and had invaded Greece; the Germans seemed poised for thrusts either through Spain into North Africa or into the Balkans and the Middle East; from Gibraltar to Suez, the land, the passageways, and the waters were problems for the British. Once he had decided to go to the Mediterranean, it then seemed wise to go to London first in order to get acquainted with British plans and intentions. The President reportedly suggested that he should find an occasion en route to confer with General Maxime Weygand, France's commander in chief in Algiers, and "explore with him the possibilities of some form of Franco-American action in North Africa."[6] This mission is perhaps what Knox and the State Department had in mind when they asked him to go to "North-West Africa."[7] When he visited with Secretary Stimson, his itinerary and its purpose made the secretary's "mouth water": Donovan was going "to take another look around and see what is really up in Gibraltar, Malta . . . Syria and Egypt—or else it was Greece and Egypt—and then he hopes to get down into Central Africa and to meet General Smuts of South Africa, coming up to see him."

"Incidentally," wrote Stimson, "he brought up the question of his own fortunes after he got back in regard to a command post in the Army. I told him of the change of conditions which have taken place in regard to the 27th Division (and how he could not interfere) with . . . that Command. Donovan was very nice about that and said that what he wanted more than anything else would be the toughest Division of the whole outfit."[8]

The news of the trip was first communicated to London by Lord Lothian who cabled on 27 November that Colonel Knox had asked him if Donovan, "who has done splendid work for us since he visited England can pay a short visit to the Middle East front."[9] Two days later, in London, Foreign Secretary Halifax wrote Lord Beaverbrook, the minister for aircraft production, that he had "learnt from a private source in the United States that Colonel Donovan (now Major General Donovan) is preparing to pay another visit to England to be followed by visits to certain places in the Mediterranean and to Casablanca and Dakar."[10] It is difficult to conclude who the "private source" was, if it was not Donovan himself or Stephenson, and equally mystifying is Lothian's rather premature promotion of the colonel. Not until 4 December did Lothian report that Donovan was going to England; in changing the request for travel arrangements, the ambassador noted that Donovan is "one of our best and most influential friends here with a great deal of influence both with the Service Departments and the Administration."[11]

In London the British were happy at the prospect of his return. Duff Cooper minuted: "He is a close friend of mine . . . I think he was very satisfied with the arrangements we made on the last occasion."[12] Halifax noted that Donovan had been very helpful to the British, thanks to the welcome which had been accorded him earlier; he was so thoroughly reliable that "certain secret information" had been released to him. The Army Council considered his visit of "the greatest importance from the point of view of Army supplies from the United States of America." Lothian, cabling again on travel plans, hoped no difficulties would arise "as he is such a valuable champion of our cause and is on the inside of all pro-British activities." To this the Foreign Office sent assurances that Donovan was welcome both in London and the Middle East.[13]

The real test of British acceptance was pinpointed by Sir Archibald Sinclair, secretary of state for air, who agreed that Donovan "is a good friend of ours" but noted that the favorable impressions he took away were due to the "frankness of our conversations. . . . We showed him a great deal and took him very largely into our confidence—I think we have had no reason to regret doing so." Unless we do so again, he continued, "the effect will be deplorable." The problem, he said, is that "the Prime Minister and Lord Beaverbrook have recently expressed strong views against giving the Americans secret information. I think, therefore, that you should perhaps mention this project to the Prime Minister and obtain from him directions on how far we should take Colonel Donovan into our confidence."[14]

Britain's intelligence chief in New York stepped in at this point with his own impressive recommendation, which was communicated to the secretary of state for foreign affairs, Lord Halifax, by Sir Alexander Cadogan: " 'C' [Menzies] tells me that Mr. Stephenson, who travelled over with Colonel Donovan, has impressed upon him that the latter really exercises a vast degree of influence in the administration. He has Colonel Knox in his pocket and, as Mr. Stephenson puts it, has more influence with the President than Colonel House had with Mr. Wilson.

"Mr. Stephenson believes that if the Prime Minister were to be completely frank with Colonel Donovan, the latter would contribute very largely to our obtaining all that we want of the United States."[15]

The prime minister's reaction will be noted shortly. Here only one other reaction of the British to the trip needs to be mentioned. J. V. Perowne, obviously remembering the confusion attending the announcement of the Mowrer-Donovan trip, minuted "but we ought to know whether Colonel Donovan is coming on behalf of the Secretary of the Navy or the *Chicago Tribune!*" [News][16]

This time Stephenson did travel with Donovan. London was told: "Mr. Stephenson, Passport Control Officer at New York, will be the fourth in the same plane to Lisbon and both he and Colonel Donovan are most anxious that it should be arranged for them to travel together from Lisbon to London." In London arrangements were made "to see that Mr. Stephenson obtains accommodation on the Lisbon-London aeroplane with Colonel Donovan." Lisbon, in turn, was notified of the importance of the visitor: "He is most friendly and useful to this country. Stephenson, Passport Control Officer at New York is accompanying D[onovan]."[17]

Together they left from Baltimore for Bermuda on 6 December on what the press called a "secret mission tied to France." Donovan was described as traveling "incognito . . . with two others, one a Frenchman," one Desgarges, whom rumor connected with a possible approach to Weygand. Donovan was said to be traveling under the name of "Donald Williams," even though his luggage bore his own initials. The third member of the party was a "Mr. O'Connell." Years later Stephenson insisted that he was "Williams," and anyhow, "O'Connell" fitted Donovan's background rather than his own![18]

In Bermuda, the schedule called for a change to the Atlantic Clipper which had taken off from LaGuardia and was to make a short stop in Bermuda. The weather in the Azores was so foul, according to Stephenson, that "the waves of Horta" kept the travelers waiting at Bermuda for eight days. Despite their impatience and the high-level travel resources that normally could be called upon, the travelers had to wait upon the waves. One can only assume that some of the intervening time must have been spent by Stephenson showing Donovan quite a bit of BSC's Bermudian operation, especially some of the intricacies of intercepting the mail.

London Clears the Tracks

The prime minister let it be known that he wanted to see Donovan as soon as he arrived.[19] He landed on 16 December, and two days later the two lunched at No. 10 Downing Street.[20] Donovan told Churchill there was a need for a "study on the economic, political and military factors to see if there could not be developed a type of doctrine that would be common to both countries." Churchill, as Donovan described the encounter shortly after returning to the United States, seized upon the idea and gave him as traveling companion "the best man in the Cabinet Secretariat," Lt. Col. Vivian Dykes of the Royal Engineers, "who has been present at meetings of the Joint Board and combined arms." Churchill also gave Donovan all the studies that had been done on the Mediterranean and Middle East situation, studies which, Donovan noted, covered all the parts but did not include "a comprehensive view combining all points as part of one strategic front."[21]

Whether or not Churchill needed Stephenson's urging to be frank with Donovan, the prime minister was just that. A "book" message to the field ordered that "every facility" be afforded Colonel Donovan, who has "great influence with the President" and who "has been taken fully into our confidence." The message makes clear that the trip was financed by the SIS: "Colonel Dykes has been told to draw on His Majesty's Embassy (or Legation) for funds which should be charged to the funds of the Assistant to the Oriental Secretary (or the Passport Control Officer)."[22]

There is some argument about another message which was allegedly sent at Stephenson's dictation by the director of naval intelligence, Admiral Godfrey, to Admiral Andrew Cunningham, the commander in chief of the Mediterranean Fleet. Godfrey has denied Stephenson's description of its sending. Nevertheless, the sentiments and the endorsement certainly reflected Stephenson's attitude:

> Donovan exercises controlling influence over Knox, strong influence over Stimson, friendly advisory influence over President and Hull. . . . Being a Republican, a Catholic and of Irish descent, he has following of the strongest opposition of the Administration. . . . It was Donovan who was responsible for getting us the destroyers, the bomb-sight and other urgent requirements. . . . There is no doubt that we can achieve infinitely more through Donovan than through any other individual. . . . He is very receptive and should be made fully aware of our requirements and deficiencies and can be trusted to represent our needs in the right quarters and in the right way in the U.S.A.[23]

The day after he lunched with Churchill, Donovan had a long conversation at the Foreign Office where he made it clear that his "primary object" was to obtain a coherent picture on the spot of the British position in the Near East and Mediterranean. He had stopped in London first in order to get acquainted with Britain's plans and intentions and to study "the whole picture of our war effort, with particular reference to the Atlantic." As he saw it, the British were taking a "severe plastering" on the seas, and American policy ought to be aimed at remedying this situation. He told his interlocutors that he would make a report to the American people who attach "great value" to a verbal rather than a written report.[24]

Before leaving London, he publicly declared that on returning from his first visit he had reported that the British people were "resolute and courageous." Now he would add, he said, that they were "confident." Aside from admitting that his trip was official, he evaded questions about its purpose, saying only: "I accept as the truth that shipping is the most urgent war problem facing Britain now."[25]

Back home, on 27 December, a sharp reader might have noticed a nine-line item at the bottom of the page that Donovan had left London the day before "for an undisclosed destination. . . . Friends said that Colonel Donovan had not left for Ireland, the United States, or the Continent, but was making a 'private trip.'"[26] Again, however, a delay was encountered, and four days' waiting at Plymouth gave him a good chance to see some of the training of a unit of commandos about which he got quite excited and was to write a long paper to Secretary Knox.[27]

Donovan Sees Everything

This is not the place to write a detailed account of Donovan's journey (fig. 6), which must be reckoned one of the most extended, varied, and important trips taken to scenes of World War II action by any American, certainly up to that time.[28] He had left Baltimore on 6 December and was not to return home until 18 March. In that time he traveled from Portugal to Britain, and then he was off to Gibraltar and Malta, to Cairo, which he reached on 7 January, to the Western Desert of Libya, back to Cairo and off to Athens, Sofia, Belgrade, then back to Greece and the Albanian front, next to Turkey, Cyprus and Palestine, back again to Cairo and soon off to Baghdad, in Cairo once again, and then began a homeward journey which still had him stopping at Gibraltar, Malta, Spain, Portugal, and Ireland, and back to England again before finally heading for the States.

As befitting a representative of the President and one who had the full confidence of the prime minister, Donovan saw everybody, everybody, that

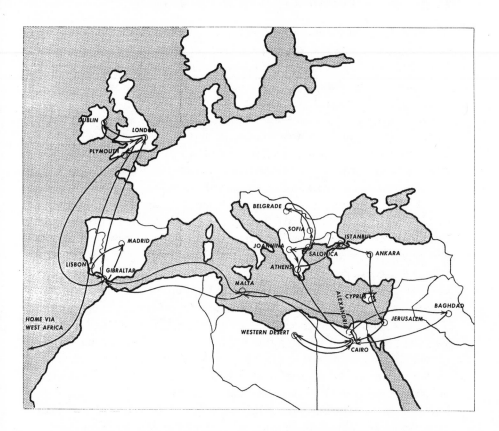

Fig. 6. Donovan's travels to London and the Mediterranean, 1940–1941

is, except General Franco, who was "very busy," and General Weygand, because the Germans made it clear they did not want Donovan on French-controlled territory.[29] Otherwise, Donovan saw and talked at great length with King Farouk of Egypt, King George and Premier Metaxas of Greece, King Boris of Bulgaria, Prince Regent Paul of Yugoslavia, his chief ministers and several generals, the Mufti Haj Amin al Husseini, Foreign Minister Suñer in Spain—whom he treated exactly "as if he was a German"[30]—and Premier de Valera in Ireland. He saw no end of British generals and admirals, including Wavell, Dill, Wilson, Cunningham, and Tedder.

Wherever he went he busied himself with what was on peoples' minds. In Gibraltar, preparing defenses was the order of the day; the thinking was that the Germans could not take the Rock, but control of Spain would deny Britain the use of the harbor. In Malta, he found praiseworthy the defense efforts being put forth by "an old sapper," General Dobbie, "a Cromwellian soldier who goes around carrying a Bible in one hand but a damn good sharp sword in the other." In Libya and Egypt he was impressed by the quality of Britain's military leadership: Wavell, whose model is General Allenby, who writes well, and has "an excellent force with him," General "Jumbo" Wilson, a big, husky fellow with a fine eye for ground;" a corps commander named O'Connor, "an active, driving kind of fellow, which was evidenced by the way he pulled off that final advance on Benghazi"; and Admiral Somerville, "who was the fellow who did the firing at Oran and [is] really a high class man."[31] In Cairo he had a long talk with Brigadier Shearer, the deputy chief of military intelligence, who showed him "some of his Intelligence Establishments ('Y' and 'M')."[32] In Palestine he was surprised to see how quickly "the Jewish boys got on to the rhythm of the drill," whereas the Arabs, "being more dull by nature, had quite a time trying to keep step." In Iraq he talked with the Mufti and others, all of whom wanted to talk with him in order to get arms. "They were a little discouraged on that when we finished our talk."[33]

It was the Balkan world, along with the problem of supplies for Britain, and protection of the supply line, that preoccupied him. In Greece, his talks with the leaders covered Greek preparations, strategy, and tactics for the resistance they were determined to offer to any German advance. They covered also the supplies needed by the Greek army: antiaircraft guns, mountain guns with ammunition, Ford trucks, donkeys eleven hands high, uniforms, shoes, and socks. His visit to the Albanian front impressed upon him the ruggedness of the Greek soldier, his simple but eloquent emphasis on liberty, and especially, the fact that he was making his fight "with a rifle, a rock, and a mule."[34] In Athens, and everywhere he went, he delivered his own message that Britain was fighting, that America would support the democracies, and that the President himself was being given "overwhelming support" in this regard.

Bulgaria and Yugoslavia were critical points because of their exposed position vis-à-vis German moves to the southeast. At Sofia he had a celebrated hour and a half meeting with King Boris in which that monarch, already secretly committed to Hitler, merely smiled when Donovan, endeavoring to ascertain the Bulgarian attitude, summarized it as meaning that the Bulgars would delay a German passage as long as possible, then permit it under pressure, but not participate with the Nazis. Sofia also provided Donovan's celebrated loss of his wallet and passport, which were snitched from him either while he was conversing with the King or back in his hotel room when the lights were unaccountably turned off.[35] While the theft was subsequently the subject of many jokes, it had no serious consequences, even though the British quickly picked up a report that secret documents of theirs had been lifted from him; and there followed the usual flurry of telegrams reflecting "acute concern."[36]

Yugoslavia gave him a good opportunity to appreciate all the imponderables of the critical Balkan situation. Would Germany intensify political and economic pressures or attack? Against whom? Where? When? To what extent? The Yugoslavs, he was certain, would not permit German passage, but would they intervene if the Germans moved to and through Bulgaria? "While not without hope," Donovan was "impressed with the weaknesses and divisions of the Belgrade regime."[37] Yugoslavia provided him with another celebrated event, this time alleged responsibility for the anti-Nazi coup pulled off in Belgrade shortly after he left the country. Donovan wrote "No" to this charge, and Langer and Gleason concluded: "There is no evidence . . . to show that either American or British influence played an important part in this dramatic overturn." Even so, the occasion was grist for the Nazi propaganda mill.[38]

The Balkan situation was the cause of the high point of Donovan's trip, namely, his meetings in Cairo with British leaders as they wrestled with the question of whether and how to help Greece resist a German onslaught. The British consulted him as a representative of the President, as someone who was passionately interested in their welfare, and as a clear-sighted strategist—as one who had been on the ground, talked with the leaders, understood the issues and fully appreciated the consequences of action and inaction. He was on his way to the Sudan when a message from Foreign Secretary Eden asked him to wait in Cairo for the arrival of himself (Eden) and General Dill, chief of the imperial general staff.[39] On the day they were to arrive, Donovan had dinner alone with General Wavell, who then outlined what he intended to tell Eden and Dill.[40] Donovan favored British help to Greece and had been a vigorous supporter of the British effort, in vain as it turned out, to form a Balkan alliance to forestall a German move. He was present with the British leaders when the decision was taken to send not only supplies but also British soldiers back on to the continent to help their Greek ally. Not unappreciative of the value of his support, they asked him to go to London to present his study of the Mediterranean before the Council of War.[41]

That study had just been written by Donovan and is one of two long papers that he sent to Washington. The first of these papers was "the substance of information that I have obtained from a great many different kinds of people." The report summarized major attitudes about the likely course of the war; the "main idea" he found throughout the Near East was the belief that Germany, to achieve a decisive victory, had to invade and conquer Britain. This entailed destruction of the British position in the Near East and the maintenance of the Nazis' own position in Southeastern Europe, and Donovan then outlined the various options that lay at hand for the Germans.[42]

His Mediterranean study was a different kind of paper in that it not only discussed possible and probable developments but prefaced them with a brief outline of his theory of the Mediterranean as a "no man's land," and supplemented them with his own strong advocacy of American support of a Balkan alliance. The Mediterranean, he had decided since his trip in July, was not so much the east-west line of communications that was traditional in British thinking as it was now "a no man's land between two lines on a strategic front running from Spain to the Black Sea. Germany holds the northern or European line except at the two ends. Britain has gained control of much of the southern or African line." It was now up to Britain, he argued, to work from inside the Mediterranean, to gain control of that sea, to retain her salient in Greece, and to hold on to the Balkans, while keeping Germany out of Spain, as well as North Africa, at the other end of the "no man's land." Arguing and urging like a lawyer in court, he declared the President should lend his name, which held such appeal in the area, and his support to a league of Greece, Turkey, Yugoslavia, and, if possible, Bulgaria, against the Nazis.[43] This was not to be, but that is another story, as is the painful consequences of the decision on Greece.

His visit to the Iberian Peninsula enabled him to contrast the economic campaign needed there with the military campaign called for at the eastern end of the Mediterranean. Ever concerned with the socioeconomic aspects of warfare, Donovan found that the only way of keeping the Germans out of Spain was to ship in food. He had talked with Dr. Alexis Carrel, then studying the effects of near-starvation in Spain, who told him the Spaniard was living on eight hundred of the eighteen hundred calories that an ordinary human required.[44]

Throughout his travels, Donovan had met and talked with several military and naval intelligence people, just, it must be stressed, as he had talked with all kinds of specialists in the fields of strategy, tactics, aircraft, ordnance, transportation, training, health, and anything that pertained to the winning of the war. What contact, however, did he have with such outfits as SIS and SOE? The former was paying the bill for his travels, and Dykes regularly contacted the passport control officer. In Athens this was a man named "Edge." In Sofia, Donovan "met Smith-Ross, our P.C.O. there, and brought him back for a talk in the hotel." In Belgrade, Dykes had "a long talk with Lethbridge the P.C.O. . . . and discussed with MacDonald the D. organization which was apparently in a very bad state in Grand's time but now shows some signs of improvement. This corroborates what Alec Ross told me in Belgrade." Back in Athens, Dykes had "a long talk with Forbes . . . about our C. and D. organization in the Balkans with which he is profoundly dissatisfied like everyone else I have talked to in these parts." In Madrid, Dykes "went round to Walsh, Passport Control Officer, to send off two cables for D[onovan] and get a little money to buy a picnic lunch for myself and D." It is not too much to conclude that Dykes and all these people must have contributed significantly, at the bidding of Churchill, Stephenson, and Menzies, to Donovan's education in secret intelligence and special operations.[45]

Deeper into Intelligence

Before Donovan returned to London, he had been the subject of some Cairo-London cable traffic. Eden, still deep in making the decision on Greece, took time out on 22 February to suggest to the prime minister that on the return of Donovan to London "we show him every attention and express our gratitude in anyway possible." Eden particularly thought that Donovan would appreciate it, "and it would strengthen his hand when he gets home," if Churchill agreed to send a message to the President, through Lord Halifax, ambassador in Washington, thanking both the President for sending Donovan and the latter for the "judgment and energy . . . the real service" he had rendered to "this country and our cause."[46]

Meanwhile, another telegram from Cairo suggested that some "priming" of American correspondents in London might help to get "full publicity" out of the access given Donovan and the use he made of it.[47] On both matters, Balfour at the Foreign Office had words of caution. Donovan, he said, had come as the "personal emissary" of Knox, not of the President; indeed, while he had the confidence of the President, he was not one of his intimate associates. "We have, moreover, heard from the Embassy in Washington that Mr. Cordell Hull is slightly jealous of Colonel Donovan." Balfour thought a message of appreciation could be sent to Halifax, who could then send it on to Knox, who, in turn, could decide on sending it to the President. As for the press, Balfour pointed out that Donovan "is himself determined to do everything to promote our cause" but had made it clear that he would handle the press in his own way. He did not want to see American correspondents before seeing FDR lest they misrepresent the strong position he had taken in support of the British in the Near East. Balfour cautioned that Britain did not want to make it appear that Donovan was taking a stronger line than the United States might wish.[48]

On 25 February, a Foreign Office minute indicated that "some time ago" Ambassador Halifax was told to convey Britain's thanks to Knox, because Donovan was *his* emissary. "But if Colonel Donovan himself would like a message of appreciation sent to the President, we should be only too glad to send it. We could confirm that this would meet his wishes when he arrives." The prime minister, at the end of January, had sent a letter of congratulations to Donovan. The last available item on this suggestion is Sir Alexander Cadogan's recommendation that the matter be taken up with Donovan when he arrives, because he "is a person with whom we can discuss matters with entire frankness."[49]

Donovan had planned on returning to London even before Eden, Dill, and Wavell had asked him to do so; Eden, indeed, had politely made such a visit a precondition for letting the colonel go to the Middle East front.[50] Donovan got back to England "just at the time that Eden and Dill had worked things out in the East, and it [the decision to aid Greece] was put up to the War Cabinet. They asked me to go before the Joint Board, made up of the Representatives of the different arms and the economists from the Ministry of Economic Warfare . . . I then went to luncheon with the War Cabinet and with the Chiefs of Staff."[51] What he told them is not known; but, given half a chance, he must have outlined his Mediterranean strategy, and surely he endorsed the decision to send troops into Greece. Several days later he described that step to American officers as "a very daring and audacious thing," calculated to make the Germans pay for everything they took.[52]

Once back in England, however, he found other items of war dumped on his doorstep, and these were items which linked him more closely to Stephenson's kind of activity. Some of this, the commandos, he had seen while waiting at Plymouth. He had seen much more of highly specialized guerrilla units training and operating in Libya. He was greatly impressed by the employment of parachutists who had been trained in England, then based briefly in Malta, and finally dropped into Italy in order to destroy an aqueduct. "The net effect was that all through Italy was spread this fear of the British parachutists coming into the country."[53]

In London he was thoroughly briefed on the organization and operation of the Special Operations Executive. He had a meeting with its head, Sir Frank Nelson, who in response to his request for "a few brief details," sent Dykes a note on the soe training schools, a short description of "our Board of Directors—so to speak," and a "brief outline of system adopted in this country" for special operations.[54] Nelson said the board was composed mainly of businessmen; this "Brain Trust" met every morning for an hour to consider projects, which were then turned over to the intelligence and planning department and then to the director of training and operations.

The special training schools, some of which he visited, were conducted by soe's M Section. They trained foreigners as either "desperadoes" for specific raids or sabotage in their own or other countries, or as "organizers and agents" to be sent to enemy-occupied countries to organize Fifth Column activities. Depending on which category an individual fell into, his training varied from four weeks to indefinite. The "desperadoes" went to "depots" where the unfit were weeded out and then to "paramilitary schools"; the others continued on to "finishing schools" where they were trained in security organization in hostile territory, the use of agents, propaganda—whispering campaigns, rumors, and so forth, "political training"— anti-Nazi underground political movements, and "organization of subversive warfare."

In describing the "system" Nelson's aide-mémoire covered organization, collaboration of the Foreign Office, secret funds, cooperation of the military services, and training. He listed some of the assistance currently needed: diplomatic bag facilities, secret wireless facilities, civilians to be infiltrated to spread anti-Axis propaganda, interference with Axis export trade with South America, and—of particular interest to Donovan and the United States—the recruitment of foreign elements in the United States and South America who could be sent back to enemy territories, and the intensification of counterespionage in the Western Hemisphere and the Far East.

Another person Donovan met was the director of the postal and telegraph censorship department, ministry of information, Mr. E. S. Herbert. Much of his work must have been covered by Stephenson when he and Donovan were sweating out the "waves of Horta," because, as has been pointed out, Bermuda was a vital mail and communication link between the hemispheres. What Herbert now gave Donovan was information on his major problems with the United States. The first concerned efforts to obtain the State Department's assistance "in getting as much control as possible of enemy communications with the Americas." This involved the routing of American planes and ships in such a way as to bring the communications under British control. The other problem related to "preparation for co-operation of British and U.S. censorships in the event of U.S. entering the war." On this point Herbert outlined the basic requirements of a mail cen-sorship system and referred to what had been shown or told to Hoover and Clegg of the FBI and to army and navy officers.[55]

A third person close to Stephenson's field, Lord Swinton of the Secu-rity Executive, also had business with Donovan. The problem that con-cerned Swinton was the effort of the Nazis to get Allied and neutral seamen to desert their ships in U.S. ports and thus seriously hamper the British shipping program. What Swinton wanted was some means of preventing seamen, when arriving in the States, from claiming the pay due them and deserting, even though they had signed up for a return voyage. "It would be a great help if discipline and the observance of contracts of service could be enforced by . . . United States courts."[56]

Donovan Alarms G-2

Donovan had been away from home for three-and-a-half months of exact-ing travel, inspection, consultation, and exhortation. On 19 March he came home full of news and views and with a long list of "things to do" (fig. 7). Without anticipating this subject (See Chapter 8), one must note here some of the impact of this trip on his thinking about intelligence and the "di-rective idea" that Stephenson had "continually pressed upon him" and "ar-gued" with him.

Less than three weeks after he had returned, he had said and done enough to give rise to this report which General Sherman Miles, assistant chief of staff for intelligence, sent to General Marshall, the chief of staff: "In great confidence O.N.I. tells me that there is considerable reason to believe that there is a movement on foot, fostered by Col. Donovan, to establish a super agency controlling *all* intelligence. This would mean that such an agency, no doubt under Col. Donovan, would collect, collate, and possibly even evaluate all military intelligence which we now gather from foreign countries. From the point of view of the War Department, such a move would appear to be very disadvantageous, if not calamitous."[57]

This report is the earliest document found which links the name of Donovan with such a plan; and however much one may take issue with words and lines, with facts and intentions, it is clear that ONI and Miles

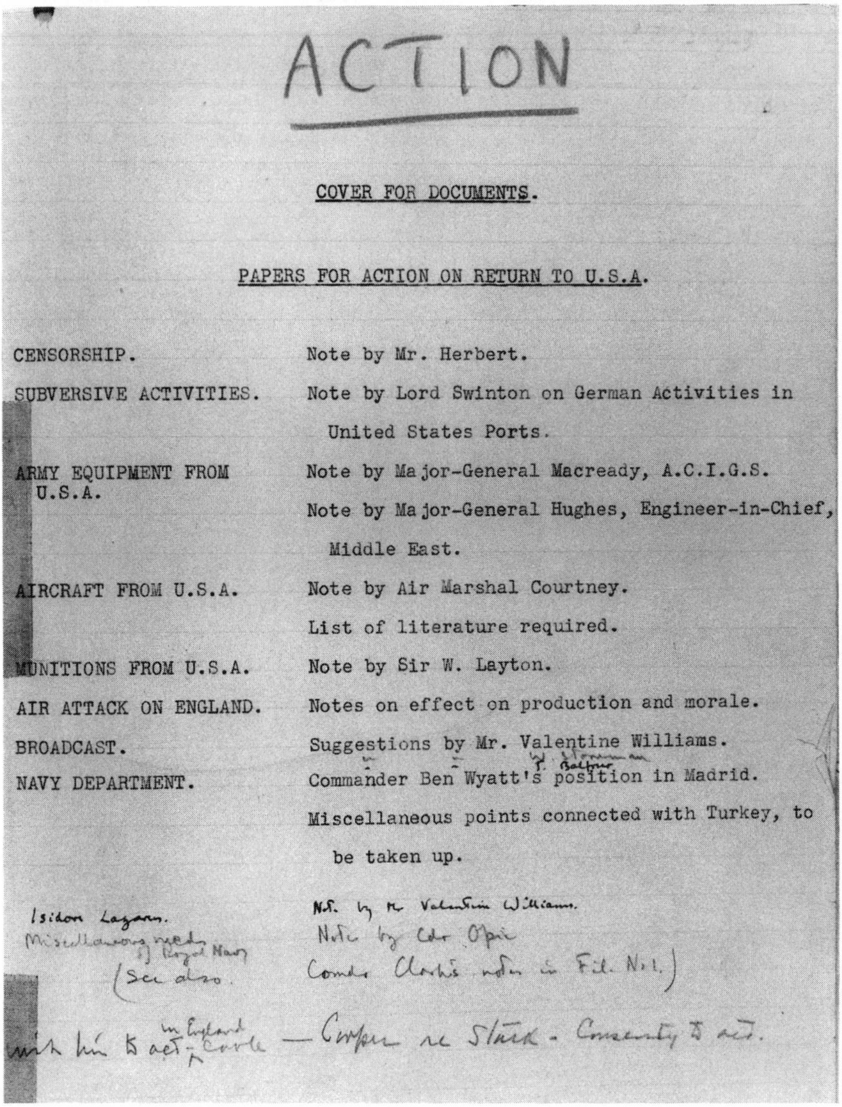

ACTION

COVER FOR DOCUMENTS.

PAPERS FOR ACTION ON RETURN TO U.S.A.

CENSORSHIP.	Note by Mr. Herbert.
SUBVERSIVE ACTIVITIES.	Note by Lord Swinton on German Activities in United States Ports.
ARMY EQUIPMENT FROM U.S.A.	Note by Major-General Macready, A.C.I.G.S.
	Note by Major-General Hughes, Engineer-in-Chief, Middle East.
AIRCRAFT FROM U.S.A.	Note by Air Marshal Courtney.
	List of literature required.
MUNITIONS FROM U.S.A.	Note by Sir W. Layton.
AIR ATTACK ON ENGLAND.	Notes on effect on production and morale.
BROADCAST.	Suggestions by Mr. Valentine Williams.
NAVY DEPARTMENT.	Commander Ben Wyatt's position in Madrid.
	Miscellaneous points connected with Turkey, to be taken up.
Isidor Lazarus.	N.B. by Mr Valentine Williams.
Miscellaneous needs of Royal Navy	Note by Cdr Opie
(See also	Comdr Clark's notes in File No. 1)

with him to act in England — Cooper re Stark - Consensus to act.

Fig. 7. Part of Donovan's agenda on his return home, March 1941. (Courtesy of U.S. Army Military History Institute, Carlisle Barracks, Pa.)

had hold of a very important truth, a very real possibility, and—from their point of view—a very real danger.

To appreciate the cleverness of the move which this knowledge prompted Miles to recommend to Marshall, one must first see what was happening in MID, ONI, and the FBI, for it was a problem of theirs which soon caused Roosevelt to look for a coordinator of intelligence.

7

. _ . _ . _

Roosevelt and the Intelligence Agencies

SO FAR IN THIS NARRATIVE, ATTENTION HAS BEEN FOCUSED ON STEPHEN-son's need for the establishment of an American counterpart to his BSC, and on Donovan's growing familiarity with the British and the newer challenges and responses of modern warfare. Meanwhile, President Roosevelt and the investigative agencies had been grappling with the new threats to American security posed by Axis warfare. The FBI, the army's Military Intelligence Division, the navy's Office of Naval Intelligence, and the Department of State felt themselves in control of the situation, and their activity and atti-tude constituted a large share of the domestic climate within which both Stephenson and Donovan had to work.

FDR Brings the Agencies Together

The President apparently took the first step in the coordination of intelli-gence, in the context of pre– and post–World War II developments, when on 26 June 1939, in a well-known order, he told the "directors" of the FBI, MID, and ONI "to function as a committee to coordinate their activities." He told them that they were to control and handle "the investigation of all espionage, counterespionage, and sabotage matters," and that no other U.S. investigative agency was to be so involved. These other agencies were to be told to "refer immediately" to the nearest FBI office "any data, information, or material that may come to their notice bearing directly or indirectly on espionage, counterespionage, or sabotage." This memorandum was sent to State, Treasury, Commerce, and the postmaster general, as well as to War, Navy, and the attorney general.[1]

The engine that was supposed to make this system operate was the assistant secretary of state for administration, who, at the time, was George S. Messersmith. Aside from being a career officer of stature and experience, he had most recently served the President in the field of coordination by successfully incorporating the foreign services of Agriculture and Commerce with that of State. Some time in the mid-fifties, Messersmith dictated a memoir on how he came to be asked by the President "to coordinate the activities of the investigating agencies" of the government.[2]

It happened "some time towards the middle of 1939." Messersmith connected it with the visit in June of the British king and queen. Presumably it occurred before the issuance of the President's memorandum. In any case, Secretary Hull relayed the President's request to him. FDR "had been concerned . . . for a long time with the duplication of activities between the investigating agencies" of the government; he found that the three agencies often followed the same matter at the same time and were "constantly crossing each other's tracks." The duplication, the President felt, was costly as well as wasteful, and in those serious times, it was essential that we have the best possible information.

The President made clear that he wanted not elimination but coordination of these agencies' activities. "The President was of the opinion," recalled Messersmith, that "if the heads of these agencies, under the leadership of one person, coordinated their activities through regular contact, the efficiency of performance would be greatly increased." For personal reasons Messersmith did not want to undertake the job; he was also deterred from doing so because of the "zealous" way in which these agencies protected their interests and because of the "further peculiarity [that] no one trusted the other." He was "extremely doubtful" that anything could be accomplished, but the President, not unmindful of the difficulties or the long hours Messersmith was already working, nevertheless wanted him to make "at least an effort to see what could be done."

The assistant secretary discussed the matter separately with each agency head, then invited them to dinner and a conference. The director of the FBI did not appear. The others listened respectfully to Messersmith's elaboration of the President's initiative, but the "atmosphere was cold and formal. The antagonisms were not personal. . . . They represented the attitudes of their respective agencies." Without Hoover, moreover, the meeting was useless, and another meeting was set for the following week. This time

Hoover appeared, thanks, according to Messersmith, to a personal presidential directive. This time also "the atmosphere eased up a good deal," and agreement was reached on Messersmith's plan, which called for regular weekly meetings. Through the months that followed, there was established "an effective machinery of exchange of information, allocation of work; and this constant close contact . . . in itself was, of course, of inestimable value." All realized the wisdom of the President's directive. In retrospect Messersmith emphasized his belief that this initiative was the "original idea which finally led to the formation of the Central Intelligence Agency."

Whatever the accuracy of the above account, especially in its details and its emphasis on Messersmith's role, it is clear that the FBI, MID, and ONI commenced regular meetings in which the assistant secretary of state, at first Messersmith, and then, when he went to Cuba as ambassador, his successor Adolph A. Berle, acted not exactly as the chairman but more as an overseer and link to the President. Their meetings went under the heading of the "Interdepartmental Intelligence Conference," which, throughout 1939–41, was chaired by Hoover, whose office kept and distributed minutes to MID, ONI, and State. It was to this group that Hoover reported the desire of the British Purchasing Commission "to set up an intelligence unit in the U.S." The first significant organizational outgrowth of the IIC was the development in June 1940 of a Special Intelligence Service, which was run for all three agencies by the FBI, and which was to be the first cause of friction between General Miles of MID and Hoover.

The idea of the service was the result of efforts of the conference members to work out a delimitation of the responsibilities of each of the agencies in the light of the President's directive of June 1939.[3] Apparently there was little difficulty on the basic delimitation: to the FBI was assigned responsibility for investigation of cases—of espionage, counterespionage, sabotage, and subversive activities—involving civilians in the United States and its territories excepting the Panama Canal Zone, Guam, Samoa, and the Philippines. MID was to handle the military establishment, including its civilians, and to cover the Canal, the Republic of Panama, and the Philippines; ONI was to have comparable duty with regard to Guam and American Samoa. What gave the conference difficulty was the coverage of these cases outside the United States and its territories.[4]

On 31 May Hoover pointed out that until recently the bureau had not extended its activities into foreign countries. "He explained confidentially that upon the instructions of the President the Bureau was arranging to detail men to Mexico City and Havana, but that this was the limit of the Bureau's operations in foreign countries." Who then was to be responsible for the investigation of subversive activities directed from foreign coun-

Fig. 8. The U.S. Director of Naval Intelligence,
Rear Adm. Walter S. Anderson, January 1941.
(Courtesy of U.S. Naval Historical Center, Washington, D.C.)

tries? "It was the consensus . . . that a decision should be reached as to the identification" of the agency which should handle this work. Miles thought State's opinion ought to be solicited and "an immediate decision" requested from Mr. Berle.[5]

At the meeting on 3 June there was undertaken a discussion of "a special Intelligence Service" possibly to function at this time only in the Western Hemisphere. Admiral Anderson of ONI (fig. 8) had pointed out at the previous meeting that "naval attachés are never allowed to maintain paid informants,"[6] and on this occasion Miles emphasized that the attachés were not to be compromised. The conference agreed that trends in South America, especially Colombia and Venezuela, had to be watched very closely. Berle stated that if MID and ONI wanted the FBI to establish a Special Intelligence Service on the east coast of South America, State would cooperate. Anderson thought War and Navy ought to be allowed specifically to request the FBI to undertake activities in foreign countries, and Hoover said the bureau could undertake any work abroad requested by State. Anderson, after other subjects had been discussed, returned to the subject of an SIS and stated that the "Navy was anxious to cooperate in setting up a foreign intelligence service," and that it ought to be done immediately, especially in Mexico and South America. A subcommittee was established.[7]

A report, written on 6 June, skirted the question of who should run the service and contented itself with describing a service whose government connection should be well hidden, whose chief should operate under business cover and maintain his office in a "metropolitan industrial center, preferably New York City," and whose operatives—men of honesty, integrity, and patriotism—should not be known to one another and should be able "to meet and develop as sources of information nationals of the country in which they are to operate."[8] This proposal was endorsed by the group on 11 June when all agreed that the approval of the President had to be obtained before any other organizing activity was undertaken.[9]

With Miles in his office, Secretary Berle telephoned the President and laid before him the IIC's request for his decision on which of the three— FBI, MID, and ONI—should run the proposed foreign intelligence unit. "The President said that he wished that the field should be divided. The FBI should be responsible for foreign intelligence work in the Western Hemisphere, on the request of the State Department." MID and ONI should cover the rest of the world as needed.[10] With this decision in hand, Hoover notified the conference on 2 July that Assistant FBI Director P. E. Foxworth had been placed in charge of the SIS and that the bureau would augment its undercover staffs in Mexico and Cuba but did not contemplate stationing intelligence officers in Canada or Greenland at that time.[11]

Disagreement, however, was close at hand. On 23 July General Miles indicated to Hoover and Anderson his concern upon learning, from conversations between his officers and Foxworth and Clegg of the bureau, that the operations of the SIS were to be "encyclopedic in scope." Miles thought the President's decision related to the identity of the agency to run the SIS and not to the scope of its work. This, he thought, ought to be restricted to gathering data on subversive activities, especially those aimed at the United States.[12]

The subject was aired at the meeting on 26 July. Anderson thought there should be no restrictions on the SIS. Hoover insisted he had no intention of running into conflict with MID or ONI in the matter. Miles repeated his position, explaining that if the operations were "encyclopedic in scope," the operatives would not be able to gather that particular brand of information which the services, by their nature, could not obtain. Presumably agreement was reached on a combination of emphasis on subversive activities and no restrictions on operations of the SIS. In conclusion, Hoover indicated his willingness to let War or Navy run the SIS if either so desired.[13]

Miles, however, was not happy with the situation. He and Hoover went over the same ground in August.[14] As late as 12 October Miles brought it up again "at the risk of being thought repetitious on this point." The SIS should stick to subversive activities; there is no need for its people to try to get what the attachés "are supposed and potentially equipped to get—factual military data concerning the numbers, equipment, organization, training, etc. of the armies to which they are accredited."[15] Meanwhile, a bigger case of MID-FBI friction was in the making, this time in New York City.

FBI and MID: A Storm Breaks Out

On 1 July Miles had advised General Marshall, chief of staff, that there was "an immediate necessity to build up our intelligence system covering the Western Hemisphere." He explained that there was a great deal of information on the hemisphere available in the New York offices of the many large firms engaged in foreign trade, but that it was not available in Washington. Just as a New York office of MID proved useful in the last war, so also he thought, it was useful now. It should not be a part of the G-2 office of the Second Corps Area, because it had to serve MID directly.

Miles proposed that the office be established by a Lt. Col. William C. Crane, who had already looked over the situation in New York, and that Crane run it until he had time to select and train a reserve officer as a replacement. This proposal was approved by Secretary Stimson on 6 July;[16] the office was opened on 30 July. About September it was taken over by Major Frederick D. Sharp, who was soon to be at the center of a Miles-Hoover clash. Sharp, incidentally, was also the gentleman who was informed by Miles in October 1940 that he was soon to be called upon by W. S. Stephenson, "an Englishman . . . whose telephone number is Circle 6-8580."

Either reflecting or anticipating trouble, Miles sent Sharp a page and a half of guidance on the "function and scope" of the New York office. Its primary purpose was "to establish direct liaison with such business firms or individuals as may be of use to the M.I.D. in the procurement of information from abroad," and the information desired was to be military, political, geographic, and economic in character. "Occasionally," Miles wrote, "information . . . on subversive activity in foreign countries" might be sought; but the office was not to seek information on such activity in the United States, nor conduct any investigation of such activity. Any information that it did receive on this subject was to be transmitted immediately to the FBI, to MID, and, where necessary, to the G-2 of the Second Corps Area or the District Intelligence Office of the Third Naval District. Finally, the office had to use its discretion in deciding whether information on subversive activities within the United States, emanating from contacts of the New York office, be sent directly to the natural recipient—which was desirable—or be sent via the New York office.[17]

About the middle of January 1941, Sharp's contacts with American firms in New York were running into conflict with the FBI, which was similarly engaged in gathering information from firms with personnel or facilities in South America. Business firms were complaining, MID was told by E. A. Tamm and Foxworth of the FBI, that they were giving the same information to more than one agency of the government.[18] A subcommittee of the IIC then endeavored to work out a written agreement and "operational procedure" to obviate the criticisms of the business houses. The essence of this procedure was that Major Sharp would clear with the FBI before making any contact with a firm. Miles, however, rejected the idea on the ground that the FBI simply was insufficiently manned to provide Sharp with the kind of service he needed.

Miles then sought a meeting with Hoover in order to settle the matter, but Hoover was so busy with congressional hearings in the week of 27 January that this was not possible. The matter of a meeting was mentioned to Tamm again on 6 February, and on that day he relayed to Miles's representative, Lt. Col. J. A. Lester, waiting in an outer room, Hoover's answer that he "could not see how anything could be accomplished by a discussion as there is no basis for a discussion." Hoover indicated that nothing could be accomplished as long as MID insisted on going beyond the presidential directive of 24 June, that MID had to stop operating in the SIS field, and that if Miles wanted the June directive changed, he would have to take the initiative. Tamm further stated that when the "storm broke" about the operation of MID in the SIS field, Hoover had gone to the attorney general saying he did not want the SIS responsibility and was willing to give it to MID, ONI, or both.[19]

The attorney general was not the only top official now involved in the hassle. On 12 February Stimson wrote in his diary: "I also was much troubled to hear that Edgar Hoover has been making trouble at the White House over General Miles—my G-2—and Marshall is much troubled over it too as Hoover, apparently instead of coming to me, goes to the White House with his complaints and poisons the mind of the President and I am going to have a show down to it if I know the reason why [sic].[20] The next day Marshall went to Stimson "in great perturbation" because of a message he had received from the White House through General "Pa" Watson, secretary to the President, asking who General Miles's successor would be! Stimson told Marshall to tell Watson that he, Stimson, was now handling the matter, and then he began "to hustle around" to get the facts so that he was "armed and thoroughly heeled" when he did handle it.[21]

In the meantime Hoover had sent Miles a list of charges against MID. These pertained not only to the operation of Sharp's office, but also to MID activity which Hoover charged would extend "subversive coverage of the military establishment into civilian plants and life," to alleged MID dissatisfaction with the FBI's form of coverage in industrial plants, and to MID efforts, according to Hoover, to acquire information on subversion in plants directly from the plant authorities themselves.[22] This letter was taken by Marshall to Stimson, whose account of what happened follows:

> [The letter] was a very childish, petulant statement which seemed more like [from] a spoiled child than [by] a responsible officer, calling attention to all sorts of little things which ought to have been the subject of mutual collaboration and a telephone call rather than a formal letter. This same letter had been sent to the Bureau of the Budget and probably had gone to the President. I went over it carefully with one of the Assistants of G-2 and got a statement made of the respects in which the letter was erroneous—and there were many of them. And then I called up Bob Jackson, the Attorney General, and told him of my situation and asked him if he would meet me and talk it over. He was very nice about it and said he would come that afternoon and asked me to have Knox in, as he wanted to talk about a similar matter with him, so at 4:30 he and Knox and I met and went over this whole matter. I was much relieved by Jackson's attitude. He told me that he had found Hoover a most difficult person to deal with; that he quarrelled with all of Jackson's predecessors as Attorney Generals [sic] but, however had not yet quarrelled with him. We agreed that we must make another effort to establish a proper collaboration and cooperation in a matter which was likely to be most serious and of public import at any time. If there are quarrels between the three Federal Agencies which the people are relying on to protect them against sabotage, just as we are entering on this great development of munitions, we are likely to have a great deal of trouble. Well, the cooperation of my two colleagues was so good that I felt very much relieved and am looking forward to my interview with the President with more hope.[23]

Apparently Stimson did not or was not able to get in touch with the President, but the intervention of higher authorities seems to have had the usual stabilizing effect. Miles took strong exception to some language and ideas in a proposed outline of operational procedures and denied that business firms had been complaining about duplication but concluded that "M.I.D. would be glad to cooperate with F.B.I. and O.N.I. in the New York Area (which is the crux of the subject under discussion) to the extent of free exchange of information and consultation on contacts." He added the two important provisos, however, that the three agencies had to maintain offices so located as to facilitate the work and "that such cooperation is on the basis of equality and implies no recognition of the primacy of any agency in responsibility, function or operation."[24]

This seems to have been the basis on which the disagreement was papered over, for thereafter there were regular meetings in New York of the local representatives of the FBI, MID, and of ONI, whose representative, Wallace B. Phillips, will be discussed shortly, and of the army and navy district offices. A meeting on 7 March may have been the first of these. On 10 March, Sharp, writing to Miles, referred to "the meeting in the F.B.I. office between the various branches of the service." Those present included D. E. Sackett, head of the New York office of the FBI, Captain Roscoe C. MacFall, the ONI chief, Colonel Frank Ross, G-2 from Governors Island, and "Mr. Soucy, head of the Baltimore Office, F.B.I. (who, it is understood, will hereafter be in close liaison with Mr. Phillips and myself), and four other members of the F.B.I. from cities adjacent to New York."

Upon Sackett's request, Sharp outlined the work of his office, the information sought, and named some of his contacts. He explained that, operating under a directive, he had made preliminary arrangements with Pan American Airways and American Export Lines to meet incoming planes and boats in order to interview arrivals from foreign countries. He assured the group he was doing nothing in the subversive field other than forwarding whatever information came unsolicited to him. He also explained a program of reviewing manuscripts and magazines for "certain static information" of interest to the War Department. Finally, in response to his pointed queries, the group assured him that his activity did not duplicate or interfere with their work.[25]

If this local interdepartmental intelligence conference thought it now had control of the situation, it had another thought coming. Just as President Roosevelt had installed an engine, in the person of Assistant Secretary Messersmith, into the IIC in Washington, so also was he about to install—to everyone's surprise—an engine in the New York local, and this in the person of Commander Vincent Astor, United States Naval Reserve.[26] To see how this happened, it is first necessary to see what the navy was doing in New York throughout this changing and somewhat turbulent period.

More Trouble: ONI and Vincent Astor

Admiral Anderson, like Hoover and Miles, was very much aware of the need for getting not only more information but also more sources of information. The international situation had obvious grim implications for the navy at home and abroad. Anderson had been a vigorous advocate of the establishment of the SIS, especially in South America. At the time of its authorization, he had told the IIC that he had already commenced a program of sending out retired officers to seaports in order to get acquainted with shipping operations, industrial conditions, and important persons who could supply needed information in times of emergency.[27]

Anderson went even further and established his own SIS, but years later was to remark that "it never got off the ground, because it was taken over by Donovan's outfit."[28] Actually it did get off the ground, although it did not go far; and it was not "taken over" by Donovan so much as it was accepted by him when the military decided late in 1941 that the new COI should run the "undercover" or "secret" intelligence service.[29] In any case, Anderson, in December 1940, hired Wallace B. Phillips, a civilian, to work as his special assistant in the development of an undercover intelligence service.[30]

Phillips was an American businessman who was a long resident of London and active in American circles there. He had been in the American Red Cross in 1940 when its representative there was David K. E. Bruce, who was to play a leading role in COI and OSS affairs in London. Phillips was authorized by Anderson, who wrote of this to Miles, to establish an office in New York as a "representative of the Director of Naval Intelligence in matters relating to its Foreign Intelligence Service." Since Phillips's work in the domestic field was strictly confined to its relevancy to his "primary duties" in the foreign field, Anderson thought it would be desirable for Phillips to be in close contact with Sharp. They had already, in fact, been in contact, and Phillips had learned that Sharp had space for him in his office and was willing to take him in. Would the assistant chief of staff agree to this arrangement?[31]

Miles, a day later, was "glad" to oblige.[32] By 6 February Phillips, now described as "a representative of the Special Intelligence Service of the Division of Naval Intelligence," had two offices: one with Sharp at 1270 Sixth Avenue, and the other with the district intelligence office of the Third Naval District.[33]

Miles next informed G-2 in New York, Colonel Ross, that "Mr. Wallace Phillips, whom I knew as one of the leading American businessmen in London, is now doing some important work for the Navy Department, and plans to have an office in cooperation with Major Sharp." Ross was informed that he would be called on by Phillips who could be relied on "implicitly."[34]

There was bound to be some confusion about activity. When Sharp explained to the local intelligence group on 7 March that he was interviewing new arrivals from foreign countries, Captain MacFall of ONI said that Phillips "also had this type of project under consideration." Phillips informed Sharp that that was so, and that the two of them should work to avoid "possible overlapping."[35] But Miles had learned differently from Anderson's successor as DNI, Captain Alan Kirk, who had been naval attaché in London during Donovan's first trip. According to Kirk, it was MacFall who was to contact incoming travelers and Phillips was to work "solely with special agents in the field." Miles instructed Sharp accordingly,[36] and that disposed of any possible conflict between MID and ONI. However, Phillips was soon to run into real opposition from a new quarter, Vincent Astor, and while it takes us ahead of the story, it is better to consider this Astor episode before reviewing Astor's appointment as "area controller" for New York.

As far back as January, when Phillips had barely gotten to work, Astor was making an inquiry at the White House about him and his activity.[37] As soon as Astor got a handle on his new assignment, he wrote the following, in longhand, to the President, then at Hyde Park:

> One might suppose that I would leave you in peace while trying to get a rest in Hyde Park. However, here is a situation which I do not feel justified in keeping from you, for if it went wrong I believe it could result in a real scandal and be just what the isolationists would like.
>
> The situation concerns a
>
> Mr. Wallace Phillips
>
> who has lived most of his life—at least since the last war—in England.
>
> He claims to be very rich and to be great friends of Churchill and most of his war cabinet. Mr. P. apparently offered his services to British Intelligence, was turned down, and came to this country last autumn.
>
> Admiral Anderson then gave him a job in o.n.i. on a "$1 a year" basis and *without* a commission.
>
> About two months ago, the #1 man in British Intelligence came to me and F.B.I. with the following story—Sir William Wiseman had approached him and requested that he be taken back into the British service,[38] in which event he could supply valuable information obtained from a Mr. Phillips who claimed that he
>
> (a) had frequent contacts with you. [The President]
> (b) was a great friend of Edgar Hoover who gave him the run of F.B.I. files.
> (c) had access to M.I.D., O.N.I. and F.B.I. files in New York.

(a) and (b) I found to be untrue. (c) was largely true until ten days ago when I made some changes.

Phillips of course had made a very bad blunder in going to Wiseman, who is not now well regarded by the British, so I decided to keep aware of Phillips. For various reasons this proved almost impossible until ten days ago when you enlarged my responsibilities.[39]

Since then I have discovered the following from P. himself.

(a) He has entire charge of expenditures of the Navy's "Secret" fund (about $100,000).

(b) He alone selects agents to be sent abroad.

(c) He refuses to allow F.B.I. to check these men.

(d) In my opinion he pays his agents exorbitantly ($4000–$6000 per year, plus $10 per day, plus travel expenses).

What worries me is that all this is being done by a man who has no commission but only an appointment from a former Director of O.N.I.

I doubt if any dollar a year man should have authority to pay out secret funds, no matter how able he might be, and that would be especially true if he had lived most of his life in England and boasted of his English government friends.

Furthermore, in my opinion for what it's worth, Mr. P. is unreliable in his statements, indiscreet, and a social climber, which is a dangerous combination for one in his position.

I have reported the whole matter to Admiral Andrews (3rd Dist) who is just as worried as am I.

We took some action last Monday which didn't work. Before we try something new, I would like more than anything your advice, if only just 5 minutes worth. So, would you let me drive up to Hyde Park tomorrow (Monday) morning arriving at absolutely any time you say? I promise by all that's holy not to stay a moment longer than you wish.

Signing it "Respectfully, Vincent," he added a P.S.:

If Grace [Tully] could send me a message back by the car that brings this, or call me at home, of course I'd appreciate it. I shall be home all evening at Regent 7-2176.[40] (Emphasis in the original.)

Two days later, and there is no indication as to whether he did or did not see the President on Monday, he wrote much of the same to Captain Kirk in Washington. He referred to the fact that Admiral Andrews had sent Captain MacFall to Washington the preceding week, and presumably this is the "action" which "didn't work." What he particularly stressed with Kirk was the very real possibility that some newsman would get hold of the story, and as a publisher (of *Newsweek*), Astor assured Kirk that only the publisher's right to hire and fire could discourage an editor from printing the story.[41]

On 10 May Admiral Andrews took the problem of Phillips to Admiral Stark, the chief of naval operations. Phillips, he wrote, "is not the man in any way for this job and his services should be discontinued at once"; and if he had to have a successor, Andrews had available "a man of higher caliber, of better attributes to fill the job," although he did not name him.[42] In reply, Stark informed Andrews that "you should know that ONI, with the approval and knowledge of the Secretary and others, is attempting to create what we call here 'a Special Intelligence Service'." Stark went on to defend the loyalty, patriotism, and integrity of Phillips, and concluded that "Colonel Knox has determined to continue Mr. Phillips on duty."[43]

With that the Phillips question was disposed of. What makes Phillips particularly interesting to future COI developments is that he and his group of thirteen agents constituted the first COI personnel specifically organized for secret intelligence work abroad. This group was moved into COI about 15 October 1941, and Phillips was asked to prepare his recommendations as to how undercover work abroad should be organized.

Now to return to Astor and how he became "Area Controller for the New York Area" as FDR's solution to the problem of coordinating intelligence, at least in New York.

Astor Is Put in Charge

Long before the spring of 1941 Vincent Astor—multimillionaire, real estate investor, magazine publisher, ardent yachtsman, and neighbor of the Roosevelts—had been on the friendliest of terms with the President of the United States. They had first met as boys, when Franklin was at Hyde Park and Vincent just up Route 9 at Rhinebeck. They were brought together largely because Roosevelt's half-brother James served as one of the executors of the estate of Vincent Astor's father. After FDR's crippling illness, the Astor swimming pool was made available to him. The friendship, however, lay dormant until Roosevelt became governor of New York in 1928. Astor then became his enthusiastic supporter, and undoubtedly contributed generously to his campaigns.

As President-elect, FDR took his first cruise on Astor's well-known, luxurious yacht, the *Nourmahal*, and took several more in following years.[44] The yacht gave rise to "the *Nourmahal* club" about which there are scattered items in the Astor-Roosevelt papers but not enough to give a clear picture of either the membership or the major purpose. Yachting was a bond between FDR and Astor, and just as importantly, perhaps, yachting also brought Astor and ONI into close contact over the years. He had turned the

Nourmahal over to the navy in both wars;[45] but in between them he piloted it around the West Indies, along the Ecuadorean coast, and among Pacific islands, often after consultation with ONI and FDR. In 1938, for instance, he wrote FDR that he would be coming to Washington to see him and also to talk to ONI about a "planned voyage . . . in the vicinity of the Marshall Islands. If that is practicable, it should prove interesting."[46]

Business also provided a link with FDR. In this respect, Astor began, somewhere along the line, acting like a one-man intelligence unit for the President. On 5 February 1940 he sent FDR a long list of individual Russian payments made to various U.S. manufacturers as shown by Amtorg's weekly drawings on the Chase National Bank.[47] In April he was reporting to the President the possibility of obtaining "valuable information" as the result of a recent Japanese approach to Chase's Winthrop Aldrich; all that was needed was the "cooperation and encouragement" of the Department of State. At the same time he was complaining to FDR, as has been mentioned, that State had quashed FBI contacts with the British intelligence chief, Sir James Paget.[48]

In May–June 1940 he played a major role in a case, whose lineaments are not clear, which involved facilitating the return to the United States of the wife and mother-in-law of Carl L. Norden, inventor of the bomb sight. Apparently an FBI agent was to accompany Norden to Europe on the SS *Washington*, a vessel owned or controlled by Astor, but there was some fear that Norden and the agent would be taken off the vessel by British authorities at Gibraltar. Astor wrote FDR that he had told Hoover the President "wished" him to send the agent with Norden and "to go ahead" and do it. Astor also arranged for "an FBI code book to be put aboard in the custody of the Captain's safe." Furthermore, he let State know that the President was "interested" in the issuance of a passport, whether Norden's or the agent's is not clear. Finally Astor reported to the President how he had held up the sailing of the *Washington* pending "the arrival of a fake bag to go aboard right after our agent," and how this ruse fooled the newsmen who were inquiring about the ship's delay.[49]

No sooner was this accomplished than Astor was asking FDR about having his naval aide, Captain Callaghan, arrange for him, Astor, to see Admiral Stark. He realized that Stark "may be cross on account of the Norden incident . . . and therefore put off seeing me. I hope he doesn't for there is so much to be done, and maybe not too much time."[50] At the end of June Roosevelt sent Stark a memo advising him that Astor would be in to see him: "I simply wanted to let you know that I have requested him to coordinate the Intelligence work in the New York area and, of course, want him given every assistance." He spoke highly of Astor's "wide knowledge of men and affairs in connection with general Intelligence work. Please pass this on to Walter Anderson."[51]

The DNI promptly had Astor called back into service on an inactive status. When navy personnel balked on doing that, Anderson simply said the President wanted it done. Period.[52] Astor reported to the President late in December that orders had been issued "which will make it possible for me to do a job in Bermuda,"[53] where, incidentally, he had a fine home and was well known in the island's yachting circles. Early in February he was telling Assistant Secretary of State Berle, at the direction of the President, that he had three things on his mind: first, passport control between the United States and Bermuda, now that a U.S. base was being built there, ought to be instituted immediately; second, one or two FBI agents ought to be put in the construction gang at work on the base; and, third, he was "worried about the entire intelligence situation" and wanted to talk with Berle about it on another occasion. Secretary Berle concluded his memorandum of conversation with: "I gather that he is reporting directly to the President."[54]

This was on 7 February, and it was then that the Miles-Hoover clash was spilling over into the offices of the secretary of war, the attorney general, and the President. On 8 March, Astor, as often happened, had lunch at the White House; and later that afternoon, he, Berle, and Kirk met with the President and discussed the subject of Astor—already intelligence coordinator in New York—getting new authority for resolving the situation in the city.[55] On 12 March Kirk sent Callaghan a draft of an order that had been approved by Berle. Two days later this was sent to FDR, who, on 19 March telegraphed his approval from Fayetteville, North Carolina.[56] New York had a newly strengthened coordinator of intelligence just like that.

The directive indicated that "all intelligence and investigational activities undertaken in the New York Area" by FBI, MID, ONI, and State "shall be coordinated through a single agency—to be known as the Area Controller." The controller was to act as a "clearinghouse for problems," and was to "assign priorities and responsibility for the various problems" that the agency representatives were to lay before him. Hopefully, this new system would coordinate the agencies' activities and eliminate duplication.[57]

The directive also indicated that it had been issued "with the concurrence of the Departments concerned," but General Miles was quick to point out to General Marshall: "It is not known who gave the concurrence of the War Department." He said that he had heard "rumors of the possibility of such a step being taken," but he knew very little of the background.[58] Stimson did not learn of it until 25 March when he noted: "This was news to me, and I am in a good deal of doubt as to whether it is a good piece of good administration or bad administration."[59] The rest of March was taken up with Miles, Hoover, Kirk, and Astor working out the guidelines under which the agencies were now to operate in New York. On 3 April Astor felt able to inform FDR: "The position of 'Controller' of certain activities in the New York area . . . is now practically established."[60]

There is no need here to follow later developments of the New York situation or the role of Astor therein except to note some comments made months later by Major Sharp, who had, of course, been an early, active participant in the weekly meetings that were now chaired by Astor. In August 1942, he was telling an MID official of the New York setup: "These conferences are a bore . . . a great waste of time. However . . . Astor must have a job. . . . Vincent Astor, for your information, *stands very close to the great white father,* so proceed but with caution."[61] Three months later, he was going over much of the same ground with another high MID official and gave him this assessment of the early period:

> There was a definite need for some sort of coordination during the early days of this office—from September until about December 1940. At that time there was a great deal of misapprehension and misconception as to the sometimes overlapping directives of all the intelligence agencies in the New York field. This confusion was entirely straightened out, however, among ourselves, prior to the advent of the Area Controller. General Miles stated to me privately and confidentially that this thing had been forced upon him and that it was up to me to exercise the utmost diplomacy and tact in getting along with the Area Controller, and avoiding any possibility of having it said that General Miles' organization was not cooperating. This I have done so far.[62]

G-2 Again: How to Control Donovan

However jaundiced Sharp's view of the Astor position, it seems clear from hindsight that the New York situation was a clear, if unnecessary, reminder to the President of the unfinished character of the assignment he had given George Messersmith two years earlier. Hence, he returned to the problem— and many other more pressing ones—after ten days of cruising on the USS *Potomac* and just two weeks after he made Astor "Area Controller."

He had an IIC in Washington run by an assistant secretary of state and a junior IIC in New York run by an "Area Controller," but, as he told the Cabinet on 4 April, he wanted something more:

> The discussion of the conflict of the three intelligence agencies of the Government came up, viz: MID, ONI, and FBI, and all parties to the

discussion seemed to admit that a certain amount of twilight zone was inevitable and the problem was the solution of that without friction. The President suggested that he recollected that in France the jurisdiction was subdivided into three parts:

(1) G-2 Military Intelligence.

(2) The civilian agency for prosecution, the "Sureté."

(3) Over the twilight zone area, a joint board.

He also stated that the twilight zone was covered and disputes were settled in Great Britain by a gentleman known as "Mr. X," whose identity was kept a complete secret. He asked if our agencies would not confer as to the institution of a similar solution for our country in case we got into war.[63]

When this report of the President's wish reached General Miles, it very quickly, if not immediately, brought to mind the name of Colonel Donovan, for it was on this occasion, on 8 April, that he warned General Marshall that he had learned "in great confidence" from ONI that Donovan was fostering a movement to set up a "super agency" to control all intelligence.

Just as quickly he offered his recommendation for warding off this "disadvantageous, if not calamitous" prospect. Indeed, he had already "consulted both F.B.I. and O.N.I. on this matter," and they apparently concurred in his belief that "Col. Wm [sic] Donovan's name should be proposed to the President as the coordinator between the three intelligence agencies in any conflict which may arise *within the field of counter subversion* (prevention of sabotage and espionage)." He went on to say that the proposal of Donovan for the position the President had in mind "should . . . clearly indicate a limitation of his field of activities to counter subversion." This was the only field, he explained, in which "conflicts between the three intelligence agencies can arise"; and even here, he added, there has been "very little real conflict"—thanks to the agreement of the last summer which "I drafted."

Miles then attached to his memorandum the draft of a letter to be sent to the President, after it had been concurred in by the secretary of war and the attorney general. This embodied his nomination of Donovan for what amounted to an "Area Controller" on the national level. The letter suggested to the President that "the instructions under which the referee would act . . . be carefully drawn, in the first instance by the three intelligence agencies for the approval of the three Cabinet officers and for submission to you." He explained that the agencies' qualification for drawing up these instructions had already been manifested by their successful negotiation of the 1940 agreement whereby, he said, "the twilight zone" had been reduced as much as it could be.[64]

As will be shown, this particular proposal never did reach the President. Whether it would have been acceptable to him is conjectural. Certainly as far as Donovan personally was concerned, it would have been laughed out of court. In any case, with the linking of Donovan's name to the President's request of 4 April, the fat was really in the fire.

8

·—·—·—

A Green Light
on COI

DONOVAN'S ACCOUNT OF THE ESTABLISHMENT OF COI IS SUCCINCT, but it is also devoid of enlightening detail and not without some confusion. In September 1943, he wrote: "Five months prior to the outbreak of war, a Committee of Cabinet members was appointed by the President to enquire into the matter [of an independent intelligence service]. That committee consulted with the writer of this paper who studied the problem, and prepared a report with certain recommendations which were accepted and put into effect by Presidential order."[1]

Two months later, he told a war college audience: "When I came back, I found that there had been a committee of the Cabinet appointed to look into the intelligence situation . . . so that a Cabinet committee had been appointed to enquire into it. They talked with me and I made certain suggestions. As a result of that, there was set up what was called the Coordinator of Information."[2]

The element of time is not clear in these accounts. "Five months prior to the outbreak of war"—that is, about 7 June—a committee was formed; on the other hand, "When I came back"—18 March—"I found . . . a committee had been appointed." There is no explanation of why the committee consulted *him*. Nor, interestingly enough, is anything said about the President. To try to straighten out the time, as well as reconstruct the event, one must begin with Donovan's return home on 18 March.

Cabinet Consults Donovan

On that date Knox informed the White House by phone that Donovan had landed in New York, and General Edwin "Pa" Watson then asked the President whether he wanted to see Donovan before they left the next day on their cruise on the USS *Potomac*. Knox was told the President would see Donovan for fifteen minutes the next morning, Wednesday, the nineteenth.[3] Knox, of course, accompanied Donovan to the White House; also present was Harry Hopkins, and the fifteen minutes apparently ran from 9:30 to 10:30.[4] What did they talk about? Aside from small and unrelated talk—and that could have been considerable,[5] the emphasis, with or without Hopkins present, must have been on the Balkan situation, the British problem in Greece, and the very pressing question of shipping—with which Donovan himself, as will be seen shortly, was both deeply and personally involved. The presence of Hopkins, whom Sherwood described as "the recognized and designated representative of the President in all considerations of production, transportation, raw materials, priorities, allocation, etc.,"[6] strongly suggests that shipping and supplies must have taken up much of the hour. It has been said that when Donovan "reported [to the President] on his mission to the Mediterranean," he "suggested the creation of a new agency" to carry out these five special functions: open, or "white," propaganda, "secret, or 'black,' psychological-political warfare," sabotage and guerrilla warfare, special intelligence, and strategic planning.[7] In the time at hand, Donovan could hardly have gone into these subjects in any detail.

The President left town that afternoon by train—and it was from North Carolina that he sent back his approval of Astor for the New York job—and set sail from Florida the next day for a cruise which kept him away from Washington until the morning of 1 April. During his vacation "the President . . . studiously avoided doing any more official work than was absolutely necessary."[8] Did he see Donovan between his return and the Cabinet meeting on 4 April? There is no evidence on the point, and one is left wondering whether Donovan figured at all in the President's mind when he discussed the friction among the investigative agencies.

While the President was relaxing—fishing, fixing up his stamps, playing poker, enjoying cocktails and dinner with Watson, Ickes, Hopkins, Jackson, Dr. McIntire, and Steve Early—Donovan was caught up in the Washington whirl of briefings and getting things done. He had already been with Knox. Next he was at the War Department visiting Stimson; "We talked for an hour, or an hour and a half, and it was very interesting," noted the secretary. Donovan has "played quite an important part diplomatically in the situation during his trip, and he and I stood over the map for a long time talking only in the way in which two old friends who are both interested in military affairs can do it." Donovan's talk, while it did not develop anything new, observed the secretary, "was rather encouraging to me and he looks at the whole situation just as I do. He thinks we should begin now to convoy the British shipping—the situation which is the blackest spot now in the big panorama of action."[9]

The next morning, at Stimson's invitation, he addressed "the Officers of our Department" and gave them the account of the trip to which reference has been made in Chapter 6. He concluded with strong emphasis on shipping as "the dominant point" on which the British had to decide whether to cut down on food or on the munitions of war. If they allowed their food stocks to be depleted, "the food situation for England will be a very serious one in the early winter of this year." For the United States this situation posed the question of allowing our supplies "to go down the drain" or of protecting them en route.[10]

In the meantime, Donovan was so wrapped up in this problem that Henry Morgenthau thought he had taken over Hopkins's responsibilities while Harry was cruising in the Bahamas. That is what the secretary of the treasury told his staff at a meeting on 20 March. Philip Young heard it differently; he "understood Donovan to say this morning he was just taking over on this Middle Eastern list which he had, not on the broader problem." The secretary countered: "Well, certainly when Donovan left here, I gathered from him that the matter is entirely in his hands," and so Morgenthau ordered that he be given all the help he needed.

At this point, the secretary paid fitting tribute to the colonel: "He is the first man I have talked to that I would be willing to really back. I saw what he did last summer. But what I said still holds true. Anything you can do to help him, because he certainly is—[sic] he has been for a week actually in the trenches up in Albania. He was down in Libya when they took that last town, whatever the last town was. He was with Wavell for over a week. He was with Eden in Cairo. He has been twice in England. He has been in Spain and he has been in Portugal. I think he knows more about the situation than anybody I have talked to by about a thousand percent. And he is not discouraged."

To all this Harry Dexter White commented: "That is all good preparation for Washington." When asked to explain, he replied: "I mean, he ought to be at home in all the fighting that is going on." To this the secretary said: "Well, he is a fighter, don't worry."[11]

On 22 March Donovan told General Marshall that he had gotten on well with the G-2 of Wavell's forces, and this officer had suggested that he would be happy to explain their intelligence procedure to an American intelligence officer. Marshall then relayed this information to General Miles with the suggestion that he get in touch with Donovan. To this Miles replied that Donovan had given "me the same information."[12] Donovan also had already had "a long talk . . . with officers of this Division."[13]

On 25 March Donovan accompanied Secretary Knox to a two-hour meeting with Stimson, Marshall, and Stark, on the one hand, and a British delegation of Admiral R. M. Bellairs, Captain Victor Danckwerts, General E. L. Morris, and Air Commodore J. C. Slessor, on the other. These were the officers then in the United States for a very secret, prolonged round of Anglo-American staff talks. On this occasion, they had, according to Stimson, a "rather effective and interesting" discussion of escort duty, the British food shortage, and methods of convoy.[14]

About the same time, Donovan received help from Archibald MacLeish of the Library of Congress on the speech that he was to give to the nation on a nationwide hookup of the three networks on 26 March.[15] He gave the people essentially the same country-by-country report he had given the officers of the War Department; but more importantly from the point of view of those who favored strong action in support of Britain, he argued vigorously that America was not actually threatened only because Britain was not beaten. He warned that aiding Britain meant making certain that the goods we made available actually got there. With obvious reference to the controversial point of escort duty and convoys, he asked, "Are we going to deliver the goods?"[16]

He had any number of odd jobs to take care of for other people. Britain's director of postal and telegraph censorship had given him a problem to take up with the State Department. So also Lord Swinton had asked him to do something about the subversion of British crews in the United States. In Ankara he picked up three items to take up with the navy: sending Turkish officers to Annapolis for some training; stationing a navy radio man in Istanbul or Ankara in order to receive daily State Department releases; and accrediting the naval attaché in Turkey to Greece also. In Madrid he was asked to do something about strengthening the naval attaché system in Spain and Portugal. In London he was asked to urge "Mr. Hoover's F.B.I. [to] get after" one Isidore Lazarus, alias Lee Lane, a Rumanian Jew then in prison in the United States, and get from him the story of his collaboration with top Nazis and of his "fleecing" of Jews who wanted to leave Germany.[17]

That the President's committee consulted him is not surprising. He had studied the Fifth Column and written on it. He had talked with Britain's intelligence chiefs and seen some of their problems, their operations, and their training establishments. He had seen commandos, guerrillas, and parachutists. He had collected more raw intelligence from more sources in more places than perhaps anyone on the scene, and he continually related all this data to strategy and tactics, to the problem at hand, to defense and victory. Perhaps the committee of Cabinet members "consulted" him, but his very activity invited that consultation.

The "consultation" took place at one of those meals, this time a luncheon,[18] which Donovan was in the habit of hosting as a standard way of doing business. This probably occurred shortly after his return, although the opening quotation in this chapter seems to link it closely with his report of 10 June. Other than holding this meeting, the committee seems to have been a casual thing. The President never mentioned it again or called for a report. There is no mention of it in either the Stimson papers or *The Secret Diary of Harold L. Ickes*. One exception to these assertions will be noted shortly.

After Stimson passed his notes on the 4 April Cabinet meeting to Marshall, the latter passed them on to Miles with the suggestion that he prepare a study for the secretary "in case the question again arose."[19] It was this suggestion which brought forth Miles's proposal of 8 April to make Donovan coordinator in countersubversion cases. This was sent on to Stimson. A note, apparently written by John J. McCloy, reminded Stimson that he had read Miles's report but had "not acted on it" and suggested that it be brought up at the Cabinet meeting on 25 April.[20] Nothing came of this.

One member of the committee specifically consulted Donovan, and not surprisingly that was Knox. For the secretary, Donovan wrote a four-page document which is significant in that it is Donovan's first paper on intelligence, at least the first that has been found. The purpose was to describe "the instrumentality through which the British Government gathers its intelligence." He laid down basic principles which should guide in the establishment and operation of such an organization in the United States: first, it should be above party; second, it should be controlled by the President; third, it should have its own secret funds; fourth, it should not take over the duties of MID, ONI, or FBI; fifth its functions should include sole charge of intelligence work abroad, the coordination of the activities of the military and naval attachés abroad, and classification and interpretation of all intelligence for the President; and lastly, the organization should have an advisory committee of the secretaries of War, Navy, State, Treasury, and the attorney general.

Having outlined these principles, Donovan then added the reminder that he had been speaking of intelligence in the narrow sense. Modern war, he said, operates on more fronts than battle fronts. Here he referred specifically to communications in the sense of "the interception and inspection (commonly and erroneously called censorship) of mail and cables; the interception of radio communication; the use of propaganda; and the direction of subversive operations." To this list he added the covering line: "On all of these factors I have obtained first hand information which I think better not to set down here." He finally returned, at much greater length, to a description of the British system, which he broke down into two parts: the production sections corresponding to such departments of government as Foreign Office, War Office, and Home Office, and the distribution sections, which organized intelligence work abroad.[21]

Thus by the end of April the subject had been formally treated by Donovan, but also by that time it seemed to have died on the vine. The reasons will explain the role of Stephenson at this time.

FDR's Other Problems

Contrary to what Miles seemed to say or imply, Donovan personally had no desire to run a new organization, unless it were a commando or guerilla organization. He still wanted to lead troops, and, fresh from Grecian and Libyan fronts, he felt the desire strongly. Stephenson has insisted that Donovan stoutly resisted the idea that he himself should run the organization which Stephenson envisaged as an American counterpart to his own BSC. Those who knew Donovan well insist that he never would have asked for anything like that for himself.[22]

The committee may well have felt that the situation which provoked the President's query on 4 April had been resolved. Stimson, for instance, was sitting on Miles's memorandum. On 12 May, the secretary and Jackson discussed the state of relations between G-2 and the FBI, and both agreed that there was no longer any friction between Miles and Hoover. Stimson added that in that case he was not going to replace Miles, who, he thought, was doing "very good work in all the organizational duties" of MID, and Jackson agreed with that conclusion. On 20 May he told the President the same thing, and the President agreed with his decision to keep Miles.[23]

For his part, the President never seems to have been really seized of the problem. He saw it as a problem of reducing "the twilight zone," whereas what Stephenson had in mind was an organization to conduct worldwide, offensive, clandestine operations, and what Donovan had in mind was even larger in conception, an organization that would include operations, the coordination of intelligence, and even strategic planning. When Miles and Hoover were pacified, the President had to be sold the new idea of a "coordinator."

The President's position, in the spring of 1941, was also greatly conditioned by other factors and problems which seized him and his Cabinet officers. In truth, some of the Cabinet thought he was not sufficiently seized of the problems. When Stimson and Jackson were agreeing that relations between G-2 and the FBI had improved, they were also agreeing, along with Knox and Ickes who were present, on "the general apprehension on our part about the indecision and lack of leadership of the whole war movement—the whole crisis."[24]

That crisis was the worsening position of Britain, the President's indecision, and the confused mood of the people. Britain had suffered military reverses in the Middle East, and following the passage of Lend-Lease the Germans struck hard at merchant shipping. The President seemed to do nothing: he had been on a cruise; he had then been incapacitated by a lingering low-grade infection; if he was not ill, he was inaccessible except, grumbled Ickes, to Harry Hopkins; and to the country he was enigmatic, especially when his press conference of 28 May deflated the sense of direction and action given just the night before by his declaration of an unlimited national emergency. For Roosevelt, leadership was a question of timing, and he preferred his own sense of timing to that of others; more important, perhaps, was his apparent judgment against provocative acts which, in his opinion, could only worsen the total situation.[25] Whatever the reason, despair gripped many; if he had had a voice that could influence people, Ickes would have quit the Cabinet and taken to the airwaves.[26]

The President's interest in a "referee" for the intelligence agencies was also but a small aspect of the larger problem of readying the government for defense and—if and when it came—war. The Reorganization Act of 1939, two years in the making, had set up the Executive Office of the President and thereby given FDR "the administrative flexibility essential in time of crisis."[27] With the outbreak of war, and especially after the end of the "phoney war," the President began establishing those "war agencies" which were to number 136 before the war was over. Of these, thirty-two were established before COI.[28] What this meant in the doing was the confused and controversial delimitation of new problems, new jurisdictions, and new channels of coordination, as well as the selection of the right people to run them. What else did Harry Dexter White have in mind when he spoke of "all the fighting that is going on"?

The President had just scored a great victory on 8 March when, after two months of furious national debate, the Senate finally passed the momentous Lend-Lease Act, but it was to be weeks before the new administrator, Harry Hopkins, had an agency to back him up and months before the Lend-Lease Administration was actually set up. In the meantime, the activist members of the Cabinet—Stimson, Ickes, and Knox—had been agitating and meeting to "do something" about countering the Fifth Column at home, building up the "morale" of the population, and encouraging home defense. The day the President spoke of the "twilight zone" he met with Bureau of the Budget officials on the executive order setting up the "so-called home defense activities," and the President, who had Mayor LaGuardia in mind, said he wanted at its head someone "who would attract attention as a good ballyhoo artist and speechmaker." Smith of the Budget, who noted the President was talking about details, pointed out that what was needed was "some leadership in the Federal government for this whole field."[29]

This subject brought up the name of Donovan. On 17 April, the Budget people discussed the draft order for civil defense with FDR a second time. They "tossed in some names from a list that we had made up. The only name that clicked to some extent with the President was that of Bill Donovan."[30] Later that same day, at the Cabinet meeting, Stimson again brought up "the question of a bureau for constructive counterespionage work," and Donovan was mentioned as a possibility along with Frank Bane, Edgar Ansel Mowrer, Max Gardner, Ambassador Bullitt, and LaGuardia. Finally, Vice President Wallace was asked to act as temporary chairman of the bureau.[31] Eventually, on 20 May, the Office of Civil Defense was established with LaGuardia at its head.

Without going into all the details of the other problems and organizational activities gripping the President and his Cabinet, suffice it to say that Donovan's plan was not high on their list at this time. The same is not necessarily true, however, of MID, ONI, and the FBI, which were still seized of the implications of the 4 April request of the President, Donovan's plan, and a new proposal for a Joint Intelligence Committee.

Opposition to a Coordinator

On 27 March, a week after Donovan's return, the former military attaché in London, Colonel (now Brigadier General) Lee prepared, at Marshall's direction, a proposal for the establishment of a "Joint Intelligence Committee." Gen. Lee's proposal was born of his experience in London, where he saw the mounting pile of information flowing out of the city into Washington and the incoming requests from Washington for information on the developing situation. Lee saw clearly that some new mechanism for the coordination of information was necessary, and he thought a JIC was the solution.[32]

His proposal was forwarded to Marshall by Miles with a covering memorandum. The gist of this was that Miles agreed with Lee's definition of the problem; he referred to the fact, for instance, that MID had never seen the cables that Donovan had sent in; but he thought Lee's proposal would erect an organization that would dwarf anything in existence and would simply compound rather than solve the problem. Hence he proposed instead that the agencies concerned with this problem get together and work out some solution. He therefore drafted for the secretary a letter to be sent to eight agencies: State, Treasury, Navy, Commerce, Office of Emergency Management, Administrator for Export Control, Office of Production Management, and the Maritime Commission.[33]

Meetings were held on 5, 19, and 26 May. Discussion centered on information coming from the British Empire, and the proposal was made that each agency set up a "clearing house" for the exchange of information. The representative from State reported to Under Secretary Welles that he thought MID was engaged in "a fishing expedition," and "several other representatives" agreed with him. In other words, MID was satisfied with the present system of liaison but wanted it extended "to see if it could obtain additional and more expeditious information" from the other agencies.[34]

The recommendations that issued from these meetings and were drafted and redrafted throughout June are a masterly example of taking much time to do nothing. In forwarding the second draft, Miles, on 17 June, rather apologetically admitted that what was being proposed, while "a distinct improvement," was the maximum that now could be attained. With obvious reference to Donovan, he wrote: "There is, I understand, some advocacy of much more radical steps . . . to correct the present lack of systematic liaison between the various agencies."[35] The recommendations, which were finally agreed upon by the committee on 7 July, established a system whereby each agency retained complete control of its own information, released whatever it wanted, designated one or more offices within the agency as the "clearing house" for exchange with other agencies, and agreed on the definition of "secret," "confidential," and "restricted."[36]

Just to complete the record, Lee's original proposal of a Joint Intelligence Committee was not completely lost in the shuffle of paper that produced this agreement. On 12 June the British Military Mission in Washington established a local JIC to correspond to the JIC in London; W. S. Stephenson was one of the seven members on the committee.[37] On 23 June Admiral Stark forwarded to Knox a detailed report on the London JIC: "Translating this British set-up into our own organization would make such a JIC responsible, in effect, to the Joint Board." On 14 July Miles and Kirk recommended the establishment of a JIC[38] in a move calculated "to forestall intrusion into such privileged matters by the President's Coordinator of Information, 'Wild Bill' Donovan."[39]

Meanwhile, the IIC was busily defending its garrison. On 15 May Miles, Hoover, and Kirk signed a report on their joint coverage of "the field of espionage, sabotage, counterespionage, subversive activities, and violations of the Neutrality Act." At their meeting on 21 May, it was agreed the report would be sent to the President, and so the next day it was forwarded to "Pa" Watson by Hoover in the belief that the President "would be interested in the carefully coordinated program presently being carried out" by MID, ONI, and the FBI.[40]

That same day Miles wrote Marshall that the IIC had agreed that a coordinator for the three services was not needed, that such an officer, if not restricted to the role of "referee," would be a "positive detriment" to the services' work, and that "there is every reason to believe that a coordinator named by the President would attempt to operate in the entire field of intelligence. This would mean that he would to a large extent control the collection and evaluation of military and naval intelligence required by the two armed services, a highly undesirable state of affairs." Miles recommended therefore that "no steps be taken in this matter unless the President again revives his project," and that if he does revive it, then it should be "discouraged" by the three Cabinet officers concerned. Finally, if worst comes to worst, then the coordinator must have no control over military information and must be restricted to the role of referee in countersubversion cases.[41]

Just to make certain that their position was clear, the three signed another joint memorandum on 29 May. Their review of two years' work under the directive of 26 June 1939 left them with the "considered opinion" that "coordination between the three Services is working satisfactorily. The inevitable 'twilight zone' . . . has been progressively narrowed." They further agreed that the "useful role" of a coordinator could only apply to "the now almost non-existent" cases of a conflict of authority in the countersubversive field. Moreover, they stressed that a coordinator would get in the way of the agencies' separate activities that lie outside "the scope of their coordinated activities." Their concluding sentence was unequivocal: "The appointment of a Coordinator of the three Intelligence Services is unnecessary and would entail great complication in, if not serious detriment to the National Service, [sic] while offering only negligible advantages."[42]

Stephenson "Manoeuvres"

They were not tilting with a windmill. On 5 May Stephenson had cabled Menzies that he had been "attempting to manoeuvre Donovan into accepting the job of co-ordinating all U.S. intelligence." SIS has described this telegram as "the first actual reference" to Stephenson's efforts in this direction.[42]

Years later, Sir William recalled that "in April of 1941" Roosevelt had begun to give some thought to expanding American secret activities, but "no decision was made for some time despite various pressures." Stephenson said he had "enlisted the help of several avenues of influence at the White House. Winant and Sherwood were the most persistent and effective, I think. There were others who kept the subject alive. Vincent Astor is one who comes to mind."[44]

At the same time, Stephenson was encountering opposition from certain London quarters which were animated by "a certain aura of suspicion understandably associated with old established organizations whose lifeblood is the undiluted quintessence of cynicism." These circles, in the SIS, would have been "horrified" had they known the extent to which "I was supplying our friend with secret information to build up his candidacy for the position I wanted to see him achieve here." To counter this attitude he had to enlist the help of Churchill and rely on the continuing assistance of General H. L. Ismay and Sir Desmond Morton in the prime minister's "immediate entourage." Subsequently: "Our friend began to send up to the Summit papers designed to stress the lack and need of establishing undercover services equivalent to I [Secret Intelligence], O[perations], and PWE[Political Warfare Executive], Economic Warfare, external CE [Counterespionage] and other related activities. *Of course my staff produced the material for these papers and they were usually sent up in practically the original form.* There was always only one objective so far as he was concerned which was: 'I must garner all I can from any source which might be of help to my country in what I see so clearly lies ahead of it.' " (My emphasis.)[45]

Stephenson recalled, however, that Donovan was not initially taken with the idea of directing "the new agency that we envisaged"; and it was not "by any means a foregone conclusion that he would be offered the appointment." As late as 1969 Sir William observed that Donovan "wouldn't reach for the job, felt he shouldn't seek it, any more than he did for the New York governorship in 1946. Donovan was a proud man. But he was a natural for the job." As far as Stephenson was concerned, Donovan had unique qualifications: the confidence of the President, Hull, Stimson, and Knox; some understanding of the conduct of secret activities; the vision and drive to build an organization; and a demonstrated willingness to cooperate with BSC.[46]

What, in fact, was Donovan himself doing about this matter during April and May? He had had the Cabinet committee for lunch. He had sent a paper to Knox. He has been quoted as saying, in regard to plans for an intelligence agency: "I talked to anybody who would listen," and the name cited as an example is Ambassador Winant, who, however, did not return to the United States for a visit until the first days of June. The record is sparse.

Stephenson has said that "our friend" was sending papers "to the Summit" on the need for undercover organizations; he had sent to Knox his paper of 26 April; on 10 June, apparently on request, he sent Roosevelt his very important recommendation for the establishment of COI; but not until 3 July did he send his long paper on the British Commandos. Other than these papers, it is difficult to know what papers Stephenson had in mind.

An interesting but somewhat puzzling account of Donovan's activity in April and May has been made by one historian of Britain's economic block-ade of the Axis and reminds one of Miles's description of the movement being fostered by the colonel: according to this historian, Donovan "was preparing far-reaching plans that would give him control over the adminis-tration of economic warfare, secret service, and political and psychological warfare." Donovan was also described as proceeding with a comprehensive plan of his own; and "many of the draft memoranda designed by Colonel Donovan to become presidential orders setting up a new emergency agency were shown to Mr. Hall" who headed the embassy's economic warfare department. This last sentence with its "draft memoranda," "presidential orders," and consultations with Hall—if it has any substance—is either a repeat of Stephenson's papers heading for the "Summit" or a clue to undis-covered documents.[47]

Despite Stephenson's "manoeuvering" and whatever Donovan was doing, nothing much was accomplished in May. On 9 May Vincent Astor sent to FDR a clipping from the *Herald-Tribune* in which Major George Field-ing Eliot decried the lack of *real coordination* among the FBI, G-2, and ONI in regard to thwarting enemy agents and Fifth Columnists and called for the establishment of "a really efficient counterespionage service." What is needed, Eliot argued, is "*a special intelligence service* to act *as co-ordinator*, responsible directly to the President, acting with his own authority, and provided with personnel to conduct investigations of its own when neces-sary." Eliot also called for "a competent, intelligent, well-trained espionage service as distinct from sabotage, for work in enemy countries." The empha-sis above was provided by Astor, who told the President that Eliot's article "would seem to indicate that anonymity can be attained, at least for a while. We may not be very brilliant up here," he went on, "but I do guarantee that, in spite of what Major Eliot may think, there is co-ordination, very little friction, and, incidentally, lots of hard work, too." That Astor thought his operation was what Eliot had in mind is indicative of the distance that was still to be traveled.[48]

A more pertinent letter was written two weeks later by Secretary Knox, and it takes us back to the "hero in search of a role." To Justice Frankfurter, who could always be relied upon to help Roosevelt fill empty slots, Knox unburdened himself: "Frankly and privately, I am a little disappointed that the Administration is not making better use of Bill Donovan's services. He has made such tremendous sacrifices and contributed in such an outstanding way, that it seems strange to me that some very important job is not assigned to him. I am getting to be a little sensitive about urging him because it looks as if I were trying to find something for him to do, which is not the case. I am impelled solely by the conviction that his services are of the highest possible value to the country in this crisis."[49]

Surely Knox intended Frankfurter to do something about the situation, but alas, there is no indication he did. The situation was to change radically in ten days, but Winant, not Frankfurter, will be seen to be the engine of change.

In the meantime, Donovan was one of millions who were given new hope by Roosevelt's proclamation of 27 May of an unlimited national emergency. "My dear Mr. President," he wrote FDR, "permit me to say that your speech was superb and hit right on the button." This evoked a handwritten note, possibly from General Watson and at the President's request, telling Steve Early to "prep[are] a little line to Bill."[50]

It must have been while Donovan's letter was in the mail or on the President's desk that the President and Henry Morgenthau were actually talking about a job for Donovan—administrator for the state of New York for the Defense Savings Program. On 2 June the secretary told Harold Graves, one of his officials, that the President, who had been in Hyde Park since the twenty-ninth, "said try Donovan first, but he didn't think he would take it . . . Farley second and third, Swope." Morgenthau then directed: "I tell you what to do. You take Donovan and if he turns you down, I'd like to do Farley myself."[51]

Three days later Donovan was informed by mail that "the President has suggested that we should draft you to serve" as administrator. "This," said the secretary's letter, "would be a full-time job," and he agreed "enthusiastically" with the President, who thought the job would present "an unusual opportunity for public service in these critical times."[52] In 1969 Stephenson observed that he could have gotten "a dozen men on Wall Street to handle that job but only Donovan could handle the COI job." Stephenson thought that it probably was the secretary, and not the President, who suggested Donovan, and at the latter's suggestion Stephenson talked with Morgenthau.[53]

The job offer was to hang fire for two weeks, much to the impatience of the secretary, for Stephenson's "manoeuvering" and Donovan's "talking," unproductive in May, were about to register triumph in June. Stephenson has been quoted as naming Sherwood, Winant, and Astor as three men through whom he worked on the President. These three certainly had both influence with and access to the President. Astor was at the White House on 24 April and 5 June. On 16 June, Donovan was reported "trying to sell [Astor] on the idea [of combining FBI, MID, and ONI] so that he in turn would sell it to the President."[54] Astor's position, however, is a little cloudy: when Stephenson recalled that "Vincent Astor is one who comes to mind," his dictation, subsequently scratched out, went on: "but he leaned toward the Hoover camp." There is no question but that Astor was a firm supporter of the bureau at this time, and he may have had ambivalent feelings towards the projected organization. Stephenson's memoir, however, does leave Astor as one through whom he worked.[55]

Sherwood was in even a better position than Astor to push the new organization, and he had some personal interest in seeing it come to fruition. On 16 June Sherwood wrote Morgenthau: "I'm waiting on the anxious seat for materialization of the job I want most to do."[56] The same day he was sending Donovan a list of names of people "for the work we discussed . . . yesterday evening at your home." These included Edmond Taylor, Douglas Miller, E. A. Mowrer, H. R. Knickerbocker, and Raymond Gram Swing, and clearly they were talking about radio propaganda, or what came to be the Foreign Information Service in the new COI. Certainly Sherwood had Winant in mind, when he also wrote: "Yesterday evening at your house was a wonderfully interesting one. I saw the Ambassador again today. He's a honey."[57]

Sherwood, who had only lately become a presidential speechwriter and a valued one at that, had also become a frequent overnight guest at the White House. He and Mrs. Sherwood were house guests for three days beginning 23 April; he was there again for three days on 7 May; and while the speech of 27 May was being drafted he was there for six days; he left the day before Roosevelt took off for Hyde Park. Sherwood apparently was not at the White House, however, in the important first half of June.[58]

The former governor of New Hampshire, Ambassador Winant, is apparently the man whose arrival on the scene brought things to a head. A confidant of the President, Winant returned from his London ambassadorial post, which he had taken in February as Kennedy's successor, talked with the President at Hyde Park, and was invited to stay at the White House. FDR returned at 8:45 on the third, and met with Winant from 11:40 to 12:45.[59]

This was the first of at least five scheduled meetings that Winant had with the President. They met again the next day, had breakfast together on the sixth; they lunched on the twelfth, and on the fifteenth Winant and Hopkins had lunch with the President in his bedroom.[60] Winant's role has been stressed by Stephenson, and Donovan is apparently the source of the observation that Winant "went to the White House and urged the President to adopt the Colonel's plan—and to make the Colonel himself responsible for carrying it out."[61] It is worth emphasizing at this point that the ambassador, who was spending so much time with the President and whose autobiography makes clear he saw everybody else in Washington at the time, was also at Donovan's home, surely for dinner, when COI was being born.

Some time in these first ten days of June—while Morgenthau was awaiting Donovan's answer on the bond job, Donovan was asked by the President to submit his recommendations on the organization he had in mind. This Donovan did on 10 June in a well-known memorandum (fig. 9)[62] in which he argued the inadequacy of existing machinery for "analyzing, comprehending and appraising" such information as was available on enemy intentions and resources, both economic and military. His recommendation was the establishment of "a central enemy intelligence organization *which would itself collect, either directly or through existing departments of Government, at home and abroad,* pertinent information" on "potential enemies," their armed forces, economic organization, supply channels, troop and popular morale, and their foreign relations. (My emphasis.) As an example of the situation and his solution, he cited the need for bringing together all the information, scattered throughout the government, "upon which economic warfare could be determined." This and other information should be analyzed not only by army and navy officers but also by research scholars and others professionally trained as economists, psychologists, technicians, and students of finance.

Donovan cited the need for developing psychological warfare against the enemy, and in this field he said radio was the most powerful weapon. True it was not perfected as a weapon, but this could be realized by planning, and planning required information. Finally he sketched briefly the layout of the organization: a "Coordinator of Strategic Information," responsible to the President, assisted by an advisory panel of the heads of the FBI, MID, ONI, and other government departments, and drawing "much of the personnel" from the army, navy, and other branches of government.[63]

At this point two other persons get into the act: two Britishers whom Stephenson and his deputy Ellis consider would-be usurpers of their own claim to having taken "the first steps" to "establish a contact with the President, Mr. Hoover, and with Donovan for collaboration in security and intelligence matters."[64] These two were Admiral Godfrey of Naval Intelligence, with whom Donovan "got along famously,"[65] and the admiral's aide, Commander Ian Fleming, of future James Bond fame, whom Donovan had met during his recent trip. They had arrived in the United States on 25 May on a secret mission; the admiral, in mufti, had alighted from the *Dixie Clipper* only to run directly into photographers' flashbulbs, meant, however, not

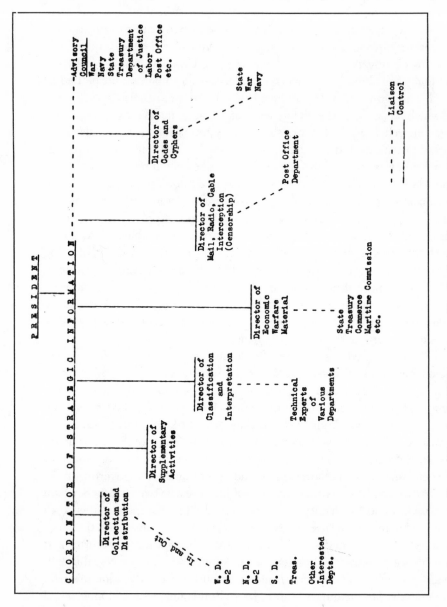

Fig. 9. Sketch of COI as approved by President Roosevelt, 18 June 1941

for him but for the well-known but not necessarily—given the time—more newsworthy Mme. Elsa Schiaparelli.[66]

Godfrey had come as representative of all the British services with a special mission to press upon the United States the integration of the intelligence services. He stayed in New York, how long is not known, at Donovan's apartment.[67] His story is that he had been getting nowhere with the services until finally Stephenson, bringing in Sir William Wiseman, suggested he had to tell his need to the President. This was arranged through Wiseman asking Sulzberger of the *New York Times* to lay it on with Mrs. Roosevelt. His meeting with the President took place at a White House dinner party on the evening of 10 June. Driving home, he "felt doubtful if he'd really made his point, but within three weeks" Donovan had "$3,000,000 to play with as head of a new department."[68]

At the time Godfrey apparently was not aware of Stephenson's own activity in relation to Donovan: "Godfrey's view now is that he and Fleming overrated at the time their part in briefing and boosting Big Bill, while underrating the skillful preparatory work done by Little Bill Stephenson."[69] Fleming's part allegedly centers on his drafting of the memorandum of 10 June. In 1957 Fleming wrote: "in 1941 I spent some time with [Donovan] in his home writing the original charter of the oss"; and in 1962 he referred to "my memorandum to Bill on how to create an American Secret Service, . . . the cornerstone of the future oss."[70]

Fleming did write two memoranda for Donovan at this time. The second of these, dated 27 June, can by no means be called "the original charter of the oss," but it certainly can be described as a memorandum "on how to create an American Secret Service." Actually, while it is a most interesting document, none of its specific suggestions were implemented by Donovan.[71]

This second document referred parenthetically to "my previous memo," but this has so far not been recovered. Is this what Fleming claims to have written in Donovan's home? Certainly Donovan was the type of person to ask people to put their thoughts on paper, and there is nothing implausible about his soliciting help from Fleming. One who knew Donovan well has asserted that however much he welcomed others' ideas and drafts, Donovan always wrote his own important papers; and in any case he would never have sent *to the President* such an important document as "the original charter" of oss had it been written by someone else, and a Britisher at that![72]

The days from 10 to 18 June were days of waiting. On the eleventh, Grace Tully sent word to General Watson that the President "wants to see Ben Cohen before he goes back to England. He will be here longer than the Ambassador. Also Bill Donovan."[73] In the light of the meeting on 18 June it seems reasonable to conclude that FDR wanted to see Cohen and Donovan *together* about COI. On 13 June, Morgenthau, sweating about his war bond job, told Graves that Donovan, who was coming to see him, wanted "to tell me something about the President first." On the seventeenth the secretary was telling his secretary, Mrs. Klotz, to remind him to call up Donovan: "I want to have him give me a yes or no on whether he is going to take the chairmanship in New York State. I am not going to wait any longer." At 9:10 that morning the following conversation took place:

> MORGENTHAU: Hello.
> DONOVAN: Good morning, Henry.
> M: Bill?
> D: Yeah.
> M: I hope you won't think I'm unduly restless.
> D: Oh, no.
> M: But we have to get started in New York.
> D: Well, look Henry, I'm down here today because I'm sup-
> posed to have a date this morning...
> M: uh uh.
> D: That's the reason you haven't heard from me.
> M: I see.
> D: I'll get a hold of you just as soon as I get through, Henry....
> I sent word by Frank the other day because I thought that
> was the quickest.
> M: Frank?
> D: Frank Knox.
> M: He didn't tell me anything.
> D: Oh that God—
> I told him to tell you, but I haven't seen him yet.
> M: No, he never said anything.
> D: Well, I thought that was the quickest way of getting it to
> you.
> M: He must have forgot.
> D: I'm sorry, Henry, because I was trying to get that word to
> you.
> M: Good, well, you think between now and sunset?
> D: Oh, even if I don't hear, I will call you.[74]

Donovan did not call, either before or after sunset. He clearly had other things on his mind.

The next day at 12:30 Donovan, Cohen, and Knox met with the President. He "accepted in totem" [sic] what Donovan had proposed. The deed was done when Roosevelt wrote in a large hand on the cover sheet of Donovan's 10 June memorandum: "Please set this up *confidentially* with Ben Cohen—Military—not O.E.M. (Fig. 10.)[75]

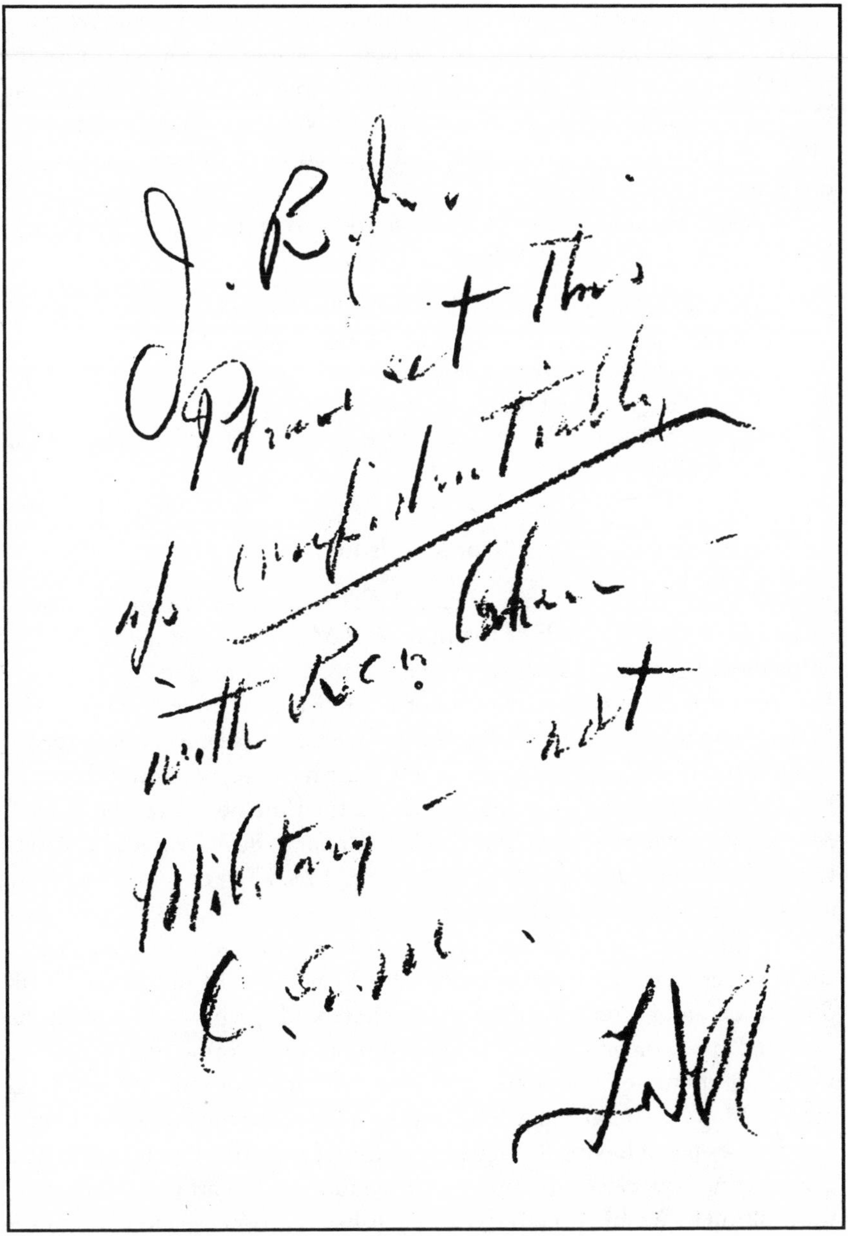

Fig. 10. FDR's instruction to John B. Blandford, Jr., assistant director of the Bureau of the Budget, on setting up COI

The "confidentially" presumably meant that Donovan would have access to the President's secret funds. "Military" meant that it was to be established by virtue of the President's authority as commander in chief and that Donovan would be commissioned a general. "Not o.e.m." kept it out of the Office of Emergency Management and thus ensured Donovan secrecy of operations.

Several weeks later Donovan wrote to his friend and new representative in London, William D. Whitney:

> It is sufficient to say that I told the President that I did not want to do it and that I would do it only on three conditions:
>   1. That I would report only to him.
>   2. That his secret funds would be available.
>   3. That all the departments of the government would be instructed to give me what I wanted.[76]

"Our Man Is In"

When Donovan left the White House, with much hard work ahead of him, he had little time to think of the impatient Morgenthau, but the chief of British intelligence could not have been far from his thoughts.

At 4 P.M. Morgenthau finally got hold of Donovan's secretary, a Mr. Mahar, who told the Treasury Secretary: "Well, I guess he must have forgot about it today while he was here. . . . He must have forgot about it because I was with him all the time and almost till the time he got on the plane." Morgenthau, wanting "a yes or no," asked Mahar to have Donovan call him that night. A day later "Donovan telephoned Mrs. Klotz evening of 6/18/41 and said he could not take the position."[77]

In the meantime Donovan must have been closeted with Stephenson. On that very day, the latter proudly cabled London: "Donovan saw President to-day and after long discussion wherein all points were agreed, he accepted appointment. He will be co-ordinator of all forms [of] intelligence including offensive operations equivalent SO2 [part of soe]. He will hold rank of Major General and will be responsible only to the President. Donovan accuses me of having 'intrigued and driven' him into appointment. You can imagine how relieved I am after three months of battle and jockeying for position in Washington that our man is in a position of such importance to our efforts."[78]

Lest the skeptic question the authenticity of this telegram, one must state that *The Quiet Canadian* is the only unclassified source in which any mention of the 18 June meeting has ever been found. In classified documents it showed up only in the working papers of the Bureau of the Budget as it went about drafting the formal notice which was issued on 11 July 1941. Finally, as of 18 June Colonel Donovan was to become Major General Donovan, but the unhappy military managed to spike the promotion.

The citation accompanying the award to Stephenson of the Medal for Merit reads in part:

> Sir William, as Director of British Security Coordination . . . gave timely and invaluable aid to the American war effort . . . in the field of intelligence and special operations. *At every step in the creation of these instrumentalities* Sir William contributed assistance and counsel of great value both to the government of the United States and to the entire allied cause. In a duty of great responsibility he worked tirelessly and effectively to advance the efficiency and competence of American organizations which provided for the American Government . . . the same strategic services furnished to the British Government by British organizations of similar nature.[79] (My emphasis.)

"At every step" can be taken literally.

9

....·-

A Postscript

THE DEED WAS DONE WHEN ROOSEVELT SCRIBBLED HIS INSTRUCTIONS
to the Bureau of the Budget. Three weeks later, on 11 July, the Coordinator of Information was officially established. A year later on 13 June, COI
was reconstituted as the Office of Strategic Services, a supporting agency of
the Joint Chiefs of Staff. On 1 October 1945, OSS was abolished, but some
branches, salvaged by the State and War departments, provided the foundation in 1946 for the Central Intelligence Group, which gave way in 1947
to the present Central Intelligence Agency. All this, however, is another
and much longer story.

This part of the book has simply been concerned with the role of the
British in the events that led to that meeting on 18 June 1941 at the White
House. Credit has always been given the British for their assistance in the
organization and *operation* of COI and OSS. Here I have extended that credit
for assistance to the *conception* and *establishment* of COI. Stephenson has, in
fact, spoken of BSC as "the parent" of COI.[1]

That the British were happy in 1941 with their offspring is unblush-
ingly evident in this extraordinary assessment written by Desmond Morton: "Another most secret fact of which the Prime Minister is aware but
not the other persons concerned, [sic] is that to all intents and purposes U.S.
Security is being run for them at the President's request by the British. A
British officer sits in Washington with Mr. Edgar Hoover and General [sic]

Bill Donovan for this purpose and reports regularly to the President. It is of course essential that this fact should not be known in view of the furious uproar it would cause if known to the Isolationists."[2]

This part has also been "an essay on origins." These, even when pushed hard, are most always elusive. Few passages so aptly exemplify the misconceptions that can arise—even among the informed—on the ultimate *Why* of things as does this comment, also from Morton: "In point of fact . . . I am assured by those concerned that the setting up of o.c.i. [Office of the Coordinator of Information] was almost entirely in the nature of camouflage for American secret activities."[3]

What Morton failed to appreciate was that he was referring simply to the *British motive* in bringing coi into being. That was, at best, only half the story. The other half was the *American motive* in setting up an organization which was not just a "cover" but was truly, as events were to show, a viable mechanism for the coordination of strategic intelligence.

Another way of putting the same thing is to stress that this paper has been the story of the fruitful but equal collaboration, in the institutionalization of a complex idea, of Stephenson and Donovan, "the two Bills."

PART THREE

·····

Questions
and
Controversies

10

·—·—·–

The FBI:
Run by the British?

HAD SPACE PERMITTED IT TWENTY-FIVE YEARS AGO, THE PRECEDING COI essay might well have included the following account of a British offer to help J. Edgar Hoover run the Federal Bureau of Investigation. Even so, when it was written shortly afterward as a contribution to CIA's *Studies in Intelligence*, its publication was turned down by the editorial board on the grounds that it would "needlessly rile" Hoover who, then at loggerheads with CIA on unrelated matters, would see it as agency criticism of the bureau's prewar record.

Now much rewritten, the story adds a new chapter to the story of Colonel Donovan's trip to London in July 1940, enhances the singularity of Stephenson's cultivation of the colonel, and shows how zealously but unsuccessfully the State Department tried in 1939–40 to frustrate British efforts to get a foot in the American intelligence doorway.

An Unemployed MI-5 Deputy Chief

The reader will remember the state of confusion in which British officials had been thrown by the sudden arrival in London of both Colonel Donovan and newsman Edgar Ansel Mowrer.[1] Who were they? Whom did they represent? And what should be done with them? The answers already given took care of Donovan's part of the story, including his return to Washing-

ton and the next year of his life, but left Mowrer in London pressing Lord
Swinton, the new security chief, for news of the suddenly fearsome Fifth
Column. Now, picking up Mowrer's trail, we begin with Swinton and then
meet the hitherto unknown British official who would soon offer to assist
or even reorganize the FBI.

Mowrer knocked on Swinton's door about 15 July, four days before
Donovan's arrival. Born Phillip Cunliffe-Lister in 1884, Lord Swinton was
at the peak of a varied career in business and government when on 27 May
1940 the War Cabinet simultaneously set up the very secret Home Defense
(Security) Executive and made him chairman. The executive consisted of
representatives of the Home Office, MI-5, MI-6, and the commander in
chief of the Home Forces. Its job was coordinating all British security activities in the United Kingdom and, to some extent, in the colonies and
territories. In particular, Swinton was instructed by Churchill to locate and
"eliminate" any Fifth Column in the land.[2]

Meant to be very secret, the executive was quickly uncovered by a parliamentary reporter from the socialist *Daily Herald*. Calling it "our 'secret
weapon' against the Fifth Column," he described it on 16 August as "a mystery committee of distinguished gentlemen . . . hard at work . . . in a big
'hush-hush' job for the government." He understood that Lord Swinton
was a member, if not the head, of the committee. With tongue in cheek, he
assured his readers that the committee's "zealous men" would be "discrimi-
nating in their snooping." The revelation provoked a parliamentary "storm"
that was only ended by Churchill's "angry 'No!'" to any question about the
committee.[3]

When Mowrer showed up at his door, Swinton asked Viscount Halifax, the foreign secretary, for guidance on handling him, especially since he
promised to be a frequent visitor. Swinton said that he had already given information to the U.S. government on the Fifth Column and asked whether
he was to treat Mowrer as "a high official" of that government. Finally, he
reported that he had put Mowrer in "contact with Sir Eric Holt-Wilson,
who has just retired, and who has a complete knowledge of all the Emergency procedures."[4]

Before formally meeting Sir Eric, let us first return to Ambassador Kennedy's complaint on 12 July that Harvey Klemmer of his office was already
investigating the Fifth Column, had seen Home Secretary Sir John Anderson, and had been to Scotland Yard. Klemmer was probably the recipient
of the information Swinton said he had given the embassy. In any case, the
ambassador said he needed no help in his investigation from any outsider
like Edgar Ansel Mowrer.

For the British this was confusion in a classical style. On one hand

Kennedy's Harvey Klemmer was quizzing the home secretary about the Fifth Column, and on the other hand Mowrer, representing Frank Knox, the two-hatted navy secretary and Chicago publisher, was seeking the same information from Swinton at the Security Executive. Was it simply lack of American coordination?

Hardly so. When Klemmer, whom Kennedy had brought from the Maritime Commission to London as his "right hand man," was asked years later whether the Kennedy initiative was prompted by Mowrer's presence in London, he burst out laughing: "Hell, yes! That's the way Kennedy operated. Kennedy called me in and said: 'Get to hell down to Scotland Yard and find out about the Fifth Column!'" So Harvey Klemmer, a shipping expert and jack-of-all-trades with seven years as a newsman, three in public relations, and a second book due out in 1941, quickly called on Scotland Yard. There he saw some "top official" who, however, minimized the threat from the Fifth Column.[5]

The confusion was quickly dissipated. Lord Swinton had already put Mowrer in touch with Sir Eric Holt-Wilson, and now on 15 July he sent Sir Eric to see Kennedy, who of course immediately turned him over to Klemmer. A few days later Sir Eric politely informed the embassy that Lord Swinton, "the Director of Security Services," henceforth wanted Mowrer out of the picture and the embassy's Harvey Klemmer to deal only with Sir Eric.[6] Sir Eric? Who was he?

Unlike Lord Swinton, Sir Eric was as little known then as he is today. Also unlike Swinton, Sir Eric was at rock bottom. He had just been retired (that is, fired) as MI-5's deputy director. Knighted in 1933, he had been fired suddenly after twenty-eight years of distinguished service. Also axed at the same time was his boss, Sir Vernon Kell, who had run MI-5 since its establishment by the Committee of Imperial Defence in 1909. Though humiliated, Kell was posthumously bracketed in postwar years with Britain's storied World War I intelligencers—Adm. Sir William Reginald ("Blinker") Hall of naval intelligence, Sir Basil Thomson of Scotland Yard, and Comdr. Sir Mansfield Cumming, who was Kell's counterpart in the Secret Intelligence Service. By contrast, Holt-Wilson has hardly been as publicized as here in these few pages—barring the following notable exception. This was the short-lived, extensive, and appreciative coverage given him in Compton MacKenzie's *Greek Memories*, which was banned almost as soon as it was published because it committed so many violations of the Official Secrets Acts. Not the least of these was the revelation of the names and identities of Cumming, Kell, and Sir Eric.[7]

Both Kell and Holt-Wilson, laboring in near anonymity, had developed and perfected a system, begun with their investigation of German espionage in the United Kingdom, for card-indexing—identifying, monitoring, and controlling—anyone engaging in clandestine activities prejudicial to the security of the armed forces of the kingdom and eventually of the Empire. Holt-Wilson's specialty was the preparation of laws, regulations, handbooks, and the numerous judicial and administrative forms required by the police and security services.

Despite their records, both men had fallen afoul of the new Churchill government, and their MI-5 became the public scapegoats for two disasters: the German sinking, in October 1939, of the battleship *Royal Oak* inside Britain's naval base at Scapa Flow, and the explosive wrecking, in January 1940, of the Royal Gunpowder Factory at Waltham Abbey in Essex. Their sacking was part of Churchill's reorganization and expansion of Britain's intelligence and security services. At the center thereof was Lord Swinton, who proceeded to "purge" MI-5 and thereby garner notoriety as its "butcher."[8]

Although Swinton had probably engineered their sacking—Kell was sixty-seven and in bad health, and Holt-Wilson was sixty-five though available for work,—he also probably seized the Mowrer-Klemmer connection as a chance to ease Holt-Wilson into a new career. Also, as Sir William Stephenson caustically observed years later, "Swinton was always trying to place people who would help him with votes."[9] Whatever the case, Swinton sent Sir Eric to meet Kennedy and Klemmer, both of whom could use some enlightenment on tracking down spies and saboteurs.

Sir Eric Applies at the FBI

Klemmer's immediate objective, of course, was to whip out a report on the Fifth Column that would put the ambassador one up on Donovan and Mowrer, who were running their own investigations. Thus on 1 August, a few days after Mowrer had left for home and two days before Donovan did likewise, Kennedy sent Washington Klemmer's report, with seventeen documents on MI-5 and the laws and regulations on such matters as aliens, munitions factories, and official secrets. Irrelevant to us now is his substantial and, as history has shown, correct discounting of the seriousness of a subversive threat to Britain's security. What is relevant is his presentation of Holt-Wilson's proud assessment of MI-5's accomplishments and his readiness to help extend the merits of its system to the United States.[10]

So impressed was Klemmer that he immediately declared that "the English have done a very smart thing in connection with counter-espionage, which might well be copied by the United States." He added, just as importantly, that for the first time in history the representative of a foreign government, namely Harvey Klemmer, was privileged to be given "complete details of the British system." On this last point a more seasoned observer, Ernest Cuneo, would have cautioned Klemmer, as he once warned me, that "the British may have taught us everything we know [about intelligence] but not everything *they* know."[11]

Nevertheless, Sir Eric did give Klemmer an overall view of the Security Service and what he called the "Imperial Security Service." That name has not been found outside Sir Eric's curriculum vitae and may be his creation. Whatever the correct name, however, it was MI-5 writ large.[12]

MI-5's central function, reported Klemmer, was the maintenance in London of "a central index of suspicious persons." This was a worldwide roundup of 4.5 million names of persons suspected of anti-British activity. Next to secrecy, the key to the service's success was "centralized control." The Army, Navy, and other government departments had their own intelligence units, but these were "brought together in the over-all organization." This MI-5, wrote Klemmer, was the only counterespionage activity "ever mentioned in the newspapers," but it was, he said, "merely one cog" in the "super machine" whose existence was apparently completely unknown to the public. Even the Germans had "no inkling" of its existence.[13]

This "machine" encompassed the entire British Empire. It was "an ambitious collaboration of Chiefs of Police from all over the Empire, of representatives of the armed forces, and of officials from various government departments." It had begun as "a clearing house" in 1909 and had been extended in 1915 to all British territories overseas except India. Territorial governors "entered into active correspondence and co-operation with this central Security Service." In 1931 responsibility for "the civil side of the national security" was added to the service's military responsibility, and thus was formed "the consolidated Imperial Security Service, with one Central Record Office and Registry for the whole Empire"—a goal toward which Sir Eric said he and Kell had labored for twenty years. It was only two years later that Sir Eric was knighted.[14]

Officials assured Klemmer that "some such system would be valuable for the United States." More than that, he said the retiring Sir Eric "would be glad" to furnish whatever further information might be desired. Sir Eric was "even willing" to go to America to help set up a centralized organization if it were wanted. Underwriting the offer, Klemmer said again in conclusion that "the British are very keen about their centralized Security Service." It was "the only way to co-ordinate the activities of the various agencies." However, he admitted that the service had still not provided "a complete solution" to the problem and had had to establish "an inter-departmental committee [Swinton's] authorized, in extreme cases, to confer directly with the Prime Minister."[15]

Sir Eric's offer was reminiscent of British concern in the Great War about the ability of the United States to protect the war supplies that were produced here and shipped to the Western Front. At that time, late 1915, Britain's new MI-6 secretly sent the thirty-year-old Sir William Wiseman to New York to set up a branch to ferret out and frustrate German saboteurs. Wiseman subsequently established close connections with government agencies even before the United States entered the war. A generation later Britain was again worrying about the security of America as the "arsenal of democracy" and was again using overt and covert means to bolster American security. Sir Eric's offer, really an opportunistic response to both official and unofficial American invitation, was only the fourth, or perhaps fifth, such effort in 1939–40.

The first effort could have been the approach made in September 1939 by Sir William Wiseman himself, then a New York banker, to Adolf A. Berle, Jr., the president's friend and an assistant secretary of state. Ostensibly an innocent visit, it struck Berle as "fantastic" that Wiseman, whom he held active in British machinations in Washington in World War I, should be calling on him at the moment. Whatever Wiseman wanted, and it was, thought Berle, probably only his patriotic effort to get back into the Great Game, Berle was put on his guard.[16]

Certainly there were two definite British attempts early in 1940 to improve their intelligence capabilities in this country. One of them was the attempted linkage, as early as February 1940, of British intelligence and the FBI through FDR's multimillionaire friend, Vincent Astor. As described in Chapter 5, Astor complained to the President that State had frustrated his efforts to work with Sir James Paget, passport control officer and the chief of British intelligence in New York.

The other effort, recounted in Chapter 3, was the request of those two representatives of the Anglo-French Purchasing Commission, Hamish Mitchell and Charles T. Ballantyne, to get a British undercover service established in this country. On that occasion, Berle, echoing the FBI, strongly objected to any such action but was willing to look at any information they might provide. He thought the British "may know things that we ought to know promptly."[17]

Next there was a third effort undertaken in April–June by William Stephenson as the representative of both MI-6 and Prime Minister Winston Churchill. This effort, the theme of my COI essay, was then unknown to the watchful Berle and apparently everybody else in the State Department. In fact, it was effected behind State's back by the collaboration with Stephenson of both the FBI's Hoover and President Roosevelt. Since it was unknown to State at the time of Sir Eric's offer, I shall leave further consideration of it to this chapter's ending.

Sir Eric's offer was, then, the fourth in the series, even if it has the appearance of merely an unemployed British official looking for a new job. It seems unlikely that the former deputy chief of MI-5 would have been allowed to render to the FBI the fruit of his twenty-eight years of secret service without some official approval and instruction. While the hand of Lord Swinton is the only government one showing, his sponsorship surely made it official.

When months later someone in Washington was curious as to how such a person as Sir Eric could be spared for service in a foreign country "in these crucial times," there was no disparaging his capabilities or years of service. He was only a poor administrator, had reached retirement age, could not be subordinated to his juniors, and in any case new blood was needed. The last was the answer.[18]

The State Department's "Headache"

When Kennedy's 1 August message—along with Klemmer's Fifth Column report, those seventeen documents, and Sir Eric's offer—reached State, there was no answer until 29 September. Then, James Clement Dunn, one of three advisors on political relations, informed Herschel V. Johnson, the counselor in the London embassy, that acceptance of Sir Eric's offer was "not deemed advisable at this time." He might have said what he said earlier about the approach by Mitchell and Ballantyne: that no foreign secret service should be allowed to operate here but that "cooperation" with such an organization was a Justice matter. As it was, he explained, perhaps defensively, "the nucleus" of the organization Sir Eric had in mind "has been in operation [here] for some time." After all, there was the Office of Naval Intelligence (ONI), the Military Intelligence Division (MID or G-2), and the FBI, which had recently created a "Special Division" for this purpose, and of course the department was cooperating with them. He was referring, first, to the vaunted but modest coordination of the intelligence agencies that Roosevelt had ordered in 1939 and, second, to the FBI's new "Special Intelligence Service," which was commissioned to provide the other services with specified coverage of spies and saboteurs.[19]

America's own fear of Fifth Column activities had galvanized the government into taking action both to counter any threats as well as to prevent the resurgence of any World War I vigilantism. In 1938 the FBI had revived its

General Intelligence Division, originally the Radical Division, to smoke out communist and fascist subversives. FDR's 1939 action and the FBI's new SIS were aimed at further coordination of the security and intelligence services. In May 1940 Roosevelt transferred the Immigration and Naturalization Service from the Department of Labor to the Department of Justice to help ready the country against the Fifth Column. In June a top FBI official, Hugh Clegg, was named to head a new "national defense investigative unit."[20]

Such activity was undoubtedly in Dunn's mind when he went on to explain to Johnson that the FBI was extending the benefits of its training to police officials from around the country and was strengthening the security of industrial facilities. Even so, wrote Dunn, the American system for selecting and organizing police officials differed markedly from that in Britain. Moreover, there was another, but troubling, difference—namely, "the flare for publicity" that in this country tempted an FBI agent, in particular one Leon G. Turrou, to make a spectacle of himself by selling his ghost-written stories in the middle of the *Rumreich* spy case in 1938. That case, an investigative and judicial fiasco, spurred Roosevelt's 1939 emphasis on improving coordination.[21]

On a happier note, Dunn informed Johnson that he was "glad" Lord Swinton wanted to deal only with the embassy and not with any Edgar Ansel Mowrer, who had collaborated with Donovan in writing articles on the Fifth Column. These Dunn found "very general in character" and containing "little . . . not already known." After all, he wrote, "it does seem ironical that a newspaper correspondent would be commissioned" to work on the Fifth Column when for twenty years there had been maintained a "service of cooperation . . . between the Embassy and the appropriate officials in England for exchange of mutually advantageous information."[22] Dunn was referring to an exchange begun during the Great War and since carried on by State, on behalf of the FBI, with both MI-5 and Scotland Yard. Probably MI-6 was also involved, but for the better part of those twenty years its hand was kept secret from the United States.

Dunn's letter would seem to have disposed of the matter, but such was not the case. Others had gotten into the act. State's desk officer for the United Kingdom, Robert B. Stewart, had apparently received an information copy of the ambassador's incoming letter. Unaware of Dunn's letter, Stewart sent Dunn a memorandum wondering "what should be done" with Klemmer's report and Sir Eric's offer. Ordinarily Dunn would have said "I've taken care of it." Unfortunately for the final outcome of the case, he had received a reply from Johnson in London that put Sir Eric back on the agenda. Johnson had not informed Sir Eric of Dunn's decision because in the meantime Sir Eric had sent him a detailed six-page account of his career in the "Imperial Security Service." An impressive vita, as well as evidence of Sir Eric's eagerness to begin life anew in the United States, made Johnson suggest that Dunn "may want me to give him some other sort of message."[23] Back to square one.

Prodded by Johnson, Dunn now had second thoughts. Despite his earlier confidence in American intelligence, he thought that Adolf Berle ought to take a look at the matter. One, "a question of policy is involved." Two, he was not familiar with the "counter intelligence services . . . in Washington," although he knew there was "a plethora of such services" proliferating everywhere in town. Three, and surprisingly, he thought Sir Eric's offer required "special consideration by the highest authorities," by which he probably meant both the secretary and the attorney general.[24]

Berle, who was State's intelligence liaison with the White House, ONI, G-2, and the FBI, had a simple view of the matter. On 18 November, two days after Dunn wrote him, he emphatically answered that "I am frank to say that I do not like the idea of having a Britisher come over here to set up a Security Service." His reason was equally blunt: "Control of the police system is the last thing a sovereign nation wants to give up." Of course, if the FBI wanted to use Sir Eric as a consultant, fine, but otherwise Berle had "a radical objection to having him come over here to organize the service." After all, said Berle, mistaking Holt-Wilson for Kell and summarily belittling their work, "Sir Eric . . . was in charge of this from 1912 through [sic] and the result was anything but impressive."[25]

Berle had another objection: the offer would "extend still further British influence inside our own government." Those who knew Berle would have chalked up that comment as much to his alleged anti-British feeling as to the merits of the case. Of German descent, he had suffered as a Harvard student during World War I because of his refusal to change his name or sign anti-German manifestoes. In 1919, angrily breaking with the U.S. delegation at Versailles, he bitterly pilloried Britain's "twisted policy." Twenty years later, when recording Wiseman's visit, he was again denouncing that British record of, as he saw it, "half truths, broken faith, intrigue behind the back of the State Department, and even the President." He held Wiseman complicit in that trickery and now supposed that the Englishman thought him "the easiest mark."[26]

It is not surprising, then, that Berle reminded Dunn of the two earlier occasions when the British "made a similar attempt." One, he said, was the "unofficial suggestion" made to Hoover that he and "the British intelligence service [Sir Francis Paget] 'coordinate' and conduct a continuous exchange of information, without passing through the State Department." The other was the British offer, from Mitchell and Ballantyne, to lend the FBI a few experienced intelligence people.[27]

On 2 December Berle had more advice, this time from the department's "gumshoe man," Raymond L. Murphy, who for years meticulously compiled files on Soviet, and then Nazi, propaganda and subversive agents in this country. Dismissing Klemmer's report as of "no great value" and too generalized in character, he faulted it for containing nothing on the modus operandi of clandestine Nazi agents and firms. He thought the seventeen documents of some academic interest but irrelevant to American laws. Perhaps, he suggested, they should be sent to some other department.[28] "You mean," someone could be imagined asking incredulously, "that after five months they have not been sent to any other department? Not even to the FBI?"

Apparently not, for as late as 31 March 1941 J. Edgar Hoover, who had heard of Klemmer's report, was telling State the bureau "had no record" of ever having received a copy. That being so, the bureau surely had not yet received the seventeen documents, or copies of them, perhaps even a peek at them. So much for improved coordination. Even stranger is the fact that as late as 4 February 1941 Johnson in London was cautioning Dunn in Washington not to let the FBI know that the two of them had been corresponding about Sir Eric Holt-Wilson.[29] Just as strange is the fact that apparently State never once consulted the bureau about Sir Eric's offer. One might charitably hypothesize that State, aware of Hoover's jealous regard for his bureau's ability and reputation, chose not to "needlessly rile" him by offering him an Englishman to reorganize it.

Still, Raymond Murphy found "one very regrettable feature connected with these documents," namely, that it seemed to be "the Department's headache now." The headache was Sir Eric, who wanted to work for us in England or come here "to instruct us as to establishing a Central Security Service." However, Murphy, like everybody else, also wondered about the Security Service's record and thought our agencies had the situation in hand. Nevertheless, "the question of rejecting" Sir Eric's offer was "still before the Department."[30]

Passing the Buck to Justice

Meanwhile another matter involving British intelligence caught the attention of both Berle and the FBI. At some moment it might have looked to the former like another British effort to get its foot in the doorway. In any case, on 5 December Berle recorded in his diary that Sir William Wiseman, in to see him again, indicated he "wanted to get back into the service." The outbreak of war had indeed reactivated the former warhorse, now fifty-five. From late 1939 on Wiseman was advising, meeting, overnighting with, and writing papers for Britain's Ambassador Lord Lothian in Washington. In May, Lothian asked Churchill to see Wiseman. While the meeting apparently did not occur, Wiseman did lunch with Lord Halifax at the Foreign Office. Wiseman was involved in some negotiations that struck State and the FBI as appeasement-oriented and violative of our neutrality laws. While he was soon vindicated—thanks largely to William Stephenson's intervention—State and Justice were ready, around the turn of the year, to expel him from the country as soon as his visa expired.[31] Berle was surely aware of this contretemps, which could only have further stimulated his watchfulness.

Still, as November gave way to December, State had not yet resolved the question of Sir Eric's offer. Why not? Why was it still a "headache"? Dunn had given the inevitable answer on 29 September. But Johnson in London, reading Sir Eric's vita, thought the department might want to send him some other message. So Dunn passed the buck to Berle, who agreed with Dunn. So did Murphy, the department's detective. Still, Berle, no indecisive person, did not repeat Dunn's earlier message to Johnson. Why not? Speculative answers abound—inertia, press of other business, deference to Sir Eric, and some nagging thought that his offer ought to be accepted.

The last possibility is not entirely groundless. Worth recounting here is the suggestion made on 3 December by lawyer Amos Peaslee, a close friend of "Blinker" Hall. Peaslee urged that Hall, the mastermind behind the Zimmerman telegram bombshell, should come here as a private citizen for a few conferences on "consolidating" U.S. efforts to combat sabotage. In this case, with its emphasis on a consultancy, State's H. H. Martin told Peaselee: "Tell him by all means to come." Because of poor health, however, Hall never did come. His countersuggestion, that he and Peaselee "fix up" the latter as "some sort of liaison" between the FBI and MI-5, never materialized either.[32]

What is pertinent here, however, is Peaslee's description of the security situation in the United States: "Sabotage is rife in this country. History is repeating itself. The press reports of fires and explosions in our industrial plants parallel almost precisely what occurred in 1915." Unfortunately, continued Peaslee, there is difficulty here getting all American agencies, "with their historic background and customs," to arrange "the necessary joint action . . . to cope with the task." Peaslee thought the job so difficult that it required "the experience, detachment, and infinite tact" that only Hall possessed.[33]

Whatever the reason for the prolonged wrestling with the question,

State finally realized it had to consult the Justice Department. Hence on 7 December Berle called Attorney General Jackson to tell him that "The British want to send over Sir Eric Holt-Wilson to tell us how to run the F.B.I." To his diary Berle confided that he made the same point—about control of the police as the last refuge of a sovereign government—that he had made "on various occasions to various people when like proposals were put up to us." A week later Secretary of State Hull, in sending the matter to Jackson, showed some annoyance with Sir Eric, Klemmer, Kennedy, and Swinton when he said that "this department was not responsible for the circumstances leading" to the original offer and hence was "placed by the English official in the position of intermediary."[34]

In reply Jackson readily agreed with Dunn, Berle, Murphy, and Hull that it was not "feasible to accept the offer at this time." However, he had a new reason for saying so: the American people would probably not take kindly to "this country's intelligence service . . . being guided by the advices of one of the belligerents." With that understatement of the day, State was at last able to turn down Sir Eric's offer to help run the FBI. The date of the news was 10 January 1941, a date that brings us back to William Stephenson.[35]

A British Foot in the Doorway

The reader will have noted that Stephenson's name never appeared in any State traffic cited in this chapter. True, it did appear in other State traffic, such as in March in the issuance of a visa for his entrance to the United States as a "Company Director" and "Government Official . . . on a mission for the Ministry of Supply." It appeared again, in June with his appointment as successor to Sir James Paget as passport control officer.[36] Otherwise, the department knew nothing of him, certainly nothing of his true mission.

Stephenson was registered at the Waldorf-Astoria Hotel in New York 15–19 April. On 16 April he met with J. Edgar Hoover at the latter's office in Washington, and then and there they reached agreement on a personal liaison, channels of communication, and pseudonyms. It is virtually certain that Hoover insisted that the liaison involve no other American agency, including the State Department, and that it have FDR's approval. Stephenson was at the Waldorf again 2–20 May and then returned to London.

It has never been fully revealed how Roosevelt's approval was obtained. Stephenson's history of his British Security Coordination says that he had "a mutual friend . . . put the matter before the President," who, "hearing the arguments in favour of the proposed liaison, endorsed them enthusiastically." The friend was probably Vincent Astor, or it could possibly have been Lord Lothian. In any case, it was done either in May or shortly after Stephenson returned here on 21 June, and it was done behind State's back because, says the same history, the FBI was under "strict injunc- tion" to avoid any unneutral collaboration with the British. Roosevelt "was very pleased and . . . a little amused," so Donovan told Hoover, "at the way in which you side-tracked the State Department."[37]

While State was unaware of the initiation of the liaison, they must have soon obtained some inkling of it from all of Stephenson's intense activity in Washington. In any case, they received a pretty clear picture of something afoot on 21 January—just eleven days after Sir Eric's case was disposed of— when the British Embassy informed them that Stephenson, hitherto the British passport control officer, was now "Director of Security Coordination in the United States." When asked to initial the message, Berle responded in his ever watchful and acerbic manner: "Why acknowledge this at all? It is a bad title— & worse to talk about. I would shut up and watch it."[38]

"Watch it" is what Berle and the FBI did. So much so that they became incensed at what they learned. So much so that they took very strong action to curb it and even contemplated forcing Stephenson's removal as director. But that effort takes us far beyond the scope of this book. Suffice it to say that while Berle was successfully frustrating the collective attempts of Sir James Paget and Vincent Astor, of Hamish Mitchell and Charles T. Bal- lantyne, and, yes, of Sir Eric Holt-Wilson to get a British intelligence foot in the American doorway, William Stephenson was, unbeknownst to them, establishing here what became a much bigger foreign secret service than any of them could have imagined. More than that, and even though Stephen- son was eventually curbed, he and his British Security Coordination, in collaboration with Bill Donovan, left behind an impressive legacy—the Co- ordinator of Information, the start of the Central Intelligence Agency.

11
·—·—·—

Three Books: From Obscurity to Fame

WHEN PART 2 OF THIS BOOK WAS WRITTEN, SIR WILLIAM STEPHENSON, "the quiet Canadian," had not yet become "Intrepid." How the transformation took place will take us from an official British history of BSC, a top secret book often quoted, highly publicized, but still hidden from public view—a sort of forbidden fruit—to its opposite, a highly successful book that not only renamed Stephenson but also ignited many controversies about him and his relations with Donovan, Churchill, and Roosevelt. Let us begin with that forbidden fruit.

The BSC History: Forbidden Fruit

The reader will recall Donovan's marginal note denying a pre–July 1940 friendship with Stephenson. It was a comment of his on a British submission to a projected but aborted history of COI and OSS. The very fact that OSS had asked BSC to submit an account of the origin of their collaboration made one think the British might have been similarly writing their own history. However, years would pass before word of it began to leak out.

On the occasion of my first meeting Sir William, I had indeed asked him about documentation for much of the Whitney Shepardson tape and Hyde's *Quiet Canadian*. He said he had no papers and doubted there were any in London. So many communications, "millions of them," had been sent to and from his office that he would have needed "a huge room to house them all." Hence, he had "everything burned." All he showed me were a scrapbook and a photograph of Bill Donovan, appropriately signed by the latter. He also gave me a copy of Hyde's book, inscribed by himself.[1]

Stephenson's answer was, at the least, a bit evasive. He did not tell me about the top secret history of BSC, which he had had written at war's end and "Copy No. (i)" of which I now know he had in his home at the time. (No reason he should have told me!) Entitled British Security Coordination (BSC): An Account of Secret Activities in the Western Hemisphere 1940–45 (hereafter referred to as the BSC History), the highly publicized but still top secret book was not publicly and fully identified until twenty years later, in 1989.[2]

The book had its remote origins in two documents completed respectively in June 1942 and March 1943; the former cannot now be located. Both were undertaken on Stephenson's orders as surveys of his agency's activities and were drawn up, as Timothy Naftali has ably explained, to be Stephenson's defenses against efforts in London to trim his personal and institutional sails.[3] As such, they seem to have been materials for, rather than early drafts of, a history.

At war's end, however, a proper history was undertaken, on Stephenson's order, and for reasons of security and economy the entire project was carried out in Canada. This was not done in any old government building in Ottawa but in a very secret place that since 1941 had been BSC's training center and backup station. It was the clandestine Camp X, which lay on the northern shore of Lake Ontario, "hidden," according to William Stevenson, "in the wilderness with black waters of a great lake for protection." It was located close to American soil so as to facilitate rapid but secret communications with BSC in New York. The spot was opposite Buffalo, just east of Toronto, near the town of Oshawa, and is now something of a shrine to Stephenson and BSC.[4]

Such a secret spot characterized the total secrecy that enveloped the book's publication from start to finish. It began with a convoy from New York to Oshawa of papers, equipment, and personnel, and ended with the distribution of the finished product. With armed guards standing by, the convoy sneaked out of BSC's Manhattan headquarters in the midnight darkness, some time in mid-1945. Traveling ten hours, it reached the border at Niagara Falls where a Canadian army captain gave his name and code number. Security guards then "opened the frontier" to this latest clanedstine movement across the border.[5]

At Camp X a team of writers, secretaries, and typists went to work. Initially the principal writers were Columbia's professor Gilbert Highet; Roald Dahl, the future writer; and Thomas W. Hill, a writer and future business associate of Stephenson's who did most of the work. Naftali tells us, however, that Stephenson found their product "too dry," and David Stafford says that Stephenson "wanted more drama and colour." Hence, it was turned over to a fourth BSC man, Giles Playfair, a former radio broadcaster, whose revision of the entire manuscript satisifed Stephenson. Printing, illustrating, and binding the history involved movements—mysterious to the local population—of personnel and materials between Camp X and nearby Oshawa, where staff lived and often worked.[6]

Because the BSC History was not intended to be a bestseller, its print run was restricted, according to Stafford, to twenty copies. These were bound in leather, each in a special box, with a lock specifically ordered by Stephenson. When this was done, all the papers were burned, with BSC officers standing by as guarantors of the operation. Because authorities thought that that was the proper way to handle wartime secrets, these historically valuable documents are now lost to history.[7] All that remains, beside fading memories and pieces of paper here and there, are those twenty copies. Or are they twenty?

Years later Stephenson told me that he had had three copies printed, one for Churchill, Roosevelt, and himself. Unfortunately this is not convincing. Roosevelt had died on 12 April, a month or so before the writing project, dated "1945," had begun. Hence a copy could not have been sent to him. Also, I doubt that Stephenson would then have given such a document to any foreigner, even FDR. In any case no copy, or any record of any copy, has been found in the Roosevelt library in Hyde Park or among the many Churchill papers.[8] Stephenson certainly had "Copy No. (i)"—and more of this anon.

As for the twenty copies, they were all reportedly sent to Stephenson, who took possession of ten for himself, Churchill, and the heads of the services he represented as head of BSC. Two of these copies were lost and one was secreted in SIS archives. As for the other ten, Stafford says that Stephenson was so concerned about their security that he had them burned and that the act was carried out on a Quebec farm by Thomas Hill and his wife.[9] Whatever the fate of the twenty, none had surfaced when Stafford wrote in 1986. He himself had never seen a copy.

Even so, ten years earlier, photostated copies of "Copy No. (i)" were freely, but hurriedly and surreptitiously, given to a friend and myself. The giver's name will remain secret; suffice it to say it was not Sir William. The copies contain brief handwritten marginalia, which I have no hesitation in affirming as being in Stephenson's handwriting.[10] Surely there are other copies floating about.

The public, however, remained ignorant of the BSC History and its full and correct identity. All it ever saw were vague references to sundry papers of Sir William Stephenson. Thus Hyde informed his readers in 1962 that *The Quiet Canadian* was based on Sir William's "files and private papers." Sir William himself told Stevenson's readers in 1976 that his biography was based on "the BSC Papers," which he described as consisting of "many thick volumes and exhibitis."[11] Late in 1983 Stevenson provoked much interest when he publicly announced that he had deposited his literary papers in the University of Regina in Canada and that "the official British Security Coordination history stamped TOP SECRET [will] shortly . . . be made public." That was his intention, but Sir William "strenuously objected"; hence that bubble was quickly burst. The university denied it had any BSC papers and Stevenson changed his story.[12]

However changed it was, his original statement was the first reference to a specific BSC history. It remained such until March 1989, a month after Sir William's death, when Stevenson became the first person to admit publicly he had a copy. He was quoted as saying that to his knowledge there were only three originals—Sir William's, Churchill's, and his. He then added that there was a fourth, which he said was in my possession and which he thought I was going to publish. Indeed, when the Regina story broke in 1983, and when I did not then know of Sir William's objection to printing the book, I informed a startled Sir William of my possession of a copy and intention, with his permission, to publish it—something I then could guarantee. No, he said, "it will only help the Soviets."[13] While I doubted that effect, it was obviously his conviction, and in view of the friendship that had developed between us, it was good enough for me.

The chronology so far suggests something of a literary strip tease. The BSC *History* was slowly being unveiled. The next to the last fan was dropped in September 1989 when a *Washington Post* editor, David Ignatius, proudly proclaimed that he had seen a copy—possibly "Copy No. (i)"—had his hands on it, spent hours reading it, gave it its full and accurate title, and correctly quoted me as verifying what he said. Three years later, Ignatius's surprisingly lengthy story became the springboard for the first scholarly critique of the volume by an author who also had obviously had his hands on it. This was "Intrepid's Last Deception" by Timothy Naftali, who on the basis of it accused Stephenson of deceiving the public about his wartime career for no less than thirty-seven years. A similarly grave indictment was leveled against Stephenson in 1993 by another Canadian, John Bryden, who "examined [the BSC *History*] while sitting at the dining room table in Stevenson's Toronto home."[14] Both indictments will be challenged in Chapter 14.

The remaining fan, however, has not been dropped. Why not? The British government will not publish the book. Nor, presumably, will anyone subject to the Official Secrets Act. Others who would cannot obtain copies. A few who could refuse to do so. So, fifty years later, it is still forbidden fruit.

Hyde's *Quiet Canadian*: A "Bumpy Ride"

For about thirty years, 1946–76, that forbidden fruit had an American counterpart, a two-volume history of oss, also top secret. However, Donovan and oss had long enjoyed an increasingly popular press. In fact, as early as the late 1940s they had been featured in no fewer than seven books. Not so BSC and Stephenson. They received no public mention, beyond reference to the Medal for Merit, until 1952. Then began what William Stevenson described as "a bumpy ride" in the efforts to write an unofficial Stephenson biography.[15] Ironically, as we shall see, Stevenson's own very successful effort hit the biggest bump.

In 1952 a Canadian journalist, McKenzie Porter, broke the BSC story in *Maclean's Magazine*. His article was a grab bag of exciting second- or third-hand stories about a mysterious millionaire who, from a Manhattan penthouse, masterminded the spiking of "Hitler's guns" in this hemisphere. Stephenson thought it "not up to much" because Porter had had to "pick up bits and pieces where he could find them."[16]

While the article made no great public splash, it made others think about a Stephenson biography. Porter himself offered Stephenson the first thirty thousand of royalties on such a book. Henry Luce offered him one hundred thousand "plus, plus, plus" as an advance on the story. The idea apparently caught on with Stephenson who, about 1954, suggested to his former BSC subordinate, Montgomery Hyde, author of more than a dozen books, that he write a Stephenson and BSC book. Hyde declined the offer, because as a member of parliament he was "too busy being a politician."[17] Five years later Stephenson turned to his former deputy, Colonel Ellis.

While Dick Ellis lacked Hyde's literary record, he had much else to his credit: World War I military service; some proficiency in Russian, German, Turkish, Urdu, and Persian; thirty-five years in MI-6; some access— now as a part-time MI-6 officer—to secret records; and a scholarly bent.[18] Stephenson thought that Ellis could write a valuable history of "our" war, as well as greatly improve Ellis's financial position. Stephenson offered Ellis all royalties and an advance and promised to "order 1,000 copies himself," a promise that Ellis thought "was simply Bill trying to do me a good turn." Stephenson said he had the "necessary basic documents" and Ellis need not worry about the Official Secrets Acts because "it is all a fairly old story."[19]

A year later Ellis turned out a first draft titled "Anglo-American Collaboration in Intelligence and Security: Notes for Documentation." This was the document that Ellis, after he had undergone a hostile security scrutiny, left for me at my London hotel in 1969. When I made a copy for Angleton's deputy, Ray Rocca, we discovered the last chapter was missing. Weeks later Rocca gleefully informed me that "they"—there was no doubt whom he meant—"had gotten into Ellis's flat and recovered the missing chapter." Whatever the effort, it was hardly worth it—at least to me. While I then described the entire manuscript as "useful," I also noted that its "usefulness would have been enhanced a hundredfold had I been able to query Colonel Ellis on the data he left out."[20] In fact, the draft, really boring, had hit many bumps.

Since Ellis cited only secondary and published sources, the draft was short on names, operations, and controversies. There was no revelation of secrets, daring adventures, personal clashes, bureaucratic bungling, or sexual escapades. No one's ox was gored. There was only high praise for all the British and American intelligence and security services and their harmonious collaboration in the common cause. No wonder that Hyde told Ellis, when he read some early chapters, that it "read too much like an office history." More dismayed, Stephenson let Ellis know that he had "pulled [his] punches too much," his style was "too dry," the whole thing was not "fierce" enough, and it was too lifeless to be "saleable."[21]

Through a mutual friend, another ex-BSC chief, John A. R. Pepper, Stephenson told Ellis he "seemed . . . too inhibited" by "his former association with a certain 'Firm' [SIS]" to let himself go. Ellis admitted he had not criticized the "Firm" and had not even referred to it directly. He referred to its address, Broadway Building, only as "B——way" or "B——y."[22]

Through Pepper, Stephenson suggested that Dick turn the job over to Hyde and let Hyde use Dick's material and supplement it with his own experiences and recollections. Pepper said Stephenson wanted a book portraying himself as "a man of initiative, an innovator, who, in spite of official obtuseness and sometimes obstruction, created something out of nothing." He thought that after twenty years "we can let our hair down" about those obtuse obstructionists and about various operations in the Caribbean and South America. And do so without restraint. Ellis was not so sure. After all, he had "spent 32 years keeping my mouth shut!"[23]

Later Stephenson wrote Ellis that, with what he had done, "finishing the job would be right up [Hyde's] street." Hyde had "the style" that was "exactly right for the job," and Ellis had helpful "clearance" at the Foreign Office. The job could be based on the transcript of the tape he had done for Whitney Shepardson and could be done "quickly." With no choice in the matter, Ellis collaborated quite promptly with Hyde, who at the time was teaching history in the University of the Punjab in Lahore in Pakistan.

Ellis had wanted a fifty-fifty collaboration with Hyde, but the latter thought coauthorship not feasible. Nevertheless, he told Stephenson that, in recognition of the work Ellis had already done, he hoped Ellis could be "taken care of in some mutually satisfactory way."[24] Ellis certainly thought there was an understanding on reimbursement, but he would soon be complaining about Stephenson's failure to pay up, even to answer his letters.

Meanwhile, Ellis sent his manuscript, books, and notes to Hyde in Lahore. However, he was reluctant to send "the original material (the copies of official reports, etc.) by post" and explained that "in the first place I shouldn't have them, and secondly they are close to the bone and contain much that is not publishable." Later Ellis told him that "Bill has a lot of material in his safe (including the famous secret report in book form)." About the same time Ellis said he had "gathered together a mass of notes including [a] copy of the original BSC report."[25] Ellis's letters make it clear that the "files and private papers" mentioned by Hyde and the "BSC Papers" used by Stevenson included more than just the BSC History. If not burned, these other documents are still more forbidden fruit.

In any case, by September 1961, Hyde, Ellis, and Stephenson—wartime colleagues—had a happy reunion and business meeting in New York. Hyde told Sir William he thought Dick found the meeting "very useful." As for himself, he was "extremely thrilled about our project"—though he sang a different tune later. Sir William was very "pleased" that Hyde was "keen on the 'book project'" and particularly pleased that it was now in his "capable hands, where it should have been in the first place."[26]

Also in Hyde's hands was "a copy of the Bible," which Stephenson handed over to him. In turn Hyde gave it to his wife Mary to put in "a safe fire proof place" in Sussex while he returned to Lahore to wind up his affairs. He assured Stephenson he looked forward "with more than usual eagerness to getting down to it." He must have done so, because, soon hurrying to finish the book—he apparently became disenchanted with it— he was borrowing freely from it. It was, of course, The Quiet Canadian, and titled so not just because Robert Sherwood had so named Stephenson but also because Sherwood had once told Stephenson that that should be the title when his story was told.[27]

By the time the book was finished, Hyde was anything but "extremely thrilled about our project." He had hit no end of bumps, of which the chief ones seemed, on the basis of Ellis-Hyde correspondence, to have been made by Stephenson. To be remembered, however, is that Ellis, beset with many problems, was having his own bumpy ride with Sir William. In any case, when Stephenson saw the British edition, he apparently suffered a sea change.

According to Ellis, Stephenson had formerly wanted him to be "forthright" and "fierce" in his book in attacking all those on both sides of the Atlantic who had caused him trouble. He had told Ellis "in effect, that the book must be full of blood and guts, *spare no one* (particularly B——way and SM)." (SM was Brig. Gen. Sir Stewart Menzies, MI-6's chief). Ellis told Hyde that Stephenson had wanted the book "full of 'meat' and violent attacks on all and sundry." Now Ellis pictured him as "moaning because he has been smoked out of his hole," fearing that Hyde was offending too many people, and wanting Hyde's book "watered down" to Ellis's original style.[28] Quoting another ex-BSC colleague, Sydney Morrell, Ellis described Stephenson as "quite seriously disturbed" about the book, wanting "substantial changes" to it, and being "alarmed at having entered the public domain . . . [he] seems to want to hide himself!" Indeed, Stephenson, fearing an adverse effect on Anglo-American relations, told Hyde he was "unalterably opposed" to publication in the United States. He also wanted Hyde to stop publication in "that hotbed Reykhavik" so as to foil "a Comie plot" [sic] against British-Scandinavian relations.[29]

At this point what can be said on Stephenson's behalf? Morrell fingered an obvious explanation: Bill was in "poor health," "was very forgetful," and had lost "most of his old friends" as a result of "his retired life & that damned tel lex [sic] of his!" (As every friend of Sir William knew, he scattered telexes like Rockefeller dimes.) Certainly at this time, 1962–63, Stephenson was obviously suffering consequences of his stroke. Ellis wrote "he is not well and . . . his old sangfroid has deserted him." Ernest Cuneo, who was Donovan's liaison man with Bill Stephenson, said Stephenson "has lost his fire!" Hyde told publisher Roger Straus that Sir William "is in very poor health." Hyde also put some blame on Lady Mary Stephenson: she had "a perfect horror of publicity in any shape or form" and was "continually breathing down her husband's neck, which does not improve matters."[30]

Another explanation of Stephenson's behavior, as well as another source of Hyde's problems, was a batch of complaints from ex-BSC men, who fretted about damage to their amour propre. One was "sore" because he was not mentioned. Another complained because of what he had read about the book. Another, perhaps with more cause for complaint, bitterly protested revealing the story of his own double agent seducing his own wife. The most upsetting to Stephenson was David Ogilvy, a London businessman, who requested a look at the manuscript's treatment of him and then wanted to see the entire manuscript. Though Hyde objected, a worried Stephenson insisted on letting Ogilvy have his way, as a result of which he submitted an inordinately lengthy list of recommended changes. Ogilvy made Stephenson think that without those changes Anglo-American relations would be irreparably damaged. Hyde ridiculed Ogilvy as an "advertising agent" who sells "'Ye Olde England' to Mid-West U.S. tourists and Burlington Arcade shirts to Park Avenue." In the end, Hyde and Straus relied on the opinion of a real expert, the former U.S. ambassador to Britain, David K. E. Bruce, also a devoted admirer of Bill Stephenson.[31]

A final source of Hyde's problems was Dick Ellis himself, who used Hyde as a crying towel, even though he undoubtedly gave Hyde much help and valuable commentary from inside and outside MI-6. Ellis's first problem was a serious protest from Rome. The Italian government complained that Hyde's treatment of the alleged seduction of the Italian naval attaché in Washington, Adm. Alberto Lais, by a BSC agent had London's "official blessing." The agent was the lifelong promiscuous "Cynthia," BSC's most publicized sex success. Her seductive charms allegedly resulted in BSC's acquisition of vital naval intelligence. Some of the fallout of the case, however, hit Ellis because of his allegedly inadequate involvement in clearing Hyde's manuscript.[32]

Ellis's second problem was a consequence of the Lais flap. It was his job with the Foreign Office, in the "I.R.D.," presumably an MI-6 "weeding" department. Once on "the suspended list," he informed Hyde in November 1962 that his employment had been "terminated . . . effective at once, on grounds that I am too compromised! It may be revenge." Of course he was "very annoyed as [the job] was very interesting & useful and brought me" an extra £600 per year. That loss was part of his money problem. Galling, as well as painful, was Stephenson's failure to respond to his pleas for the compensation that had been promised him. He thought he was due "a douceur."[33]

Meanwhile, Hyde had his own money problems. He was peremptorily dunned by Sir William's secretary for the repayment of a £600 advance. (And this happened at the very time Hyde was paying out £4,000 for settlement of a suit brought against him by the Lais family.) Hyde was "extremely astonished" at Sir William's demand. He sharply reminded the secretary that "the idea of the book, which has caused me such a costly expenditure of time, energy, anxiety and money . . . did not originate with me and that I was invited by Sir William to write it."[34]

Meanwhile, the QC had reached the bookstores, in Britain in 1962 and in the United States in 1963. It had been "a bumpy ride," however. It was bumpy for Ellis, whose manuscript was rejected and who had had to beg for compensation for his troubles. It had also been bumpy for Hyde, who had felt put upon by Stephenson,—who had dunned Hyde—and who had been sued by the Lais family. It was no less bumpy for Sir William, who had come to regret having anything to do with the book and who at the same time was, by all first-hand accounts, undergoing painful physical, mental, and psychological recuperation from a major stroke. In 1964 he retired to Bermuda, still "a quiet Canadian."

Stevenson's Book: "Off Like a Rocket"

Then came William Stevenson. He and Sir William, according to the latter, had "established complete rapport even at [the] ends of overseas cables with [the] speed of light."[35] Between them there was, indeed, much that quickly bound them together. Both were Canadians, though the former was born in London, in 1925. Both had been fighter pilots, though in different world wars. Both were individualists, though Stevenson's medium was literary. Both were anti-communists, champions of American-British-Canadian values, and defenders of intelligence and special operations. And both had the same strong emotional commitment to their common ideology.

Their bond undoubtedly had its remote origin in the fact that at the end of World War II Stevenson, a Royal Navy Air service pilot, was briefly attached, almost meaninglessly, to Sir William's BSC. Thereafter, the younger man went into journalism, wrote books, and produced TV documentaries. His first field took him for fifteen years to such foreign hot spots as China, India, Kenya, Korea, Indochina, Malaysia, and Afghanistan, where he covered East-West conflicts, guerrilla wars, and national revolutions. In the meantime he wrote fiction and authored several political commentaries. Then, roaming no more—or much less than before—he settled down in Toronto to produce, direct, and film TV documentaries. That field brought him back, in the early 1970s, to his earlier contact with Sir William.[36]

The two Canadians now shared two interests, one a documentary and the other a book. The first was a documentary on Sir William, initially proposed by Ian Fleming. It also had a bumpy ride, but its ups and downs need not concern us here. Suffice it to note that the dramatic conception that drove the TV project was essentially the same as what later animated *A Man Called Intrepid* (hereafter AMCI). That conception, he told Sir William, was looking at the two world wars and the interwar years "through one pair of eyes—your own." To that end he had done so much filming and acquired so much footage on Sir William and admiring ex-colleagues that he confidently asserted that "no story in this century equals the one contained in all those cans of film."[37]

The other interest connecting the two men was Stevenson's account of the search for the missing Nazi chief Martin Bormann, whom Stevenson considered more monstrous than Hitler. This was *The Bormann Brotherhood*, in which Sir William slips in and out mysteriously while his former agents in Latin America guide Stevenson in his search. Here the important relevancy is the book's dedication: "For Intrepid." While "Intrepid" had been the cable address for MI-6 in New York, and while Sir William had long used it in postwar years as his,[38] it had never been publicly identified with him. One might say then that this use was "Intrepid's" moment of conception; his birth would come with AMCI.

The book contained more than "For Intrepid." An explanatory line said it was he "who made this journey through a terrible chapter in history possible." Realizing those words were not really self-explanatory, Stevenson explained privately to Sir William that they could be taken in two ways: one, if it were not for men like him, there would have been a different end to the war; and two, if Stevenson had not felt Sir William's "support and encouragement," he would not have finished the book.[39] The latter comment, not an uncommon one for Stevenson, reflected not so much flattery as respect and affection. It was easy to like Sir William. Nevertheless, the comment, especially when coupled with Sir William's alleged decisive effect on the war's outcome, evidenced the very high, if not extreme and ultimately very controversial, regard with which Stevenson would ultimately write his Intrepid book.

Before we turn to that, however, we must first watch, with some surprise, the reappearance on the scene of Stephenson's old friend, Dick Ellis. The latter may have been down, but he was not out. He had suffered that hostile interrogation in the mid-sixties, been practically convicted of treason, and probably suffered a diminution of his pension. He had not been hanged, however, as he had been assured would have been the case in wartime. Rather the government allowed him, for whatever practical reasons — a simple cover-up or weak evidence, perhaps — to live out his life under his private dark cloud. Had he lived long enough — he died in 1975 — to experience the revelations by Pincher and Wright, that cloud would have become a public cloudburst.

Be that as it may, and despite his failure to write a Stephenson book, Ellis had returned to the task, probably on his own initiative, and had a rough manuscript completed by April 1972. Titled "The Two Bills," it was the story of the wartime intelligence partnership of Donovan and Stephenson.[40] In coverage, detail, and style it was not much better than his earlier venture, but it did have one new distinguishing feature. It portrayed Sir William not as the representative of the MI-6's Sir Stewart Menzies — whom Sir William contemned — but as Prime Minister Winston Churchill's personal representative in the Western Hemisphere. This portrayal would be enlarged upon in AMCI and would become, as will be shown, one of that book's most controversial features. In Ellis's hands, however, it and the manuscript went nowhere.

Well, almost nowhere. At one point Bantam Books had apparently agreed to publish it in paperback but then wanted it first published elsewhere in hardcover. To this end, as well as in the review and revision of the manuscript, Ellis sought help from Sir William and such friends as Hyde, the writer Roald Dahl, aviation writer Arch Whitehouse, Bill Stevenson, and, yes, this writer. I was asked to write the foreword, was sent the manuscript, but went no further because Ellis had meanwhile run into so many problems that he once again exhausted the patience of Sir William, ultimately the decision maker in producing Stephenson books. Fearing that Ellis's "faulty sparkplug" and "fiddling delays" might hold up Stevenson's TV show, Sir William reached agreement with Stevenson and Ellis in March 1973 that Ellis would once again play second fiddle, this time to Stevenson, who would take over "The Two Bills."[41]

In doing so, Stevenson could hardly have taken a second look at it. It was too far below his mind, imagination, literary style, world view, and political commitments to provide him assistance or inspiration. The latter was already found in the work Stevenson had done on that up-and-down TV show. It was Sir William, "an unusual man" who symbolized "the individual struggling against mass movements and their controllers." He was a man, said Stevenson, whose military, inventive, entrepreneurial, and industrial talents and skills—reflective of recent developments in modern technology—fitted him to be the link in the secret alliance between Churchill and Roosevelt that saved Anglo-American civilization in the fateful days between Dunkirk and Pearl Harbor. Had he not been in New York as Churchill's personal representative, the war would not have ended as it did. Stevenson saw "no way to over-state Bill's achievements."[42]

While Stevenson's tale would stress the role of secret armies, it was not a conventional cloak-and-dagger story. It was the story of men and women whose work could not be publicized, who had employed extraordinary methods of unconventional warfare but had done so, in the midst of war's confusion and uncertainty, in a thoroughly justifiable manner, and whose participation therein was honorable. This was a record, he thought, that had to be made straight, to be communicated to new generations who knew virtually nothing of World War II, and to be kept in mind against future necessities. Stevenson thought it a new angle, "a third dimension," in the war's historiography.[43]

Stevenson sought to write the history of the two world wars as seen through Sir William's eyes. Hence he planned the book to move in chronological fashion from episode to episode with Sir William always occupying the center stage in each. The link was some word, thought, or action that tied him to the episode. Stevenson sought to reconstruct a period or an atmosphere and admitted this entailed some subjectivism. For background he immersed himself in all the current literature, but he eschewed writing conventional history. Stevenson admitted he was not a historian but a foreign correspondent who still had his wits about him. He found it "enormously helpful" to rely on Sir William's "prodigious memory," which was "infintely preferable to scouting through dusty documents, of which many are wrong or distorted anyway." In building the story around Intrepid, he explained that he had to choose between "a densely documented account which then required a scholarship I do not possess, or a good yarn that is accurate without being dull." Some times he found "less personal material" about Intrepid than he wanted but managed "to get around some of the problems by making statements on my own authority—that is—where a judgment or comment is required."[44]

In shaping and writing the book, Stevenson relied heavily on the advice and experience of his editor at Harcourt Brace Jovanovich, Julian Muller, who had served with U.S. naval intelligence. Muller had early been captivated by the personality and story of Intrepid, was a great admirer of Britain, and saw the world as having been saved from tyranny by the Anglo-American alliance. More to the point regarding Intrepid, he felt there was "a moment when the fate of civilized man rested in [Intrepid's] hands; and that this should be made plain at the outset." He told Stevenson the book had to be either a book about the secret wars, "dry-as-dust historical stuff," or a book about Intrepid, "gripping for today's teenagers." He gave Stevenson two options: "Beef it up, make it documentary . . . stuffed with facts and references" or keep Intrepid "squarely in the middle of events." He and others reassured Stevenson there was "no requirement to dot the i's and cross the t's in detailing the historical background." That advice echoed Intrepid's hope that Stevenson, in writing, would be "lifted forward like a canoe on a fast-flowing stream."[45]

What was Intrepid's role in the writing of the book? The question is important because of Sir William's endorsement of its "authenticity," and therefore his coresponsibility for its contents. Certainly Sir William and Stevenson had established rapport with the speed of light. Certainly the former placed himself, his records, and his "prodigious memory" at Stevenson's every beck and call. The two men were in constant contact—in Bermuda, or by telex, telephone, letters, and through friends. Stevenson wrote many long letters explaining his needs, progress, and problems. In return Sir William fired off cables answering questions, identifying people, arranging travel, and offering encouragement. His cablese was witty, sportive, factual, cheery, considerate, and always inspiring. Whatever "sangfroid" and "fire" he had lost ten years earlier had now been recovered. Whatever troubles he had caused earlier were history; now he was once again the ebullient energizer doing everything possible to keep that fast-flowing canoe moving forward. Certainly, then, Sir William knew what was going into the book. However, the kind and degree of his responsibility for its alleged defects we shall consider in Chapter 14.

That fast-flowing canoe symbolized the high expectations that Intrepid, Stevenson, Muller, and everybody at Harcourt Brace had had from the beginning for *A Man Called Intrepid*. They knew, as one or other said, they had "a great story," "a terrific story," "a winner," a sure bestseller in the making. The publishers, in New York and London, could hardly wait for Stevenson and Muller to finish their quickening of the book's pace. London was confident "it will take off like a rocket." It sure did. Ballyhooed from the start, it took off in 1976 as a book club selection with a first printing of 50,000 copies, $35,000 in a major national advertising campaign, plugging by all the publishing journals, and reviewing in all the proper places, including CIA's *Studies in Intelligence*, which carried my own review.[46]

Reviews were of two kinds and from two kinds of reviewers. Those who knew nothing about the subject gave the book high praise, and those who knew something thought it was worthless. The former were impressed by AMCI's detail, documentation, and startling revelations. The latter, mainly Britishers, charged it with inaccuracies, distortions, exaggerations, and perversions of facts. Though the latter had the credentials, they had no effect on the public which, twenty years later, has not stopped buying the book. By 1993 it had sold two million copies and was in its twenty-seventh printing.

For me the book was both a disappointment and an embarrassment. As for the first, it provided none of the "dry-as-dust historical stuff" that was grist for my mill, and at the same time it spilled forth so many incredible statements, claims, and portrayals that it immediately lined me up with its critics. As for the embarrassment, that was the consequence of my friendship with Sir William, and through him with Bill Stevenson. At one point Intrepid suggested I collaborate with Stevenson, but for me, a CIA staff officer, that was not feasible. At another point Stevenson asked me to appear in his TV documentary, but CIA frowned on such publicity. Thus the friendly relationship among the three of us was such that I found myself embarrassingly congratulating them not on the book's story but on its financial success.

Finally, Sir William was no longer "the quiet Canadian," a shadowy spymaster hiding himself and his secrets. He was now "Intrepid," still in hiding, but this time from untold millions whom he fascinated. There were more approaches—for interviews, visits, comments, advice—than he at eighty could or cared to handle. He shuffled most of them onto Stevenson, but even so he had until his last days a steady stream of visitors—generals, admirals, politicians, members of parliament, and congressmen. He garnered more recognition in his last fifteen years than in his previous seventy-eight. Most dear to him was the honor of the Companion of the Order of Canada, which had long been denied him for petty reasons. Particularly appropriate were two celebrations of his new name. The first occurred when HMS *Intrepid*, docking in Bermuda on 10 January 1976, made a presentation to the new Intrepid, and the second took place on 22 September 1983, when the U.S. aircraft carrier *The Intrepid* was the stage on which the Veterans of Strategic Services awarded Sir William the William J. Donovan Medal.

Finally, his name recognition was so great, and its implications so obvious to him, that, by his order, his death on 31 January 1989 was not announced until after he was buried lest well populated little Bermuda be overwhelmed by a heavy influx of foreign visitors and media.[47]

Donovan:
A British Agent
During World War I?

THIS BOOK HAD ITS INSPIRATION IN THE SURPRISING AND INTRIGUING suggestion in Hyde's *The Quiet Canadian* that in 1940 MI-6's Bill Stephenson converted Bill Donovan into London's "man in Washington." This development was initially and greatly facilitated, so it was claimed, by the existence of a Stephenson-Donovan friendship that long antedated both the outbreak of war and the collaboration of the two men in that year.

The validity of that claim was, it seemed to me, convincingly refuted by the evidence presented in the COI essay. However, as will be shown, Stephenson not only never backed off that claim but later collaborated with William Stevenson in producing a remarkable explanation of the friendship's origin. On top of that, another author, Anthony Cave Brown, has used this new explanation as the springboard for a new and much more serious claim that Bill Donovan was actually run as a British secret agent as far back as 1916 and remained on British intelligence books for years thereafter.

It clearly behooves us, therefore, to revisit the issue. That means exploring for the first time Stephenson's first account of the origin of his friendship with Donovan and then taking up the new explanation and author Brown's exploitation of it.

A Thirteen-Thirteen Deal in 1930

When first queried on the issue in 1969, Stephenson had a ready explanation. They had met in London in 1930. They did so when Stephenson met with a New York banker, Harry B. Lake of Ladenburg, Thalmann and Company, to negotiate the purchase of the Pressed Steel Company. Stephenson explained that Donovan had come to London with Lake as his legal counsel, that they had come to Stephenson's office in St. James Place, and that they had lunched with him in his private dining room.[1]

Pressed Steel was then owned by the Edward G. Budd Company of Philadelphia. In that depression year, Stephenson explained, the Budd company was short of money. He recalled, grinning broadly, that Harry Lake liked to recount how he then sold Pressed Steel to Bill Stephenson in thirteen minutes for thirteen million dollars. The steel purchase included the Pressed Steel plant in Germany, and because of this connection with Germany, Stephenson explained, he learned of German rearmament efforts and regularly furnished such knowledge to Winston Churchill, the future prime minister. The latter, of course, was then out of office, in his "wilderness years," and was constantly, and generally vainly, warning of the rising threat from Nazi Germany.

As for the immediate bond of his friendship with Donovan, Stephenson pointed to their common World War I experience. They had both been in Fère-en-Tardenois, in France, in July 1918. Stephenson had been accidentally downed by French gunners near the southern American line where Donovan was stationed. After 1930 he and Donovan occasionally met when Donovan, in London, stopped in to see him.

Stephenson had urged me to get confirmation of his account from Harry Lake himself. As background Lake explained that during the war and on behalf of Ladenburg, Thalmann and Company he had obtained for Stephenson's British Security Coordination many foreign currencies, chiefly marks and yen for, as Lake said, purposes unknown to him. He proudly showed me the solid silver cigar box that Stephenson had sent him as evidence of British gratitude.[2]

Lake laughingly confirmed the thirteen minutes, thirteen million dollars transaction, but in his version it was more happenstance than by design. He had been in London on several missions for six months but everything he arranged collapsed. Then he ran into Stephenson at the Savoy. "Are you here on pleasure?" was Stephenson's query. "Might as well be," replied Lake. The thirteen-thirteen deal followed quickly, but, insisted Lake, it did not involve Donovan in any way, and it did not involve the German plant.

When the question of the Pressed Steel case was put to George S.

Leisure of Donovan's law firm—then Donovan, Leisure, Newton, and Irvine—Leisure and another senior partner, Otto C. ("Ole") Doering Jr., had no recollection of the case but readily accepted Stephenson's word on it. However, a few days later, Leisure informed me by letter that a thorough search of the firm's records showed that the case "was never in this office."[3]

None of the above was included, as the reader will note, in the essay as completed in 1970. The reason was twofold: first, neither Lake nor Leisure supported Stephenson's claim, which rested only on his own memory, and second, Donovan's own categorical denial of a pre-1940 friendship seemed enough to cover the point. However, wanting to pursue the matter with Stephenson, I sent him copies of the two pages stating Donovan's position. In return he briefly repeated the Pressed Steel story but included several details and names that hopelessly rolled the Pressed Steel story and Donovan's trip to London in 1940 into one event.[4]

Two years later, in September 1974, while the COI essay was still classified secret, I was authorized to deliver a copy to Stephenson, by a State Department channel, and then go to Bermuda to discuss it with him and retrieve it. While I will later relate his general reaction to the paper when discussing his relations with President Roosevelt, suffice it here to say that he had only one fault to find. He did not like "one line, the one that says Donovan says he met Stephenson after *July* 1940.'" As Sir William then read it to me, I could not help but sense his unhappiness. So I asked: "Do you mean that it makes out one of you to be a liar?" To which he smilingly replied: "Yes." Well, I queried, "how do you explain the discrepancy?"[5]

His answer was disarming: "Donovan was the most honest person I have ever met. If he were in this room right now—and he might well be[!]— he would certainly affirm that we had known one another long before 1940." He offered to cable his London secretary to search the records. When I asked "Why not?" he said it was not "that big a matter," but he held to his position.[6]

To my surprise Stephenson then came up with a villain in the piece. It was, of course, not Donovan. It was the same Otto Doering mentioned a few paragraphs above. Doering and I had become fairly good friends as had Stephenson and I, and both men struck me as being as honorable and honest as Stephenson held Donovan to be. Doering had been a Donovan partner before the war, his executive officer in OSS, and after returning to the firm after the war was virtually the custodian of Donovan's reputation and interests. He was as protective of Donovan as any OSS or law-firm veteran. However, Doering, said Stephenson, "was always anti-British and always trying to play down the British connection," especially any before COI was established.[7]

Doering was not so much "always anti-British" as he was "always" pro-Donovan. Thus, he generously acknowledged British assistance to COI and OSS, but he just as often ridiculed Stephenson's claim that Stephenson had the red carpet laid out for Donovan when he made his historic 1940 visit to London. Donovan, said Doering, did not need Stephenson to get him into high places in London, because Donovan had his own well-established reputation and contacts there. Doering was always quick to rebut any oh-so-subtle suggestion that Donovan was London's "man in Washington."[8]

A Chance Encounter in 1916?

There the issue rested until early 1976, when on publication Stevenson's book hit the bestseller list. Overnight, as already indicated, it turned Sir William into the world famous "Intrepid," a man of mystery, courage, and skill who operated unselfishly at the highest levels of Allied statecraft, a model of political virtue for an anti-heroic world. And this happened to him at age eighty when most such personages, having left the world stage, are not heard of again until their obituaries appear. However, Stephenson paid a price. Not only was the book flayed by the coqnoscenti as distorted, exaggerated, overblown, misleading, laughable, and fictional rather than factual, but its author and its hero were also heavily criticized. Some sympathy was shown Sir William, though—he was aged, senile, garrulous, too talkative, even misused.

Of the many points of controversy stirred up by the book, there was one that was dropped like a bombshell into the question of the Donovan-Stephenson friendship. Since I had long known the book was in the works, had discussed it with Sir William and Stevenson, and though Stephenson had read my COI essay, I was not prepared for the stunning revelation that the two of them dropped in the book as early as page five. There it was, a re-markable account—over forty years after the events, as we shall see—of an equally remarkable first meeting, not in 1930 as originally claimed, but four-teen years earlier, in 1916, during World War I. And here it is: While convalescing in England from severe gassing suffered in the trenches, twenty-year-old Bill Stephenson met thirty-three-year-old Bill Donovan, who was in England on a Rockefeller war relief mission. The encounter, a chance affair, was recalled by Donovan "in notes for a biographer," who is identified in a footnote as Whitney Shepardson, mentioned in my Introduction. This encounter is recalled by Donovan as "our first meeting, in 1916." He remembers himself "as an old man, wickedly well-fed as against this skinny kid," whose questions caused him to "pay attention." He continues for twenty-three printed lines:

We discovered a shared background that overcame the gulf between those already fighting the war and us Americans, still out of it. . . . Stephenson understood our American style that was taken, in England in the midst of a bloodbath, for brash vulgarity . . . [and he] was willing to translate the horror [of the war] into facts and figures. . . . [He] combined compassion and shrewdness in assessing German military and psychological weakness . . . [and] didn't see the war as an accident of history complicated by lunacy at the top. . . . [Stephenson] was certainly not in love with the war . . . [but] said someone had to fight this evil. . . . [He] refused to dismiss as propaganda the reports of German atrocities . . . [and] wanted to get back to the front. The doctors said his lungs would never permit [it].

"So he decided to fly," recalled Donovan, remembering more of the wartime career of young Bill Stephenson: "He wangled a transfer to the Royal Flying Corps [which] didn't ask questions . . . fudged his medical history and nobody looked too close. After five hours' instruction, he was a fully fledged combat pilot."[9]

What are we to make of this remarkable recollection? Is all or any part of it true? If substantially true, it clearly makes Bill Donovan contradict himself. It distinctly reinforces Stephenson's insistence on a long-established friendship with Donovan. It enhances the prescience and skill with which Stephenson, beginning in 1940, did cultivate and nourish a friendship, new or old, with Donovan. It also embarrasses those, like Otto Doering (now deceased), who played down Donovan's British connection before COI's establishment. Before accepting this story, however, let us look at it closely.

First of all, it is true that Donovan's alleged "biographer," Whitney Shepardson, was working from 7 August 1958 to 1 November 1961 on a history of OSS and Donovan. Evidence of this is found in the Donovan Papers, which were first stored in New York, then in 1961 transferred to CIA's Historical Intelligence Collection, and then twenty years later permanently deposited in the Military History Institute in Carlisle Barracks, Pennsylvania. But Stevenson had no access to the papers at CIA, and his book was written when they had not become publicly available in Carlisle. He has told us nothing about the provenance or location of those "notes." I have never found them in either CIA or Carlisle.

Second, did Shepardson ever interview General Donovan, as these "notes" allege? Never have I found any evidence that he either did, or tried to, interview Donovan. Beginning in 1956 Donovan suffered a series of strokes, which were soon diagnosed as an irremediable atrophy of the brain. By April 1957 he was confined to his bed and in need of constant nursing attention. Following a third stroke in March 1958, he was not expected to live much longer and, at the request of President Dwight D. Eisenhower, was transferred to Walter Reed General Hospital in Washington. There he lingered for nearly a year, often staring blankly, a dying man whose family and friends were already mourning his passing. He died 8 February 1959. Is it really likely that in the six months between 7 August 1958 and 8 February 1959, Whitney Shepardson, though an old friend, was permitted to interview the dying general about, inter alia, "our first meeting, in 1916"?[10]

Third, could that 1916 meeting have actually occurred? Beyond telling us that it took place in England in 1916, Stevenson gives us no precise details on where, when, and especially how. So let us look at the possibility. Donovan, for his part, was in London on two occasions in that year, both connected with his war relief mission. He was there the first time for thirteen days, from 27 March until 9 April. He was there the second time for "a brief stay" in mid-July when he was hurrying home, on orders from the War Department, to report for military service on the Mexican border. He was listed "on active duty" on 15 July and was "mustered into Federal service 19 July 1916."[11]

Where was Stephenson at those times? While the chronology of his military service has not been satisfactorily established, he and his biographers assert that he was badly gassed in the trenches in 1915 and hospitalized for months in Folkestone, in southeast England, about 120 air miles from London—and that late in 1917 he was back on the continent as a fighter pilot. No one has yet placed Stephenson in London or Donovan in Folkestone, in 1916.[12] So, aside from theoretical possibilities, how could the two have met?

Finally, do these "notes" ring true? One wonders whether a dying Donovan was capable of recalling this kind of conversation with a stranger forty-three years earlier. One wonders whether this invalid could recall seven different subjects of that conversation and a handful of additional biographical details about the stranger's subsequent flying career. One wonders why Donovan rather pointedly and apparently without provocation referred precisely to "our first meeting, in 1916." Are we to believe he was consciously correcting his 1944 statement and trying belatedly to cede the point to his good friend Bill Stephenson?

Since these "notes for a biographer" raise so many questions, and since they have been connected with the name of Whitney Shepardson, which is their only prima facie claim to plausibility, how can one account for them if they are not authentic? As mentioned in my introduction, Sir William knew of Whitney Shepardson's research and in 1960 dictated for Shepardson his own account of his relations with Donovan and oss. That knowledge, coupled with Stephenson's parallel but subsequent familiarity with my interest in "our first meeting," might well have served both him and Stevenson as the foundation for a putative 1916 meeting with which otherwise real or supposed Donovan comments could be associated. Certainly the very words "our first meeting, in 1916" struck me the moment I read them as a definite rebuttal of the position I had clearly laid out for Sir William.[13]

No, until those "notes" can be authenticated, the case will be left here where a healthy sixty-one-year-old Donovan left it in 1944: "Did not know S[tephenson] then. I met him only after return."

From War Relief to Espionage?

When an interesting and intriguing story appears in print, it is likely to enjoy some replay elsewhere. So it was with Stevenson's story of the Stephenson-Donovan meeting in 1916. It was not only replayed but enlarged upon by author Anthony Cave Brown, first in his 1982 biography *The Last Hero: Wild Bill Donovan* and then in subsequent public comment.[14] It was so enlarged upon that the original chance encounter became the beginning of twenty-four years of a secret connection of Donovan with the British Secret Intelligence Service. There is some irony here; this allegation of a long-standing secret link with MI-6 appears in a book whose author enjoyed the important and enthusiastic support of many champions of oss and Donovan, especially the allegedly anti-British Otto Doering. The replay merits scrutiny.

According to Brown, Donovan had "his first encounter with the British security and intelligence services" even before meeting Stephenson —namely, when the security men held up the unloading of his ship and when he and others had to register as alien neutrals at the Vine Street Police Station in London. Because of an alleged hitch in his mission, Brown went on, Donovan was left looking for another job. "Did he commence his intelligence career at this time?" asked Brown. He called the question "one of the riddles" associated with Donovan's stay in London.[15]

Relying on Stevenson, Brown said the two men had their first meeting "in London in 1916." He described Stephenson as "a Canadian with an American mother, and a captain in the Royal Flying Corps." Further, "whether [he] was in or associated with British intelligence at that time was not important—all Britons were at that time de facto British spies." Nevertheless, "the subject" of the Donovan-Stephenson conversation was "German military and psychological weaknesses."[16] Noting Donovan's denial of having known Stephenson prior to 1940, Brown nevertheless alleges that Donovan, writing his wife, said he had met and dined with "a Canadian," whose name he did not give. Brown admitted that the evidence in Donovan's papers in support of Stephenson's claim is "slender."[17]

Now, continues Brown, when Donovan had first encountered those British intelligence and security officials, in Southampton and London, they would have noted that Donovan, an American official heading for famine relief service in Belgium, "was in a position to render British Intelligence services of great importance." They would have noted that Donovan was headed for German rear areas—including "northern France," where the Germans were planning a big offensive and where Donovan, because of his legal and military training, "would have been a very desirable spy." But, asks Brown, "did Donovan work for the British at this time?" "We do not know the answer for sure," but in 1981 the CIA "revealed" that Donovan had "probably" received British "military intelligence" training in World War I.[18]

There were only two occasions, continues Brown, when Donovan could have received such training, and this period in London was one of them. How was that? Well, he had already been "spotted" twice on arrival, and because of that hitch in his mission, and before he left for the continent, he "kicked his heels in London for three weeks." That was "ample time" for the British to give him that intelligence training. What the second occasion was Brown apparently forgot to tell us.[19]

Again wondering whether Donovan "collaborated or not with British intelligence," Brown nevertheless paints a picture that leaves us little doubt as to what he wants us to think Donovan was doing. Thus, Donovan's "cautious, brief, and uninformative" letters to his wife showed he was aware of British censorship and the possible compromise of his mission, "whether that mission was legal or illegal." Thus, he "crisscrossed and entered and left Belgium extensively and frequently." Thus, "he certainly engaged . . . in political warfare" when he discussed the reconstruction of the Louvain university with Belgium's Cardinal Mercier—"Is it possible [he] had become a spy for Christ?" Thus, he made "increasingly odd perambulations behind the German lines," and his movements after he left Louvain became "no more explicable" than before—"unless he was spying." Thus, later movements, "nowhere recorded" as business related, "suggested intelligence rather than good works."[20]

What Brown wants us to see as Donovan's spying for Britain apparently ended in July 1916 when Donovan rushed home, on military orders, for service on the Mexican border. That, however, was not the end of Donovan's connection with British intelligence. No, said Brown in 1983, he was kept "on the British Intelligence Service's books for many years." So much so that during World War II the British, showing "unusual confidence" in him, backed him "without hesitation" as the "intelligence master of the United States."[21]

The Power of the Imagination

Surely Brown has told us a remarkable story about the late Bill Donovan. So let us ask here the same question that was asked earlier about those remarkable "notes for a biographer": is any of it true? Like that story, it deserves to be looked at closely.

The first thing discovered is that it contains not one single fact, verifiable or not, supportive of the proposition (however slyly suggested) that Donovan was working not for the Rockefeller war mission but for British intelligence. There is not one name, one date, one event, one organization, or one operation or activity that has been put forth to that effect. There is no evidence of Donovan's spying, no evidence of any intelligence gathered, no witness against Donovan, no German, Austrian, or American document charging or suggesting any espionage. There is no evidence that the people whom he ostensibly served, the Rockefeller Foundation, ever accused him of betraying his commitments to them. There is not even an endnote of Brown's that purports to sustain any allegations. No, the story is devoid of factual basis and therefore ought to be thrown out of court immediately.

There is a baker's dozen of demonstrable errors or inaccuracies, however, that additionally undermine trust in this account. One, author Bill Stevenson did not say that that famous first meeting occurred "in London"; in fact, he said nothing about precisely where, when, or how it occurred. Two, Stephenson's mother was, by his own account, a "Canadian girl of Norwegian descent, Christina Breckman." Three, Stephenson was not "a captain" at the time of his alleged meeting with Donovan; and four, he was not in the Royal Flying Corps until over a year later. Five, "German military and psychological weaknesses" was one of seven subjects, not *"the"* subject [my emphasis], of the alleged Stephenson-Donovan conversation.[22]

Six, the "evidence" in the Donovan papers supporting the Stephenson version of the meeting is not "slender"; it is nonexistent. Take Brown's story of Donovan writing his wife of dining with an unnamed "Canadian." Even if he said he did so dine, that is all that that proves. However, in a letter on 5 April 1916 Donovan wrote his wife that he "went to the theatre alone, sat next to two sgts [sergeants] in a Canadian regiment—Price and Riddle. I bought them supper afterwards and they talked." Seven, Donovan did not plan to and did not enter "northern France." Eight, CIA "revealed" nothing in 1981, or any year, about Donovan's "probably" receiving British "military intelligence" training; in that year a CIA author, myself, publicly quoted Emmet Crozier as writing in his *American Reporters on the Western Front 1914–1918* that Donovan [in 1917 or 1918] "had been training with British intelligence," and I immediately added "probably military intelligence."[23]

Nine, Donovan had not lost his Rockefeller job and had therefore not "kicked his heels" in London. In any case, and ten, he could not have done it for "three weeks," because he had been there for thirteen days at most: from 27 March until 9 April when he left for Holland; or eleven days, if we subtract two days for train time to London, hotel registration and check-out, and finally reaching the packet boat for Holland. Eleven, it is not true that he "criss-crossed and entered and left Belgium extensively and fre-quently": he entered and left Belgium, period; meanwhile, he concentrated on Brussels and visited Antwerp, Hainaut, Mechlin (where he met with Cardinal Mercier) and Luxemburg before being ordered by his director to go to Berlin. Twelve, there were no "odd perambulations"; his travels are plausibly detailed in a fifteen-page report to his director. And thirteen, it is insinuating and false to say, as that report disproves, that his business trips were "nowhere recorded." And for good measure, it is utterly gratuitous, as well as false, to say his movements "suggested intelligence rather than good works."[24]

So much for errors and inaccuracies. Let us turn to innuendo and speculation, of which there is another baker's dozen of instances. The reader will quickly note the half-dozen times Brown raises Iago-like ques-tions about Donovan: Did he "commence his intelligence career" at the Vine Street station? How about "the riddles" arising from his stay in Lon-don? Was his new friend Stephenson then "associated" with intelligence? Did Donovan "work for the British" on the continent? Did he "collaborate" with British intelligence? Was his mission "legal or illegal"? And what was he doing "unless he was spying"? The reader will also note the half-dozen times Brown slyly suggests that Donovan was groomed for or involved in British intelligence activity: "his first encounter" with British intelligence; his being in a position to "render" them "services of great importance"; his being perceived as "a very desirable spy"; his being "spotted" twice and having "ample time" for intelligence training; and his being kept "on the British Intelligence Service's books for many years."

Now for the fantasies. Since his story is as full of errors as it is empty of facts, it is not surprising that Brown winds up with fantasies about what Donovan was really doing when he was supposed to be feeding the hungry. First is the unlikely daydream that sees British intelligence turning a pearl into a sow's ear in thirteen, perhaps only eleven, days; that is, "spotting" a stranger—an American relief official, the future hero of "the Fighting Sixty-Ninth"—corrupting, recruiting, and training him as a spy, and then success-fully directing and dispatching him as their secret agent behind the enemy's lines. Here is the second, more impossible, daydream: Britain's secret agent is seen traveling openly for three months on this itinerary: from England to

Holland, Belgium, Berlin, Stockholm, Vienna, Sofia, Berlin, Holland, Berlin, Vienna, Berlin, Switzerland, and for the fifth time back to Berlin and all the while—forget feeding the poor—he is gathering vital current military intelligence about the enemy and all the while pulling the wool over the enemy's eyes! The grandest daydream of all, however, is the last one, the dazzling accomplishment of British intelligence, the retention on their "books" for twenty-four years and the reactivation, when they needed him in World War II, of a long-standing treasure, "a sleeper," whom at a critical moment they made "the intelligence master of the United States."

What makes Brown's fantasizing particularly incredible is the fact that only once does Brown allow for the possibility that Donovan would not "compromise himself,"[25] but that is precisely what Brown would have us believe he did. He would have us believe that Donovan, allegedly out of a job, betrayed his solemn commitment to the Rockefeller Foundation, the U.S. Department of State, and all the combatants to work in Europe in an absolutely neutral way to study relief methods and bring relief supplies (that is, food, milk, and so forth) to hungry people, especially in Poland. Brown would have us believe that Donovan betrayed the following assurance that he gave a German official about himself and his mission: "[Those] who are sent to countries at war or to neighboring countries are required to devote themselves exclusively to the objects of their mission. They are obliged to observe strict neutrality in word and act, to refrain from expressions of opinion on the issues of the war and to preserve in the strictest confidence any knowledge as to facts of actual or potential military significance of which the correct performance of their purely neutral functions may make them cognizant."[26]

Donovan provided that assurance, in the name of the Rockefeller Foundation, on 7 June 1916, weeks after he had allegedly lost his job with the foundation and was "kick[ing] his heels" in London, a juicy target for British recruitment.

Brown would also have us believe that Donovan took leave of his common sense. Let us note a few of the considerations that might have occurred to Donovan had he been offered Brown's harebrained scenario. First, ten years a lawyer, Donovan knew that wartime spying meant immediate execution in the event of capture. Second, two years married, he knew that Britain and Germany had already shot spies. Third, he surely knew that he had been forbidden by President Wilson's proclamation of neutrality of 4 August 1914 from "tak[ing] part, directly or indirectly" in European hostilities.[27] Fourth, he was fully conscious of his American military status as a captain in Troop One of the First Cavalry of the New York National Guard. Fifth, he expected to be called to his country's colors in the event of Mexican hostilities and had conditioned his acceptance of the Rockefeller post on immediate release to rejoin his troop. With such considerations surely at hand, is it likely that Donovan would have taken off on a summer sabbatical as a British spy?

No, reality must displace fantasy. Brown's account is a groundless exploitation of that imaginary Donovan-Stephenson meeting in 1916. As such, it is a piece of fiction, not of history. It is a concoction of demonstrably false and inaccurate statements, innuendo and speculation, and fantasies. It is such a fanciful concoction that it is admirable testimony to the power of the human imagination.

Echoes of Iago

Great oaks from little acorns grow, and so also in the telling and retelling of fanciful tales and daydreams. So also has it been true—was it not predictable?—of the concoction by Stevenson and Brown. In 1986 the CIA—no less—staged an exhibit entitled "With the Sixty-Ninth: Donovan in World War I." The opening ceremony was dignified by the presence not only of DCI William J. Casey and New York Sen. Daniel P. Moynihan, but also of visiting high-level Australian, British, and Canadian officers. The latter were on hand because the exhibit included panels that pertained to their countries' fighting in several campaigns, for instance, Ypres 1914 and 1915, Gallipoli 1915, Verdun 1916, the Somme 1916, and Vimy Ridge 1917.[28]

Since all of this fighting occurred before the United States entered the war and, therefore, did not involve Donovan and the Sixty-Ninth, why were they featured in a Donovan exhibit? The "most important reason" for including them, noted William M. Henhoeffer, the agency's curator of its Historical Intelligence Collection, was "Donovan's travels in Western Europe from late March through late June 1916." Further echoing Anthony Cave Brown but without naming him, Henhoeffer, an admirer of Donovan, explained that "there has been some recent speculation that his travels in German rear areas *near* Belgium and *northern France* might also have been intended for *"intelligence, not just good works."* (My emphasis.) The curator began his next sentence—most of which is irrelevant here—with a throwaway phrase straight out of Brown: "Whatever his purposes, Donovan ..."[29] Whatever *his* purposes, the curator clearly had concluded that Bill Donovan, his and CIA's hero, may well have been a British agent in World War I. Iago had done his work.

Echoing and embellishing have been carried to greater heights by Brian P. Sullivan, who did research in the Rockefeller archives on Donovan's career in both world wars. Outlining that research in a Rockefeller newsletter, he showed his indebtedness to Anthony Cave Brown. At the outset Sullivan asserted that Donovan's espionage career "possibly" began "in 1916" and then, using one of Brown's favorite devices, he said that "one of the unanswered questions regarding Donovan is whether he engaged in espionage during his first visit to Europe in the spring of 1916." "It has been suggested," Sullivan continued, that Stephenson "already worked for the Secret Intelligence Service at the time and recruited Donovan to gather intelligence for the British government on the continent." Furthermore, wrote Sullivan, "others have speculated" that Donovan "may have agreed to undertake an espionage assignment" for Cardinal Mercier. Citing Brown, Sullivan noted that Donovan's movements in March–June 1916 could be "explained only by spying."[30]

Surely it is worth noting that, like Anthony Cave Brown, neither Brian Sullivan nor William Henhoeffer has cited one single fact, name, date, organization, or accomplishment that directly or even indirectly points to any recruitment, training, control, direction, or exploitation of Bill Donovan by British secret intelligence in 1916. No, there is no factual or rational evidence of any such activity. There is only innuendo, speculation, and fantasy. Unfortunately, though deplorable, it is not surprising that such airiness can captivate otherwise sensible persons.

13

·−−·−−·

Churchill's "Personal Representative"

THE DATE WAS 12 FEBRUARY 1969—WELL BEFORE THE MEDIA HUBBUB over Sir William Stephenson's wartime role. The setting was his living room in Bermuda. The topic was his 1939-40 travels. He said he visited the United States and Canada in September–October 1939. Then early in 1940 Winston Churchill, first lord of the Admiralty, asked him to go to the States as his "personal representative." From then until his death in 1989, Sir William often spoke to me, as he had obviously done to others, of this special relationship with Churchill.[1] There are some who think he was fantasizing, even lying.

Five years later, 18 September 1974, the scene was once again Bermuda, the front entrance of the Princess Hotel. A car, driven by Lady Mary Stephenson, stopped in front. Out stepped Sir William. Handing me the copy of my COI essay that CIA had authorized me to show him, and striking a Rooseveltian pose with his head suitably cocked, he said: "In the words of FDR, 'puffectly grand!'"[2] The memory of that encounter—just the three of us—has lived on. Had he actually been so close to FDR that such posturing had become second nature? Or was he, once again, fantasizing, even lying?

This Churchill claim on Sir William's behalf was first publicly mentioned in 1952, in McKenzie Porter's article. It was then fully developed in 1962 in Hyde's QC.[3] It never provoked any denials or challenges, however, until 1976 when it—along with many other claims—was so extravagantly elaborated in Stevenson's AMCI that outraged scholars hurried into print. They denied or greatly minimized any Stephenson connection with Churchill and Roosevelt. They threw out the baby with the bath.

Leading these critics was Sir John Colville, Churchill's private secretary in 1940–41, in 1943, and from 1951 to 1955. It was he who exposed the falsity of the AMCI photo caption that identified Stephenson, instead of Brendan Bracken, as Churchill's companion surveying with him the bombed ruins of parliament. Colville had more cutting assertions: he never heard Churchill speak of Stephenson, doubted Stephenson ever entered No. 10 Downing Street, and said no one who was there could recollect his ever doing so. Hedging his position, Sir John admitted that Sir William's "name may have been mentioned to Churchill" and "was probably also known to Roosevelt," but as for a special liaison between the two leaders it was just not so.[4]

An American scholar, Warren Kimball, the editor of Churchill-Roosevelt correspondence during the war, said that "Intrepid's claim to have been the intermediary for the Churchill-Roosevelt exchanges is, on the documentary evidence, patently wrong." He noted that Stephenson's name was not mentioned in any of more than two thousand telegrams and memoranda that passed between the two leaders. Even so, he offered a partial explanation—to which we are coming—for that silence as well as for Colville's ignorance of Intrepid.[5]

What, then, was Stephenson's wartime role? Was he, as he claimed, the "personal representative" of Winston Churchill in the Western Hemisphere? Or was he simply the New York representative of the MI-6 chief, Col. Stewart Menzies? Was he, as another Canadian scholar, Wesley K. Wark, described him, merely "a minor intelligence official surrounded by a lot of mythology"?[6]

A Dual Role: Liaison Officer and Mission Chief

There is no primary source—telegram, letter, photograph, or statement by Churchill, Roosevelt, Menzies, or anyone else—that answers the question incontrovertibly. The Churchill-Roosevelt correspondence, as Kimball stated, contains no mention of Stephenson. Equally impressive is the fact that Churchill historian Martin Gilbert, when narrating Churchill's daily activities from the outbreak of war to Pearl Harbor, mentioned Stephenson only once in no less than 1,308 pages of his Finest Hour.[7] While that reference and other evidence, including an impressive statement from Donovan, will be discussed shortly, suffice it for now to admit the absence of any irrefutable documented answer to the question.

Why the silence? Sir John Colville would say he had already answered that question: Stephenson was nobody. Colville, however, has been rebutted by Warren Kimball: the fact that Stephenson was never mentioned in any memo or letter "is hardly surprising given the secret nature of his work; just as it is hardly surprising that Colville never heard the name of Britain's secret agent in America bandied about 10 Downing Street."[8] Kimball is only echoing the centuries-old truth—and jest—that the most important thing about the secret service is that it be secret!

That is the truth that dramatist Robert Sherwood appreciated when he named Stephenson "a quiet Canadian." That is the truth writer Roald Dahl had in mind when he described Stephenson as "a silent . . . kind of unknown small creature, hiding in the back of a dark room somewhere up in New York." That is the truth served by David K. E. Bruce, America's three-time ambassador, who described Stephenson as "a modest, almost anonymous, figure," whose activities were "totally unsuspected by all except a handful of individuals on either side of the Atlantic." Echoing that truth was BSC officer Bickham Sweet-Escott, who said that Stephenson "was known to the people that mattered . . . four or five in Washington . . . and five or six . . . in London."[9]

That is the truth that hides, even until today, the careers of Stephenson's subordinates. Take his deputy, Colonel Ellis, for example. Known now largely because of his alleged German and Soviet service, Ellis's career in New York and Washington has never been detailed. Publicly named but still less known than Ellis was John A. R. Pepper, Stephenson's secret intelligence chief. Totally unknown then and now is his propaganda chief, Richard Coit. None of these secret agents, like most of their predecessors and contemporaries, including Stephenson, left the paper trail beloved of scholars. Indeed, the lives of secret agents in history are almost as unknown to the public as was Ultra before the publication of Winterbotham's *The Ultra Secret*. So unknown is it that, for example, Sir John Colville, sitting in Churchill's "inner circle," could write 287 pages without naming one recognizable British secret agent—except, of course, those well-known traitors who worked for the Soviets![10]

Be that as it may, it appears at first glance that the BSC *History* has answered our question. There on page xi, in the opening paragraph on BSC's "Origin, Development and Functions," it says: "In the early spring of 1940, WS [William Stephenson] paid a visit to the United States. Ostensibly private business was the purpose of his journey. In fact, he travelled at the request of CSS [Chief of the Secret Service, Col. Stewart Menzies]." Then follows a score of quotations from Stephenson's cables to Menzies. There are none from Stephenson to Churchill. On one occasion Stephenson told

Menzies that he "should personally convey to Prime Minister" a message about Donovan's great importance to the British cause.[11] Otherwise, Churchill's name is referenced in the index only five times. Case closed?

Not yet. Where Stephenson was described as travelling at the request of "css," those initials were crossed out in my copy of the history. In their place was inserted, in the unmistakable Stephenson handwriting, "wsc," Winston Spencer Churchill. This is not the place to speculate on the when or why of the change. Enough to say that it points sharply to a different view of "the request," a view that has a pedigree worth reviewing. Simply put, there were two requests, one from Menzies and another from Churchill himself.

McKenzie Porter had written in 1952 that Churchill, when seeking a man to run British intelligence in the New World, "thought of the astute and well-informed . . . Stephenson" and "sent him to New York" for that purpose. Since Porter had not interviewed Stephenson, he surely obtained his view of things from such friends of Stephenson as Sherwood, Cuneo, Pepper, and Wiseman, whom he did interview, and who obtained it from Stephenson or someone else.[12] Incidentally, if Porter had known of the Menzies request, neither he, nor anyone subject to the Official Secrets Acts, would have dared publicize his name. For decades the sis chief was known only as "C." Still, can the bsc History and Stephenson's claim be reconciled?

Let us begin with the history's statement that Stephenson "paid a visit" to New York. Yes, he "paid a visit." As noted earlier, he obtained a visa in London on 6 March to travel here as a "Company Director" with the "Ministry of Supply." He met Hoover on 16 April, traveled to California, and returned to London on a date so far unknown. But then there was a second trip: on 3 June he was issued another visa, sailed on the S. S. Britannic, arrived here on 21 June, and did so in order "to take over the duties of British Passport Control Officer" in New York.[13] This was not "a visit" but in fact a mission "for the duration." This trip was never discussed, even mentioned, in the bsc History.

The difference between the two trips was plausibly spelled out by Montgomery Hyde. The first, on Menzies' request, was simply to "establish relations on the highest possible level" between MI-6 and the fbi. The second was much more far reaching. Because Stephenson was an aggressive innovator and entrepreneur, he had returned to London convinced that the fbi liaison was only the start of what needed to be done in the United States. He was also convinced that the task required a larger organization than New York's minuscule passport office. Far from London, it also needed strong political and bureaucratic backing to survive and grow. Stephenson, when asked by Menzies to take the job, took time to think it over, discussed it with friends, and then sought an interview with Churchill. Sitting in his old room at the Admiralty—he had not yet moved into Downing Street—Churchill "looked Stephenson straight in the face. 'Your duty lies there,' he said. 'You must go.'"[14]

That Churchill remark has had many versions, but since they have not been a subject of controversy, there is no need to recount them. Not so, however, the date, the occasion, and the locale. Where Hyde had the interview taking place in the Admiralty, AMCI had it occurring at Lord Beaverbrook's home, at a dinner attended by Churchill, Stephenson, and other "chiefs of war." When this was contemptuously rebutted by Sir John Colville, Sir William named those "chiefs" and specified the exact date of the dinner. It was 10 May 1940, the day on which Churchill became prime minister. For David Hunt, one of Churchill's wartime secretaries, that claim was so ridiculous that it destroyed "the last corroboration of a special relationship between Stephenson and Churchill."[15]

Perhaps. Perhaps not. Let us state a double proposition. First, Stephenson did represent Menzies as his nominal chief and initial point of contact in London, but, second, Stephenson accepted the offer of "C" only after Churchill asked him to do so, assured him of full backing, and promised personal access to himself. This latter claim, first made by Porter in 1952 and developed more fully by Hyde in 1962, has never been convincingly challenged, much less disproven. Still, let us offer some proof. Let us begin with its plausibility.

Donovan Work for Hoover?

When Bill Donovan, age fifty-seven, returned from London in August 1940, Secretary of War Stimson noted that he "was determined to get into the war some way or other." A hero in search of a role, he had several options, but he chose intelligence—thanks largely to Stephenson. Not as well known a hero as Donovan, Stephenson was no less determined to get into the war and, at forty-four, no less in search of a role.[16] Not a politician, not a member of parliament, he was not a likely cabinet appointee. As for the military, his honors and experience had all been of the Great War vintage. Twenty years of leadership in business and finance fitted him nicely for a managerial chieftaincy in the burgeoning war machinery. Like Donovan, however, he wanted action, and like Donovan he found it in intelligence. How did that happen?

Certainly it was not as insinuated by Anthony Cave Brown. Nor is the account spun out in AMCI any more believable. According to it, in the Great War the great "Blinker" Hall tagged the young fighter pilot, because of papers he had allegedly written on "hot pursuit" and prison camps, as a prime recruit for a future in secret intelligence. Thereafter Hall so guided his secret career that by the mid-1930s Stephenson had become "the chief of a private intelligence agency." So secret was all this that "all record of his activities was erased from the newspapers after 1935"! No documentation is offered for any part of this fanciful scenario.[17]

No, there is a more mundane explanation. It takes us back to Stephenson's Pressed Steel Company and the information he thereby gained about German steel production and then furnished to Churchill via Desmond Morton. Later, he was introduced to Menzies, to whom he provided such intelligence. In the winter of 1939–40 he played a major role in MI-6's effort to sabotage German access to Sweden's high-grade iron ore. The attempt, though strongly backed by Churchill, who surely knew of Stephenson's role, ran into so many political objections—Sweden being a neutral—that action was held up, postponed, and then aborted, much to the deprecations of Stephenson and Churchill.[18] Stephenson's involvement easily explains Menzies' asking him to "visit" the United States.

But why should anyone think that Stephenson quickly nodded yes to Menzies' offer of an indefinite overseas assignment? MI-6 was a relatively unknown government bureaucracy, regularly neglected, always underfunded, often criticized by the military, and unprepared for war when it broke out. It immediately lost stations in Berlin, Vienna, Warsaw, Helsinki, Riga, and Tallinn, and in the spring of 1940 it lost Oslo, Copenhagen, Paris, Rome, Brussels, and the Hague. Just as devastating, and most embarrassing, was the Venlo incident—the German capture in November 1939 of two MI-6 agents at Venlo on the Dutch border. Their subsequent debriefing left MI-6 almost naked to the Nazis. No, to the extent that Stephenson knew any of this about the service, he could not have thought: "That's for me!"

There was another drawback. Col. Stewart Menzies, fifty and not yet knighted, had been in MI-6 since 1915 and had become chief only on 29 November 1939, despite strong, sustained opposition from Churchill. As "C," Menzies topped a leadership that was later criticized by Lord Dacre as "of very limited intelligence." Dacre denounced the professionals under Menzies as "by and large pretty stupid," a characterization made earlier to me by Sir William. David Bruce told me as early as 1969 that "Stephenson did not like Menzies," that he considered him "a difficult man, very secretive, an army officer, a gentleman." As things worked out, Stephenson contemptuously called Menzies "my man" in London, and the sis admitted, as the reader will recall, that Menzies "was indeed always at pains to describe Stephenson as 'my representative' and inclined to be jealous of occasional communications not sent by or through sis."[19] Nothing in the record suggests that Stephenson could have been or was Menzies' cheerful spear-carrier.

Instead, the record shows Stephenson as a leader, not a subordinate. He would no more have been a station chief under Menzies than Donovan would have run the New York FBI office for J. Edgar Hoover. No, Stephenson, a wealthy industrialist who was either founder, owner, partner, or director in such firms as General Radio, Cox-Cavendish Electrical, General Aircraft, Sound City Films, Earls Court, Catalina, Pressed Steel, and Alpha Cement, was the kind of person who ran his own show. "A true top-level operator, Stephenson," said Kim Philby, "was not used to footling around at the lower levels." Stephenson, said an MI-6 officer who met him on his arrival in New York, would have become Menzies' "unpaid representative" only as "the result of a directive from Churchill."[20]

There is another side to the coin. Is it likely that Stephenson's mission here would have been made without Churchill's involvement? Yes, if Stephenson had come simply to replace Sir James Paget as control officer. No, if his mission far exceeded that of an ordinary station head. Stephenson came here not just to liaise with the FBI but with "a wide-ranging brief" to carry on covert diplomacy at the highest levels; to obtain rifles, ammunition, and destroyers; to build a secret agency; and with all effective means to subvert American isolationists, expose and frustrate Nazi agents, and bring the United States into the war. He came here when it was, as A. J. P. Taylor said, "the moment of decision for Churchill and the future of the British Empire," and when this country was more important to him than any outside Britain. Hence, Churchill surely had his say about naming a "true top-level operator" to handle all British secret operations in the Western Hemisphere, especially in the United States. In fact, Nigel West asserts that in June 1940 Churchill announced his intention, "to the astonishment of Menzies," to send Stephenson to New York and that Menzies "attempted to resist, but in the end he capitulated."[21]

The Other Side of the Colville Coin

What tradition and reason tell us about the Stephenson-Churchill relationship is borne out by impressive testimony from contemporaries, not the least of whom was Donovan himself. His single most telling point on the subject was made in 1944, in another marginal comment, this time on a portion of a draft history of COI and OSS by the historian Conyers Read. Where Read, writing about Donovan's 1940 trip to London, said that "Lord Lothian . . . arranged for Donovan to see Churchill himself," Bill Donovan struck out Lothian's name and wrote "Bill Stephenson" in the margin.[22] Donovan,

in mind when he said that Stephenson was "not used to footling around at lower levels." There is no need here to assess the total accuracy of the "fact." What matters is that it was circulated as "a fact," as a very credible "most secret fact."[27]

Let us note carefully, moreover, the identity of the Londoners who were "aware" of the secret. First was none other than the prime minister himself. Second was Morton, "who handled all Churchill's relations with most secret affairs." Third was Colonel Jacob, who reported directly to Churchill's principal military advisor, his chief staff officer, Maj. Gen. Sir Hastings ("Pug") Ismay. And fourth, because he stood between Jacob and Churchill, was surely Ismay himself.[28] So Stephenson, as "a true top-level operator," was well known to an "inner circle"—Morton, Jacob, Ismay, and Churchill.

A second point worth stressing concerns Stephenson's relations with Roosevelt and senior Americans other than Donovan. While his imitation of Roosevelt left me with an impression of his having enjoyed great familiarity with the President, he subsequently affirmed publicly that "my meetings with the President were few, and always most discreetly conducted." He said his first meeting—undoubtedly off the record—occurred a few days after his arrival, when he was accompanied to the White House by Lord Lothian.[29] This strikes me as entirely plausible, but let us look not at what Stephenson says but at what the evidence shows.

Hoover said he was authorized by the President, about July 1940, to conduct liaison with British intelligence. Sherwood publicly revealed in 1948 that it was by "Roosevelt's order" that liaison with Stephenson was implemented.[30] Then on 7 September 1940 "the President . . . assured 'C''s representative in the United States" that he could have any American intelligence he wanted.[31] On 20 April 1941 Vincent Astor, FDR's personal friend and intelligence coordinator in New York, told the President of a meeting with "the #1 man [in the United States] in British Intelligence." On 3 September 1941 it was said, probably by Adolf Berle, that "the British [intelligence] representative in the United States" said his communications facilities were being "utilized by the President in sending messages to high officials in England" and hence he could not divulge the code being used without "the approval of the President."[32]

On 24 October 1941, President Roosevelt, writing Churchill about Donovan, acknowledged that Donovan "has had most helpful cooperation from the officers of His Majesty's Government who are charged with direct responsibility for your war effort." On 27 November 1941 FDR's son James delivered to Stephenson the news not then known either in the Foreign

Office or its Washington embassy that negotiations with Japan had broken down and that action was expected "within two weeks."[33] Only twice in this chronology, which is by no means complete, is Stephenson specifically named, but in all the instances only he is the conceivable referent.

More than that, he was known to Roosevelt and willingly tolerated as a foreign secret agent causing much heartburn for State and the FBI. As evidence, here is a sample series of complaints from Adolf Berle. On 31 March 1941 Berle voiced his and Hoover's unhappiness with Stephenson's activity when he warned Secretary Hull and Under Secretary Welles that Stephenson was developing "a full size secret police and intelligence service" with officers in ten cities from Boston to Seattle. Berle thought the matter should be taken to the President. It was, at a cabinet meeting on 12 April, when Attorney General Jackson "objected to the British establishing an intelligence service here."[34] British activities so concerned Berle that on 18 September — the day Morton was writing to Jacob — he went to "see the President and got his somewhat belated blessing on my attempt to make the British Intelligence calm down here." On 27 September, Berle reminded Welles that they had recently taken up with "the British Government the fact that British Intelligence had given us documents which they had forged." On 9 October Berle told Roosevelt the FBI was concerned about all the coded messages the "British Intelligence" were sending to London for him.[35]

Such complaints need not be multiplied. Let three conclusions suffice. First, Stephenson's provocative activity must have been authorized by Churchill, however ready he was to disavow it. Second, Roosevelt's knowledge of that activity and the anger it caused his subordinates revealed FDR's own authorization of it. Third, Churchill and Roosevelt had thus reached a gentlemen's agreement on that activity, including its "dirty tricks." Hence FDR was not, as alleged, "taken in" or "deceived" by those tricks. In fact, he was complicit in them. Thus, when in October 1941 he publicly claimed to possess a Nazi map showing a Nazified South America, he could not have cared less that it was most likely a British fabrication. Though the original was on his desk, he refused to show it to reporters; it never has been found.[36] No wonder, then, that Stephenson's mission was "a most secret fact" known only to a handful of persons on both sides of the Atlantic.

A third point to be stressed is the uniqueness of Stephenson's British Security Coordination, which Berle termed "a full size secret police and intelligence service." Conceived, created, managed, and partly financed by Stephenson, it was no mere enlargement of New York's Passport Control Office; no, it was totally new in size, scope, functions, and offensive spirit. It was probably unprecedented as a foreign intelligence service operating in this country. It is just as probable that nothing comparable had ever been operated by MI-6 anywhere in the world. Nothing like it had ever been run by the United States anywhere or at any time.

Its uniqueness lay, however, not in its still secret statistics, its hemispheric expanse, or its nearly full-service secret operations, but in the integration and subordination under Stephenson of the secret and covert functions of all British organizations represented in this hemisphere. The list began with what the BSC *History* called its "four parent bodies in London"— MI-6, MI-5, SOE, and Security Executive—and continued, at one time or another, with the Ministry of Economic Warfare, the Political Warfare Executive, Political Intelligence Department, and certain Imperial Censorship functions in Bermuda, Jamaica, and Trinidad; security functions of the British Purchasing Commission; a secret international communications network; and liaison with numerous American and Canadian police, intelligence, and immigration services.[37]

What has never been recounted, because it remains unknown, is the story of Stephenson's actual survival for five years as the ringmaster of all the independent agencies that somehow came within his reach. He had encountered stiff opposition in the United States from Berle, Hoover, and Jackson, but he enjoyed Roosevelt's protection. Who protected him in London, where he surely had fought many battles? Hardly Menzies; as noted earlier, Stephenson told Ellis to "spare no one," including Menzies. He told me the queen's brother, David Bowes-Lyon, of the Political Warfare Executive, was more troublesome than Sir Eric Holt-Wilson. The likely answer was given by Stephenson himself. Recounting in 1960 how London often opposed his early buildup of Donovan, he said that he once had to "enlist the support of the great man at the top [Churchill], who fortunately for me always saw eye-to-eye with me on all the matters relating to British-American exchanges, and in his immediate entourage were some who kept an eagle eye on any suggestion of deviation from the great man's orders." Just who in Churchill's "inner circle" were such eagles? Stephenson named two: "'Pug' Ismay was one and Desmond Morton was another."[38] The inner circle again.

A final point is the aggressive spirit that characterized Churchill and Stephenson. Churchill's fierce determination to resist and defeat Nazism, to fight defensively and offensively, is too well known to need elaboration. It was summed up succinctly in his calling upon SOE to "set Europe ablaze!" Porter essentially wrote in 1952 that Churchill sought a man to do roughly the same thing against American isolationism and Nazi subversion in the Western Hemisphere and that he found his man in his friend Bill Stephenson. Stephenson certainly had Churchill's aggressive spirit, the spirit that drove him and his BSC to meddle, often outrageously, in American affairs, and which embroiled him with Berle and Hoover—but won him FDR's support. Stephenson did the job in the United States that Churchill wanted done. He did it as one who was asked to do it not by Menzies, however, but by Churchill himself. Hence it is not strange that Churchill, when approving names on the 1945 Honours List, wrote opposite Stephenson's name: "This one is dear to my heart."[39]

Sir William's claim to a personal connection with Churchill invites comparison with his claim to a pre-1940 friendship with Bill Donovan. He made both claims long ago, when all the principals were living. He made the first one in 1944, in a history of BSC and OSS relations, when he and Donovan were in close touch with one another, in full possession of physical and mental health, and on the friendliest terms professionally and personally. The second claim was made publicly in 1952 by Porter—probably on the basis of information supplied by Stephenson's friends—when Churchill was once again prime minister and Sir Stewart Menzies was only six months into his retirement as the SIS chief.

Stephenson held to both claims with unyielding tenacity. He did so privately and publicly, politely and clearly, in the face of many challenges, and in many conversations and much correspondence with me and others. He did so even though he and his biographers were unable to offer a satisfactory account of the origin of the Donovan friendship and even though he himself gave different accounts of Churchill's personally asking him to take the New York post. On the core of each claim, however, he never wavered. He held to the first for forty-five years, from 1944—despite later contradictory evidence—until his death in 1989. He held to the second for at least thirty-seven years, from 1952 until his death.

What are we to conclude about both claims? I have argued here, as I did twenty-five years ago, that he probably was in error on the Donovan friendship. It is conceivable that some day there will appear new and conclusive information, or perhaps a new line of argumentation. One writer has suggested that it seems unlikely that Stephenson and Donovan would have hit it off as remarkably and quickly as they did in the absence of a prior friendship.[40] Perhaps. In any case, to suggest that Stephenson, in making that claim in 1944, was deliberately fantasizing or lying is, in my opinion, absurd.

On his assertion of a personal connection with Churchill, it must be made clear that no one has actually disproved it, though many, as narrated earlier, have done their best to deny or minimize it. There is no prima facie evidence or smoking gun that answers the question—at least none publicly available. There may be some evidence still squirreled away for safekeeping in MI-6 vaults. Also, there is probably some in papers of Desmond Morton, who was certainly in Churchill's inner circle, and who, I know, was a personal friend of Sir William. Unfortunately, some of Morton's papers are still "subject to extended closure and will not be open to public inspection until [hold your breath] 2016."[41] Otherwise all there is is the kind of circum-stantial evidence presented here. On balance I think it favors Sir William's side of the question.

14

·—··—·—·

Thirty-Seven Years of Deception?

LET US TURN NOW TO A QUESTION THAT WAS ASKED AT THE OUTSET of the last chapter: was Intrepid a liar? Asked more or less rhetorically about his claimed representation of Churchill in the United States, this question, about that and other claims, must be reconsidered in the light of specific charges leveled against Intrepid by two Canadian authors, both of whom, especially Timothy Naftali, have already been encountered here. They assert categorically that Stephenson was a liar—a deliberate, persistent, significant, aggrandizing, and, in Naftali's case, a self-"apotheosizing" liar.[1]

The first assault, by Naftali in "Intrepid's Last Deception," was launched in 1991, two years after Intrepid's death, when Naftali accused Sir William of lying not once, not twice, but—as the word last in that title surely implies—three or more times. In fact, Naftali accused Intrepid of lying about himself for nearly four decades, over a third of his life. Indeed, the deception, trapping both the *Washington Post* and Intrepid himself, continued even after his death. The second assault followed two years later when John Bryden ended his *Best-Kept Secret* with these words: "From first to last, however, Stephenson was a liar."[2] Such a double-barreled assault on Intrepid's integrity obviously demands a response. Let us begin with Naftali.

Naftali's "Linear Progression"

According to Naftali, Sir William was so driven by self-aggrandizement that from the early 1950s he deliberately deceived the world about himself and his wartime role as the BSC chief. He "was determined to reap some reward for his secret work and set in motion a plan aimed at widespread public recognition." He had a "dream of a big biography," of "a bestselling" book, even of making money out of it. To realize the plan he helped a string of writers—Porter, Ellis, Hyde, and Stevenson—falsify and magnify the record of his wartime service as laid out in the BSC History and ultimately apotheosize himself. The result, in Naftali's view, has been a "thicket of claims and counter-claims" and "a mess of contradictions."[3]

Now Naftali is concerned not with investigating the truth or falsity of those claims—indeed, he assumes them to be false—but with cutting through them in order, as it were, to end the "controversy over the legendary versus the authentic dimensions" of Stephenson's life. To that end he studied "the various iterations of the Stephenson biography" and thereby uncovered what he calls a "linear progression from histories based on documents and recent memory to apotheosis." The result of this "progression" was the transformation of Sir William from a "second-tier" liaison officer in the BSC History into the "top-level player" of Stevenson's A Man Called Intrepid.[4]

Naftali's base point for establishing this "linear progression" is a trio of BSC documents: one, written in 1942, is lost to history; the second, written in 1943, is still locked up; and the third, the 1945 BSC History, is in its own peculiar limbo. Hence, all three documents are beyond ordinary reach. While Naftali, who had a good look at the last two, admits that their "accuracy" is not easily determined, he nevertheless faults none of them. He calls them "histories . . . based on documents and relatively recent recollection" and, as such, "a high-water mark." So high is the mark that anything important written after them—by Porter, Ellis, Hyde, and Stevenson—but not found in them he dismisses out of hand. For him those documents enjoy a pseudobiblical inerrancy.[5]

From that triadic base point, the "linear progression" took off about 1952 when, according to Naftali, Sir William decided to "break his silence" and implement his plan for recognition. He "collaborated" with Porter on the latter's "sensational" article in Maclean's Magazine. It so "brimmed with revelations" and "outstanding bluster" that it "probably boosted Stephenson's ego." It introduced two assertions about Stephenson that were not found in the BSC History—namely, that he was sent to New York by Churchill and that he played a big role in "deciphering" German messages. A

third assertion—that Stephenson had a role in the assassination of Reinhard Heydrich, the Nazi boss of Czechoslovakia—had already been raised
but left unexplored by Naftali.[6]

Other than asserting in four places that Stephenson "collaborated"
with Porter, Naftali never in his text or voluminous notes offers any proof
thereof. Well, is it true? Here is Porter's own answer in his "sensational"
article: Stephenson "is reticent . . . rarely gets into print . . . [and] dislikes
talking himself." He "never speaks to writers . . . of his wartime experiences." Even so, continued Porter, "from a wide variety of sources . . . it
has been possible to piece together a picture" of his "extraordinary career."
Moreover, as the reader will recall, Stephenson himself said that Porter's
article was "not up to much" because Porter had had to "pick up bits and
pieces where he could find them." Surely then, Stephenson did not collaborate with Stephenson—unless Porter also is to be judged a liar.[7]

But was the article "sensational"? That adjective is Naftali's favorite.
He once said the *Post* article "created a sensation." AMCI was "the most
sensational" of Stephenson's biographies (what other "sensational" biographies were there?) The two forewords in AMCI set a "more sensational tone"
for the BSC story than it had ever enjoyed. Yes, but was the article "sensational"? Naftali thought so, but he says too that it "excited little interest"
and elicited no American response, none from the *New York Times* or any
popular journals, and *Maclean's* published no letters to the editor. In fact,
indifference was also the fate of the once "sensational" *Post* story: it provoked no letter worthy of publication.[8]

Second, what about the Churchill angle, which is the gravamen of the
case against Stephenson and has already been much discussed here? Twice
Porter linked the two men, once when "Churchill" sent Stephenson to New
York, and second, when Churchill "sought a man" for the American post
and "thought of the astute and well-informed" Stephenson. Naftali never
determined the truth or falsity of that story. No, for him it was false because
it was not found in the inerrant BSC *History*. Still, what about the story itself?
Both it and the magazine are so denigrated by Naftali that one might easily
dismiss the story as not worthy of scholarly comment.[9] Porter could have
dreamed it up, heard rumors, or obtained "bits and pieces" from Stephenson's Canadian and American friends. He does not say; he gives no source.
One thing is certain: he did not obtain the information from Stephenson,
because Stephenson had not "broken his silence." That being so, the story
is no launching pad for any "linear progression" to apotheosis.

Stephenson's second new alleged assertion was a claim to having deciphered German messages. Proof lay in Porter's story that in 1943 a BSC
radio monitor on the coast of Uruguay picked up a signal from a Ger-

man submarine. The monitor transmitted the signal to New York, where it was put through the decoding machine and was passed on to the Admiralty, which informed Royal Navy destroyers. The lapse of time between the radio signal and receipt of the message by destroyers was "three minutes," and "within half an hour" the submarine was sunk. What are we to make of this story? First of all, according to the most authoritative account of German submarines lost in World War II, no submarine was sunk off the coast of Uruguay in 1943. Second, three experts have rendered their verdicts on the story: David Kahn of *The Codebreakers* fame dismissed it with an expletive. Jürgen Rohwer, the leading German naval historian, said no German submarine ever moved south of northeast Brazil, and he laughed at the thirty minutes. So did Dr. Louis W. Tordella, former deputy director of the National Security Agency (1958–74), who said Porter "simply wrote science fiction" and doubted that that alleged feat could be accomplished even today.[10]

The feat itself, however, was of little interest to Naftali. No, he saw the story as a revelation of British ability to decode German radio signals. That was "an incautious reference to Ultra; later he hyperbolically termed it a "blatant" reference. Whichever it was, it was "harmful," because "a careful" reader could interpret the great feat as proof that the British "had broken German operational ciphers." Now the reader knows that Ultra, or intercepted and deciphered German messages, was the war's most tightly guarded secret until the publication in 1974 of Winterbotham's *Ultra Secret*.[11] But Naftali would now have us believe that, no, the secret had been leaked by Stephenson twenty-two years earlier. Strangely enough, however, the leak, "incautious" or "blatant," lay unspotted by any "careful" reader until Naftali spotted it forty years later. A great leak indeed. In any case, since the story is "science fiction," so is the Ultra leak. So much for that story's place in that "linear progression."

Next in the "linear progression" is Dick Ellis, who in Stephenson historiography is a pathetic figure but who is much worse if he were guilty of that alleged Nazi-Soviet service. Still he did play a role in Stephenson's alleged "plan aimed at widespread public recognition." Ellis's aborted biographies of Stephenson and his Transcaspian history, workmanlike though the last is, demonstrated his inability to write a "sensational" and "bestselling" book about anything. Moreover, his fear of offending MI-6 inhibited him from venturing into sensitive areas. So what was his contribution to the "linear progression"? In his first manuscript, he never dared tell any decoding secrets, much less mention Ultra. He fudged the Churchill angle, but made it clear that Stephenson insisted on and received a wide-ranging brief. He never mentioned the Heydrich assassination. In his second effort he forthrightly said Churchill sent his "close friend" Stephenson to New York and again said nothing about Ultra or Heydrich.[12] Neither effort, however, ever saw daylight.

Next in the "linear progression" was Montgomery Hyde, whose treatment in QC of the Churchill issue was covered earlier. Hyde never mentioned Heydrich or Ultra, although Naftali says that Stephenson wanted the subject discussed. Biographer Hyde understandably made Stephenson the QC hero, but not to the extent described by Naftali. In his hyperbolic fashion, he declared that Hyde "changed all the references to 'BSC' in the official history to 'Stephenson.'" Not so, because, as any perusal of Hyde's text will show, both "B.S.C." and "British Security Co-ordination" pop up regularly. In any case, Hyde's book startled no one and, as Naftali admits, gained Intrepid "no lasting fame."[13]

So far, then, where is the "linear progression"? It is true that from mid-1954 until the appearance of QC Stephenson had negotiated with Ellis and Hyde on the writing of his story. Naftali will have us believe that he wanted "a big book"—"a bestselling book." If true, surely this is shameful. But the worst that has so far been quoted from Stephenson himself as to what he wanted was a wish to be portrayed as "a man of initiative, an innovator, who in spite of official obtuseness and sometimes obstruction, created something out of nothing."[14] Stephenson may thus have sinned against humility, but if this book has proven anything, it is that he spoke the truth: throughout his life he was "a man of initiative" and "an innovator" and one who in wartime "created" a remarkably large, multifaceted intelligence organization (BSC) out of a sleepy SIS backwater in lower Manhattan.

But wanting a book about himself is not the charge against Stephenson. The charge is wanting it so badly, wanting self-aggrandizement, apotheosization, that he spent over a third of his life deliberately deceiving the world about himself. From Porter—if he is thrown in for the sake of argument—to Ellis and then to Hyde there is no "linear progression." There is no transformation from a "second-tier" liaison figure to "a top-level player," no "lasting fame."

No, popular acclaim came much later, in 1976, with AMCI's publication and Sir William's endorsement thereof. With that book lasting fame came forth full blown, all at once, without warning, and without any connection with Porter, Ellis, or Hyde. The book's unreliability has been stressed enough. Here it only needs be pointed out that the fame it gained Sir William was founded on badly chronicled history. But was the bad chronicling the result of "deception"?

In Dante's Nether Hell

Before answering that grave charge, let us bring in John Bryden, another Canadian scholar. His *Best-Kept Secret* is a groundbreaking study of the history of the Canadian Communications Security Establishment, Canada's counterpart of the U.S. National Security Agency and Britain's Government Code and Cypher School. His major materials were thousands of wartime intercepts. In his story Stephenson and the BSC *History* were subordinate factors. Still, Bryden leaves no one uncertain of his assessment of both as utterly untrustworthy.

About Stephenson he is scathing: after fifty years Stephenson was "still enigmatic," and that was by "his own choice and contrivance." He "brazenly manipulated those who interviewed him" and seemed in the process to be a person who "enjoyed conspiracy for its own sake." Stephenson was not above "deceiving his subordinates." Ambitious, he "sought the company of the powerful" and was "capable of being completely unscrupulous." His claims were "extravagant" and "exaggerated or impossible." "From first to last, however," concludes Bryden, "Stephenson was a liar." Oh, yes, and all of this was masked by "an outward show of geniality."[15]

On the BSC *History* there is more of the same. Its "errors" are "legion." "It is full of errors, misdirections, and exaggerations . . . appears to have been written from someone's faulty memory . . . is often hopelessly confused" and contains "elementary errors of fact." It was obviously "deliberately cooked" to cast BSC in the best possible light. Again, it is "full of distortions, exaggerations, and falsehoods."[16]

Bryden tells us that he "believe[s]" he is "the only trained historian to have examined" the BSC *History*. He tells us that it has been unseen by the public and is "still held" by William Stevenson, who allowed only "the occasional journalist" to see it. Then in 1991, "after lengthy negotiations," Stevenson "allowed" him to "examine" it. "Having promised not to quote it without permission," Bryden "examined it while sitting at the dining room table in Stevenson's Toronto home."[17] The scene invites wonder: in front of us is "a trained historian . . . sitting"—we are not told how long—at a stranger's "dining room table," "examining" four hundred printed pages, and concluding thereupon that the book was "deliberately cooked" and Stephenson "was a liar."

A different conclusion, however, was reached by another "trained historian," one who did more than merely "examine" the book at someone else's dining room table. In fact he has studied it so much as to feel confident enough—mistakenly so, in my opinion—to declare that its every mention of BSC was changed by Hyde in his QC into "Stephenson." He had also studied it enough to make it his *point de départ* for a "linear progression" in Stephensonian historiography. That historian is, of course, Timothy Naftali, a Yale A.B. and Harvard Ph.D. As stated earlier, he had trouble assessing the history's "accuracy." He found it part "spy thriller" and "administrative history," "remarkably eloquent" and "strikingly dramatic for an official publication." It had "entertainment value," a "cheerleading tone," and was "cleverly written" in order to sell BSC as a model for the future. However, he never otherwise faulted or denounced it, as our other "trained historian" did. Instead, he found that in "the evolution of the Stephenson story" it was "a high-water mark."[18] Using the BSC *History* as a standard, he rejected whatever differed from it. As between the two trained historians, then, the ordinary reader, denied the document, might consider it a wash.

Let an untrained historian enter the lists. I have had a copy of the BSC *History* for more than a decade, have read it, reread it, and consulted it numerous times. I think both Bryden's total rejection and Naftali's unquestioning acceptance of it equally unwarranted. Some of it has puzzled me; some events are inadequately treated; the chronology is often confusing; and few SIS personnel are named. Most weaknesses probably reflect the *fin de guerre* haste with which it was written and the likelihood that chunks of it were written by other than the four named authors. In any case I never found it "full of distortions, exaggerations, and falsehoods" or "full of errors, misdirections, and exaggerations" or proof positive (or otherwise) that from first to last Stephenson was a "liar." That it portrayed BSC as an imitable success did not shock me. Nor did I judge it the last word on the subject. In short, I think it a readable, informative, valuable, but pedestrian and often dull document to be mined by historians, trained or otherwise. Someday the reader may have a chance to make his or her own judgment.

Let us now get back to Bryden's case against Intrepid. While denouncing him as the father of the history's lies, and of all those untruths repeated by other writers, he never raises any questions about the integrity of those who actually wrote the history, namely, the four authors—Highet, Dahl, Hill, and Playfair. Were they not all knowing accomplices to a pack of lies? Likewise, he never questions the integrity of Montgomery Hyde, who borrowed much from the history. Was not this lawyer, biographer, and BSC official complicit in disseminating falsehoods? And what about William Stevenson, whose *AMCI* precipitated this continuing literary brouhaha, and whom, strangely enough, Bryden hardly mentions and never once faults? Was this experienced journalist, author, and TV producer not also complicit in knavery? No, for Bryden none of these grown men, professionals, public men, is so stained.

While unequivocally stated, Bryden's case is short on proof, even an effort to provide it, even a bill of particulars. There are, in its 390 pages, only four specific allegations about Stephenson's integrity. First are the "doubts as to [his] competence and honesty" voiced early in 1942 by his American foes, Hoover and Berle. Second is a charge of "extravagant claims" made by him about the German spy threat in South America. Third is a June 1942 BSC report to London, which was "apparently" prepared by Stephenson and could "only have been deliberately deceitful." Fourth is a charge, and frankly this is fascinating, that Stephenson falsely claimed to have been the man who rescued the Soviet defector Igor Gouzenko from his would-be Soviet captors.[19]

Let the reader, who thinks the first three instances worthy of attention, pursue them in Bryden and elsewhere. The fourth, however, deserves attention now. Bryden alleges that Stephenson was responsible for inserting his name for that of the man who actually did the deed. And who was the latter? None other than the MI-6 chief himself, the then Col. Sir Stewart Menzies! And why did Intrepid do it? Because Menzies' name—the SIS's biggest secret—had to be hidden, and hence, as Bryden writes: "It appears [Stephenson] simply took advantage of Menzies's shyness to add lustre to his own reputation."[20] Bryden's proof for this astounding double claim— of Menzies' presence in Ottawa that fateful night of 6 September 1945 and Intrepid's faking of the record—is based on discrepancies in the published and unpublished diaries of the Canadian prime minister, Mackenzie King, who was prepared to throw Gouzenko to the Soviet wolves.

Bryden offers some intriguing details, but his case is still arguable. Particularly questionable, if not incredible, is the claim that the super-secret Menzies was masquerading in Ottawa as "H. Stuart Menzies." His true name was "Stewart Graham Menzies." Is "H. Stuart Menzies" a believable SIS "funny" name? Equally arguable and incredible are the action and motivation ascribed to Stephenson. His connection with Gouzenko was first reported by McKenzie Porter in 1952, when Gouzenko, Menzies, and several Canadian officials could have nailed the lie to his front door. His motivation? Since his name then had no "lustre," how could he have "added" to it? In any case, had he then been so hungry for "lustre" and so Machiavellian as to pull off that fraud, one wonders why it took him so long, twenty-four years, to achieve divinization. In short, Bryden, having examined the BSC *History* at a dining room table, has summarily imprisoned Intrepid with the liars of the world in Dante's nether hell.

Judgment Day

It is time to return to Naftali's case against Sir William. As already emphasized, Sir William's endorsement of Stevenson's AMCI brought him fame and shame. Critics deplored his underwriting of the book's tall tales and its abyss between fact and fiction. They commented, en passant, on Intrepid's talkativeness and his "romantically exaggerated claims," about "old men reminiscing" and their need for "decent modesty," and about "delusions" and "hallucinations." One critic did wonder whether "aging memories" could be "trusted as records of history," and referring to Stephenson he commented that "obsession with secrecy does strange things to the human personality."[21]

Few commentators paid attention, in trying to explain the tall tales, to the responsibility of the book's author or to that of the latter's editor, Julian Muller. Yet it is pertinent to recall what was written earlier—namely, that Muller proposed the writing of the book, that Stevenson eschewed research, and that he relied on Intrepid's "prodigious memory." Noteworthy is the fact, evident in Intrepid's numerous cables to Stevenson, that Intrepid never cited any documents to buttress his memory.[22] How then, do we explain Sir William's endorsement of AMCI?

Admittedly Naftali deserves considerable credit for being the first scholar to try to answer the question. Plowing new ground, he went beyond the critics and zeroed in on a new answer—that for thirty-seven years Intrepid deliberately and persistently deceived the public—and supported his answer with a fairly elaborate brief. Ironically enough, however, he also turned up much evidence that actually undercut that brief. This evidence strongly suggests that the answer points elsewhere—to the effects of the one or two strokes Intrepid suffered. Unfortunately no medical evidence is available for experts and amateurs to analyze. For what it is worth, then, I can say that never in my twenty years of frequent contact—personal visits, telephone conversations, and correspondence—did Sir William ever give me reason to question his mental or moral integrity. There was, from age seventy-four to ninety-three, physical infirmity and some confusion in recalling events, but no senility. There was always understanding, alertness, and initiative.

Nevertheless, Naftali has marshaled the stroke evidence for us: he suggests that it was that first "serious" stroke that may have caused Intrepid to "break his silence," and the second seemed to have "erased his memory." He apparently had had "a brain lesion." He cut himself off from old friends and exhibited "a querulousness." There was evidence of "impaired judgment," and he began to "fantasize about a Communist conspiracy against him." Naftali wondered whether in the late 1960s Stephenson was "accurately recalling the past." By the late 1970s, according to Naftali, Intrepid had an "unshakable conviction" about his great importance and, though voicing some unhappiness with AMCI, he nevertheless "remained convinced" he had been Churchill's personal representative.[23]

Correct or not, Naftali has built a fairly convincing case for holding the stroke(s) responsible for any distorted recollection of the past and therefore for Sir William's subjective honesty in holding to those recollections. It might also be added that such a disabled person would have been putty in the hands of an admiring editor and a talented writer who eschewed research and relied on his disabled subject's "prodigious memory." Naftali even says that "Stevenson created Intrepid."[24] In any case, it is difficult to understand Naftali's readiness to cast aside his own evidence of stroke damage and opt instead for saddling Sir William with a verdict of deliberate, long-standing fraud. In fact, Naftali seems to end up somewhat unsure of his own case, uncertain whether Sir William was a deceiver or a disabled victim. He notes "a pathetic shift in the old man's interpretation of the past." He also writes: "Sadly" Sir William "staked his reputation on the distorted image of his career." Even "sadder still," according to Naftali, was the fact that honors came to him only with AMCI's "exaggerated" account of his career. Why all the sorrow? If Intrepid obtained his heart's desire by deception, why is Naftali so sad? Why does he show this long-term fraud the pity and sympathy reserved for the innocent instead of the righteous indignation usually heaped upon charlatans? He seems, paradoxically, intent upon absolving Stephenson of subjective guilt.

No, Naftali's answer does not square with the honors awarded Stephenson by Britain, the United States, Canada, and the Veterans of Strategic Services. It does not square with the common conviction of those who knew him, in war and peace, as a man of great personal honor. Furthermore, its imputation of dishonor does not square with the known record of Stephenson's first fifty-six years. The answer to Naftali's search lies, instead, much less in Stephenson's head than in the overheated imaginations of those who produced *A Man Called Intrepid.*

15

· — · — · —

Too Much Gratitude?

A COMMON ENOUGH OPINION WAS VOICED IN 1970 WHEN THE BRITISH
journalist Donald McLachlan observed that "war in 1941 found the United
States with next to nothing ready for the intelligence tasks that had to be
done. Thanks to British instruction and assistance . . . the Office of Strategic Services was created so efficiently and quickly that it was playing an
important role by 1943." However, McLachlan conjoined that opinion with
an uncommon complaint when he inserted, at the ellipsis in the preceding
sentence, the words: "which American writers nowadays never mention."[1]

As proof of his complaint, McLachlan could have cited Allen Dulles's
1959 account of COI's origin with which this volume began. Not only did
Dulles never mention Stephenson, but also he never mentioned Admiral
Godfrey, the hero of McLachlan's *Room 39*. McLachlan would have found
his complaint further justified if he read William Casey's summary judgment
in 1974 that "it all began" with Donovan (and quite clearly, only Donovan).
McLachlan could well have said: so much for the "still small voice of gratitude."[2]

When McLachlan wrote in 1970, only a score of books on OSS had
been published. They were mainly personal, anecdotal tales of adventure
and derring-do with little or nothing of the historical record that interested
McLachlan and later writers. Moreover, American parochialism found
Donovan, OSS, and CIA, in the early postwar years, a fascinating Ameri-

can success story. At the same time, the British dimension to the story had not yet been publicly acknowledged, even though it had been revealed by the American medal given Stephenson and by American reviews of Hyde's QC. Not fully appreciated, much less investigated, was Donovan's own fulsome personal acknowledgment that "Bill Stephenson taught us all we ever knew about foreign intelligence."[3]

Uncommon as was McLachlan's complaint, much more uncommon, if not almost unheard, has been the opposite protest—namely, that too much credit has been given the British. Yet that is the complaint that was put forth in 1989 by another subject of the crown, Edinburgh history professor Rhodri Jeffreys-Jones, in his CIA and American Democracy.[4] Unless precisely drawn, a disagreement over the extent of credit due someone might be so subjectively argued as to render airing it somewhat futile. Here, however, the complaint by Jeffreys-Jones is so focused on fundamental aspects of the structure of American intelligence that arguing has practical value transcending scholarly disputatiousness.

Between the two opposite complaints there is this difference. McLachlan's was tossed off parenthetically, an afterthought, a slap at ungrateful Americans. Its source can be easily diagnosed, perhaps incorrectly, as McLachlan's unhappiness with American indifference to both his hero, Admiral Godfrey, and those contributions that he knew personally had been made by Britain to America's intelligence progress. By contrast, the complaint by Jeffreys-Jones is impersonal, unemotional, and intellectually grounded. It results inevitably from his conception of the basic flaw in the organization of American intelligence. But before unveiling that conception, let us hear the complaint itself.

Distorting America's Intelligence Past

Jeffreys-Jones complains that too much credit, given by CIA's advocates, and given for the wrong reasons, has had a bad effect on the structure of American intelligence. The trouble began with "the American spy's search for higher status"—in particular, Colonel Donovan's propagation in mid-1940 of "the notion of a Nazi fifth-column menace" as a way of helping "his campaign to establish a new American intelligence agency." This propagation took the form of the widely syndicated Donovan-Mowrer articles warning the American people of that menace. The articles, notes Jeffreys-Jones, "paved the way" for "clandestine ventures" in World War II and "foreshadowed" later use of the "KGB bogeyman," all of which was Donovan's way of "publiciz[ing] his case for a new agency." To that end, writes Jeffreys-Jones, Donovan resorted to "headline-grabbing tactics and dubious arguments" and to "methods" which, in his and his successors' hands, had "a distorting effect on . . . the American intelligence community." They also produced an "extravagant retrospective acknowledgment" of British help.[5]

The first thing wrong with the history by Jeffreys-Jones is that neither he nor anyone else has ever advanced any evidence of a Donovan "campaign" for a new intelligence agency when those articles appeared, namely, 20–23 August 1940. No such evidence appeared until the spring of 1941, when Stephenson's campaign for such an agency manifested itself. The second error is that the articles almost assuredly had not been written, or even partly written, by Donovan. Their author was Edgar Ansel Mowrer, a journalist who could churn out such war copy without Donovan's help. What help Donovan gave was his name. As he told Colonel Menzies: "You may have noticed that I identified my name with certain articles that were appearing. This was done at the instance of the President."[6] The third error concerns the campaign in which the articles figured. It was indeed a campaign, but it was one for national defense and preparedness. Donovan participated, but it was not "his campaign," and it had nothing to do with a new intelligence agency.

The heart of the complaint, however, is not the articles themselves. Neither is it, troublesome though they were, those "clandestine ventures" or combat with the KGB, which Jeffreys-Jones facilely labels a "bogeyman." Nor is it those "headline-grabbing tactics and dubious arguments." No, it is that "extravagant" thankfulness to the British, which was brought on not chiefly by "actual indebtedness" but for reasons that obscured the lessons of the country's intelligence history and thereby ill served its current and future needs. Those reasons are four.

First is Anglophilia, which, however, Jeffreys-Jones never explains. What he apparently means, however, as we shall soon see, is that CIA's advocates have been so enamored of their British "cousins" that they have been blind to the virtues and values of their own intelligence past. Second is "the immodesty of British intelligence veterans like Stephenson, who boasted that they taught the Americans what they needed to know, and even claimed that the CIA's paternity was theirs." Whether immodest or not, British veterans like Stephenson, McLachlan, and Malcolm Muggeridge have made such statements, but Americans like Donovan, Bruce, and Cuneo (as well as myself) have generously repaid them in kind.[7]

Third is CIA's "search for respectability and standing." According to Jeffreys-Jones, the critics of CIA said that it was "like the Gestapo or the KGB." No, its "defenders" said, "it was similar to the more reputable British secret service and, in fact, stemmed from British tuition during the democracy-saving wartime partnership." The critic cited by Jeffreys-Jones was Lewis Mumford, writing in 1970, and the defender was a former CIA inspector general, Lyman B. Kirkpatrick, Jr., responding in 1973 to Mumford's "barb." The trouble with the way Jeffreys-Jones used the exchange, however, is that President Truman, General Donovan, and David Bruce had expressed American indebtedness to the British long before the Gestapo-KGB allegation was made.[8]

The fourth reason, surely one of those "dubious arguments," was the convenience of "the legend of British help." The "legend," which "distracted attention from the American roots" of its intelligence, was the answer to the critics who wondered why a peacetime intelligence service was needed if, from a standing position, the OSS could take off so quickly and successfully. "The explanation of this 'miracle' lay, of course," writes Jeffreys-Jones, "in the crash instruction offered by the British." That was, indeed, a neat answer but not therefore unjustified. COI and OSS made up a new intelligence service that would never have come into existence or then survived—in view of the intense hostility it suffered at the hands of State, the FBI, army, and navy intelligence—had it not enjoyed Donovan's leadership, FDR's backing, and, yes, "British tuition."[9]

The unfortunate consequence of "extravagant" acknowledgment of British assistance was neglect of the roots of American intelligence, especially in the Spanish-American War and World War I. This history was explored by Jeffreys-Jones in 1977 in his *American Espionage: From Secret Service to CIA*. There he argued—to put his thesis more bluntly than he did—that CIA, as established in the National Security Act of 1947, was a mistake. The part of the past that was most neglected and should have been the model for the postwar intelligence system was the system established in 1915 by President Wilson and Secretary of State Robert Lansing and later known as U-1. Most readers, unless they have read *American Espionage* by Jeffreys-Jones, are likely to find U-1 such a new term that they might mistakenly think it an early version of the U-2 reconnaissance aircraft flown by Francis Gary Powers and shot down by the Soviets in 1960. Not so, however.[10]

The Rise and Fall of U-1

"U" was the quite ordinary State Department designation for the office of the under secretary of state. It was in use by 1921 as a result of the establishment by Congress two years earlier of the new office of the under secretary. Also in 1921 there was a U-1, who of course reported to U. There were also U-2 through U-6, all of whom reported to U-1 and then up the ladder to the secretary.[11] Such in barest form was the State office that decades later found a champion, perhaps its only champion, in Rhodri Jeffreys-Jones. What was so special about it?

At the beginning, say 1915, when World War I was spawning real and imagined threats to this country's domestic security, neutrality, and foreign relations, U was the office of the counsellor, the State Department's second highest ranking officer. Its occupant was a kinsman of President Polk, Frank L. Polk, a New York lawyer and municipal reformer who revealed a surprisingly fine hand for intelligence. It was probably at his instance that President Wilson agreed with Secretary of State Lansing that the State Department should be given central responsibility for handling the information about spies, saboteurs, subversives, and various radicals that was flooding into many departments of the government.

According to Jeffreys-Jones, Wilson's action gave State the monopoly on counterintelligence that had been unilaterally and successfully seized by the Secret Service in the Spanish-American War. That service's chief, John E. Wilkie, had asked his boss, the Treasury secretary, to request from President McKinley funds to investigate hostile Spanish activities. With the money in hand, Chief John Wilkie exercised a "central" role in running investigations freely and high-handedly. While he coordinated no other agency, he succeeded in making the Secret Service what Jeffreys-Jones calls "the pivotal intelligence agency of its day." During World War I, State "took over the [Secret Service's] coordinating role," and Frank Polk turned it into State's "central intelligence organization, U-1."[12]

U-1 was certainly State's central intelligence office, and Jeffreys-Jones has done well to focus as much light on it as he has. Information from other agencies was fed into it before being sent to State's country desks, and within the office the various U officers funneled their take to U-1. Polk and his associates—poorly recognized persons like Gordon Auchincloss, Leland Harrison, William L. Hurley, L. Lanier Winslow, Robert C. Bannerman, and Edward Bell in the London embassy—employed the day's best counterintelligence tradecraft in pursuit of the enemies at home. It was probably in recognition of their workload and Polk's leadership that Congress established the under secretary's office and thus brought the U-1 structure into existence. Still, U-1 coordinated no other agency.

When it was proposed to Wilson, Secretary Lansing said that what was needed was "a clearing house" to handle all the government's many secret reports. What he recommended, and apparently received, was Wilson's order that all such reports be sent to State, to Counsellor Polk, and that other departments collect any information requested by State. That Lansing had in mind nothing but a clearinghouse seems evident from his assurance that the new job required no more staff "beyond possibly a thoroughly trust-worthy stenographer, and if the work is unusually heavy a filing clerk." That that is all the future U-1 was is further evident in Secretary of the Trea-sury William G. McAdoo's reference a year and a half later to "a sort of 'clearing house agency' in the State Department" and in his suggestion that a "Bureau of Intelligence" be established in either State or Treasury. While Jeffreys-Jones often speaks of U-1's "coordinating" role, it comes through as a "liaison" role, as when Jeffreys-Jones himself described U-1 as "State's piv-otal intelligence liaison agency." [13]

With the war's end, U-1 continued to carry a heavy workload be-cause of the appearance of new enemies, especially agitators like foreign and domestic Bolsheviks. But within a few years State's own enthusiasm for sleuthing lessened, apparently because of uneasiness with the peace-time pursuit of troublesome citizens. Hence in 1927 a new secretary of state, Frank B. Kellogg, abolished what by then seems to have become just U-1 and U-2. With one exception all the information that had formerly gone into the U system was now redirected to its original recipients, the coun-try and regional desks. The exception was the concentration of commu-nist materials in the Division of Eastern European Affairs—specifically, in the hands of Robert F. Kelley and the department's "gumshoe man," Ray-mond L. Murphy. [14]

For Jeffrey-Jones the demise of U-1 was regrettable and disastrous. Re-grettable, because it ended State's deserved control of intelligence policy, because it ended the "central coordination of foreign intelligence," and be-cause U-1 had been a quiet, informal operation, whose demise was largely brought on by its "obscurity." And disastrous, because it split State from the other intelligence services and thus broke their "internal cohesion." The resulting vacuum was filled by powerful new agencies like oss, cia, and the Defense Intelligence Agency with—as Jeffreys-Jones sees it—their threat to civilian, democratic control of intelligence, an argument beyond our pur-view here. [15]

U-1 was not just abolished; it passed into oblivion. Except for Jeffreys-Jones it has been unremembered and unlamented—especially by the De-partment of State. Nothing was ever said of it by State during the late twen-ties and thirties. U-1 was not recalled in 1938–39 when President Roosevelt first "coordinated" the intelligence services. It was not remembered in 1941 when those services, scheming to head off Donovan, assured FDR they were satisfactorily "coordinating" themselves. It was not revived then by Assis-tant Secretary Berle, as it should have been, writes Jeffreys-Jones. It was not remembered in 1945 when President Truman, having fired Donovan, instructed State to "take the lead" in developing an entirely new national foreign intelligence system. Nor was it recalled in the next two years of discussion leading to CIA's establishment. It has not been mentioned since then. It has not been lauded as a model even by Sen. Daniel Patrick Moynihan (D., N.Y.), who has favored turning over much of CIA's responsibilities to the State Department.[16]

While U-1 itself was lost, the general structure and quality of State's interwar intelligence, as well as that of the other services, was not forgotten. In fact, it was regularly depreciated, though undoubtedly unfairly at times. Still, nothing was more symbolic of the apparent innocence of American intelligence than the often quoted line uttered in 1929 by Secretary of State Henry L. Stimson about gentlemen not reading other people's mail. During and after World War II, a string of credible witnesses—Generals Marshall and Eisenhower, Secretary of State Dean G. Acheson, and less well known authorities like Brig. Gen. George V. Strong, State's own Francis Russell, diplomat Charles Thayer, and historian Graham Stuart—may be quoted on the unsatisfactory state of American prewar intelligence. Most memorable was Marshall's regret that "prior to entering the war [G-2] had little more than what a military attaché could learn at a dinner, more or less, over the coffee cups."[17]

The concluding point is not whether CIA's partisans were guilty of making an "extravagant" acknowledgment of British assistance. Aside from a few statements by Donovan, Stephenson, Cline, and myself, there is no impressive record of repeated and fulsome gratitude to support the charge. No, the point is whether such acknowledgment, whatever it was, bore any responsibility for the failure of the country—as Jeffreys-Jones alone among historians sees it—to have remembered and revived U-1. As already indicated, U-1 was a dead past, a deservedly dead past (by all accounts except that of Jeffreys-Jones) and it had no living spokesmen—in State itself, the intelligence services, the White House, academia, the publicists, or the country at large. It was, in fact, an absolute irrelevancy, one that would never have been rescued even if there had been no Donovan, Stephenson, COI, OSS, and CIA.

Oh, yes, there was one chance, as Jeffreys-Jones himself has suggested, one chance that things might have been different—namely, if there had "lived in 1945 a person gifted with prophetic anticipation of future needs as well as with knowledge of the past." But alas, there was no such "wise person of 1945." There was "no magical seer."[18] When and where was the last one seen?

16

·-·-·-

Twenty-Five Years Later

ON 15 NOVEMBER 1944, BILL STEPHENSON SENT HIS FRIEND BILL Donovan a congratulatory letter and a wish for the future. He congratulated Donovan on the "amazingly successful" work of oss and expressed his hope that the organization would "continue in the future," that is, into the peacetime world. He also observed that "after this war you and I will probably be following our normal peacetime preoccupations."[1] That is essentially what they both did, but it was not the whole story. Having eaten of the tree of intelligence and having found it tasty, they wanted more, at least a bit more.

That Stephenson continued to be involved in intelligence was evident to me from his "Olds" project. There were other small indicators in the intelligence literature, distinct from my immediate interests, which he often sent me. There were also reports from various people about his many intelligence connections. But not until 1986 was there any public report of Stephenson wanting to carry on after the war as an intelligence chief of a new intelligence organization. He was then said by Arthur C. M. Vining, a close friend, to have asked Vining in 1946 for help in "a bid to set up and run a new Canadian intelligence agency."[2] Nothing more is known of that bid except that, while Canada did get such an agency, Stephenson never had any official connection with it or, as far as is known, with any intelligence service. No, his official intelligence career ended in 1946 with the abolition of his BSC. He had accomplished his mission—to find a man and an organization with which he could collaborate—and that was it. Hence he left behind him no institutional legacy for others to fight over.

Quite different was Donovan's experience. Three days after Stephenson sent him the above letter, Donovan sent to FDR his formal proposal for a permanent peacetime American central intelligence agency. What role, if any, Donovan then envisioned for himself in such a new agency is not known. However, he worked very hard and publicly for the establishment of CIA. As long as Harry S. Truman was President, there was no chance he would ever be asked to head the agency. It is likely, however, that he would have accepted the post of DCI if Truman's successor, General Eisenhower, a Republican and a friend, had not felt constrained to offer the job instead to Allen W. Dulles, the brother of his secretary of state. Unlike Stephenson, however, Donovan did leave behind him an institutional legacy, for the CIA, arguably the most important new American agency spawned by the war, was very much his creation.

Like any human organization, CIA has had a checkered career. It began with strong official and public support and enjoyed the popular mystique engendered by its secrecy, cloak-and-dagger operations, and dedication to unmasking the evil designs of foreign enemies. It made mistakes and committed blunders that unsettled the public; for a while its effective answer was that its failures were public knowledge while its successes had to remain secret. But the roll of history revealed so many problems that the agency was subjected to increasingly strident criticism, numerous high-level investigations, creeping congressional micromanagement, and several reformist or protective executive orders. While it still retained basic presidential, congressional, and public support, it was forced by the end of the Cold War in 1989 to justify its continued existence. It was compelled by the Aldrich Hazen Ames espionage case in 1994 to defend not only its record but even its "culture." It had never fallen upon such hard times.

In such circumstance it is tempting to wonder what "the two Bills," the men ultimately responsible for CIA's existence, would have had to say on the matter. Until his last day, Sir William was a hardliner. He would have defended CIA as the first line of defense against threats to peace and stability in the United States, Britain, and ultimately, the world. He would have defended CIA's role in espionage, covert operations, research and analysis, and as leader of the U.S. Intelligence Community.

As for Bill Donovan, the legendary hero of two world wars, he would

have argued that a solution to CIA's current problems lies not in the cogita-
tions of a senate committee or a nondescript multimember commission but
in personal leadership, in a leader with intellect, initiative, energy, enthusiasm, and courage, not a time-server. Spurning a commission, he would have
chosen a leader like himself, a man with an idea and a sense of mission.

·· — — ··

Notes

Introduction

1. Remarks of William J. Casey on receipt of the William J. Donovan Award at the Dinner of the Veterans of Strategic Services, New York, 5 Dec. 1974. The quotation appears on p. 1 of these remarks, reprinted as "The Clandestine War in Europe (1942–45)."

2. Dulles, "Donovan and the National Security," 36–37, 40.

3. Hyde joined Stephenson in May 1941 and left for service in Europe in 1944.

4. Stephenson was publicized as "Intrepid" in William Stevenson's *AMCI*. Sherwood's characterization appears in his *Roosevelt*, 278.

5. Kirkpatrick, review of Hyde's *QC*.

6. U.S. War Department, *War Report*; Darling, *Central Intelligence Agency*. For the deep-sixing, reportedly done by Dulles, see Montague, *Smith*, 104.

7. Stephenson to Troy, 16 Nov. 1968. The transcript was received 16 Dec. 1968.

8. *Times* (London), 1 Jan. 1945, 2. On Hale see Ford, *Donovan*, 4–5. Stephenson gave me the lower figure, which later appeared in his foreword to Hyde's *Secret Agent*, xiii. The higher figure, which seems exaggerated, appears in Hyde's introduction to the 1989 paperback edition of *QC*.

9. Leonard Lyons, "The Lyons Den," *New York Post*, 23 Feb. 1945.

10. *New York Times*, 1 Dec. 1946, p. 54, col. 3.

11. *The Times* (London,) 1 Dec. 1946.

12. *Ottawa Journal*, 2 Dec. 1946, 8.

13. "Know-How for Export," *Time*, 6 June 1949. Noting the number of former intelligence men in wcc, A. C. Brown commented on p. 795 of his *Last Hero*: "Whether this was an intelligence organization or a corporation engaging in commerce would be debated from time to time." However, Brown provided no information on who debated what, when, and where.

14. The 5 percent figure is found in "Sir William Stephenson in Bermuda Hotel Deal," which appeared, apparently, in the *Daily Gleaner* (Kingston, Jamaica) about 18 Aug. 1947. The "dollars" remark is in "English Chief of New Hotel Group Here Explains Policy," *The Royal Gazette* (Bermuda), 23 Aug. 1947.

15. "Arrives Here for Directors' Meet," *The Daily News* (St. John's, Newfoundland), 27 Mar. 1952.

16. The first quotation is in "Sir William Stephenson Appointed Adviser for Manitoba's Industrial Development," in, probably, the *Winnipeg Free Press*, Mar. 1954. The "semi-retirement" comes from "Province Council on Industry," *Winnipeg Free Press*, 3 Sept. 1954.

17. Naftali, "Intrepid's Last Deception" (hereafter Naftali, "Deception"). Sir William's adopted daughter Elizabeth told me on 3 Apr. 1994 that she knew nothing about the first stroke or of any records of it, and that her father never spoke of it, except to mention a few "silly things" that happened in the hospital.

18. This is in notable contrast with the health of a regular correspondent, Sir William Wiseman, whose health in those years was a matter of frequent concern to both Wiseman and Stephenson.

19. Naftali, "Deception," 81. Naftali calls it "a second major stroke." Cuneo many times spoke to me of the gravity of this stroke, but I never recall him mentioning two strokes. Hyde to Roger W. Straus, Jr., 22 Feb. 1963, in the H. Montgomery Hyde Papers (hereafter Hyde Papers). Ellis to Hyde, 10 (or 18) June 1963, ibid.

20. The event occurred 22 Sept. 1983 on the hangar deck of the USS *Intrepid*, moored in New York harbor. See my article "U.S., Canada, and OSS Vets Honor Bill Stephenson."

21. Such dialogue here and hereafter is in my personal notes or my memory.

22. Memorandum, Troy to Director of Training (DTR), [CIA], "Report on Interview with . . . Stephenson in Paget, Bermuda, 11–15 February 1969," 13 Mar. 1969, 2; in National Archives and Records Administration (hereafter NARA), record group (hereafter RG) 263, Troy Papers, box 7, folder 66. These papers, hereafter Troy Papers, are my research papers, which CIA deposited in NARA in 1987 and which are open to the public.

23. Ellis interview, Bermuda, 11 Feb. 1969. McLachlan, *Room 39*, 230.

24. Godfrey interview, Eastbourne, Eng., 4 Nov. 1969.

25. Capt. Stephen W. Roskill, in Beesly, *Admiral*, 306.

26. Telephone conversation with Rocca and Angleton, 21 Oct. 1969; Troy to DTR, "Report on TDY in London and Bermuda . . . the Donovan Project," 5 Dec. 1969, Troy Papers, box 7, folder 58.

27. Conversation with Stephenson, Bermuda, 16–17 Nov. 1969.

28. Pincher, *Their Trade*, 161–72; Wright, *Spycatcher*, 325–30. See p. 330 for the interrogators' summary judgment on Ellis. The litigation was Whitehall's unsuccessful effort to suppress Wright's book.

29. Pavel and Anatoli Sudaplatov, *Special Tasks*, chaps. 7 and 8.

30. Conversations with Stephenson, Bermuda, 12–15 Feb. 1969.

31. The Canadian article is Porter's "Private Eye."

Chapter 1: The Coordinator of Information and British Intelligence

The citations for Chapters 1–9 were written in 1969. Since then, some citations have been rendered out of date because of changes in location and filing of the documents cited. This is particularly true of Coordinator of Information, Office of Strategic Services, and Donovan papers. The COI and OSS papers have been transferred to the National Archives and Record

Administration and can be found under a NARA "entry" number or title, which is obtainable from archivists in the Modern Military Records Branch. Some of the Donovan papers are in NARA, but others have been deposited in the Military History Institute at Carlisle Barracks, Carlisle, Pennsylvania. Otherwise, citations have been updated as much as reasonably possible. Unless otherwise indicated, NARA is the repository of such cited record groups as RG 59.

1. St. Augustine, *Confessions* (New York: Dutton, 1942), 262.

2. Darling, "Origins of Central Intelligence"; Alsop and Braden, *Sub Rosa*, 9–17; Dulles, *Surrender*, 4–9; Kirkpatrick, *Real CIA*, 14–17.

3. Hyde, *QC*, 34–47, 151–56.

4. McLachlan, *Room 39*, 224–39.

5. Speech to the Erie County (N.Y.) American Legion, 11 Nov. 1939, *New York Times*, 12 Nov. 1939. Donovan said that the position of the United States did not mean "that we are not going to contribute manpower at some time. . . . In an age of bullies we cannot afford to be a sissy."

6. Entry for 6 Aug. 1940, Henry L. Stimson diary, vol. 30 (hereafter Stimson diary).

7. Gamal Abdel Nasser, *Egypt's Liberation* (Washington, D.C.: Public Affairs Press, 1955), 87. Nasser's line is in turn a modification of Luigi Pirandello's *Six Characters in Search of an Author* (New York: Dutton, 1923).

Chapter 2: Frank Knox: A Friend at Court

1. Morison, *Turmoil*, 479.

2. Grenville Clark Memoirs (MS), cited in letter from Robert G. Albion to Mrs. Frank Knox, 3 Aug. 1949, Frank Knox Papers (hereafter Knox Papers), 10,457, folder 21, box 8. For Knox's statement see his letter to Roosevelt, 15 Sept. 1939, n. 9, infra.

3. Brownlow, *A Passion*, 433–35.

4. Ickes, *Secret Diary*, vol. 2, 717–19.

5. Alfred M. Landon to A. H. Kirchhofer, 13 June 1962, my files.

6. Brownlow, *A Passion*, 436.

7. *New York Times*, 10 Dec. 1939, p. 3, col. 2.

8. "Memorandum of conversation with President Roosevelt on December 10, 1939, at the White House," 12 Dec. 1939, Franklin D. Roosevelt Papers, President's Secretary's File (hereafter Roosevelt Papers, PSF), box 59.

9. Knox to Roosevelt, 15 Dec. 1939, Roosevelt Papers, PSF (Knox).

10. Roosevelt to Knox, 29 Dec. 1939, ibid.

11. "Notes from WJD [William J. Donovan]," 5 Apr. 1949, William J. Donovan Papers (hereafter Donovan Papers), Washington, D.C. CIA job 66-595, box 1, folder 2.

12. Troy, "An Inventory of Papers," 15 Feb. 1968, Troy Papers.

13. "The Composite Presidential Diary, 1940" (hereafter Presidential diary), and the "Usher's Diary, 1940" (hereafter Usher's diary), Roosevelt Papers. These are not diaries but appointment books or logs.

14. John Balfour, commenting on telegram no. 359, 26 Feb. 1941, from British embassy, Cairo, in Foreign Office Papers (hereafter F.O. Papers), A1154/183/45/(1941).

15. Knox to Roosevelt, 17 Jan. 1940, Roosevelt Papers, PSF (Navy).

16. Langer and Gleason, *The Challenge*, 510.

17. Lobdell, "Frank Knox," 312.

18. Knox to Roosevelt, 18 May 1940, Roosevelt Papers, PSF (Knox).

19. Ibid., 21 May 1940.

20. *New York Times*, 25 May 1940, p. 3, col. 2.

21. Quoted in McCoy, *Landon*, 351.

22. Knox to Roosevelt, 27 May 1940, Roosevelt Papers, PSF (Knox).

23. Knox to Annie R. Knox, 5 June 1940, Knox Papers, box 3. Mrs. William Brown Meloney was a great friend of Mrs. Roosevelt and organizer of the *New York Herald-Tribune* "Forum." On 25 June 1940 she sent FDR a reprint from the *Tribune* of Donovan's article "Should Men of Fifty Fight Our Wars?" in Roosevelt Papers, President's Personal File (hereafter Roosevelt Papers, PPF), 6558 (Donovan).

24. Knox to A. R. Knox, 11 June 1940, Knox Papers, box 3.

25. Brownlow, *A Passion*, 445–46.

26. Knox to A. R. Knox, 15 June 1940, Knox Papers, box 3.

27. Morison, *Turmoil*, 480–81.

28. This title appears in Janeway, *The Struggle*, 140.

29. Casey, "Clandestine War," 22.

30. *New York Times*, 22 June 1940, p. 10, col. 7.

31. Rawleigh Warner to A. R. Knox, 29 Mar. 1940, Knox Papers, box 1.

32. Donovan's home was at 1647 30th Street, NW. The address has since been changed to 2920 R Street, NW. The residence is now owned and occupied by Mrs. Katharine Graham of the *Washington Post*.

33. Knox to A. R. Knox, 6 July 1940, Knox Papers, box 3. To judge from the contents of this letter, the date should read 5, not 6, July.

34. Ibid., 14 July 1940.

Chapter 3: Stephenson, Hoover, and Donovan

1. For Stephenson's life see, in addition to Hyde's *QC*: J. J. Brown, *Inventors*, 90–92; Whitehouse, *Heroes*, 236–37; Porter, "Private Eye," 66–75; Stevenson, *AMCI*.

2. Berle's remark was made in an interview in New York, 7 Oct. 1969. I have not yet found proof that Tunney and Stephenson, though they certainly were friends, won championships on the same occasion.

3. Hyde, *QC*, 11. The can opener story is probably apocryphal; Sir William did not want it used in *AMCI*.

4. *Charleston (South Carolina) News and Courier*, 22 Sept. 1924.

5. Hyde, *QC*, 24, 30.

6. U.S. Department of Justice, Immigration and Naturalization Service, form 1-404-A, Stephenson, William S., New York, 21 June 1940 (INS file A6 762816.

7. "Weekly Report of Visas Issued . . ." U.S. embassy, London, despatch 4981, 2 Apr. 1940, RG 59 (State decimal file 1940–42), file 811.111 dip/15254.

8. Letter, SIS to U.S. embassy, London, no. YP/81/1 (Historian), 10 Nov. 1969, paras. 3–5 not avail.

9. Memorandum, Edward K. Merritt to Lowell H. Smith, 25 June 1940, NARA, RG 165, file 2801-304/34.

10. Memorandum, R. P. Kramer to E. A. Tamm, 19 Mar. 1940, RG 59, file 841.24/229.

11. Hoover to Berle, 22 Mar. 1940, RG 59, file 841.24/229. Hoover also forwarded to Berle a copy of Kramer's memorandum. The IIC is described in Chap. 7.

12. Memorandum by Berle, 26 Mar. 1940, RG 59, file 841.24/229.

13. "Memorandum for Files" by Fletcher Warren, 4 Apr. 1940, RG 59, file 841.24/229. Warren recorded what Berle had told him of his conversation with Tamm.

14. Hoover to Berle, 10 Apr. 1940, RG 59, file 841.24/235.

15. Memorandum, Berle to Moffat and Dunn, 18 Apr. 1940, RG 59, file 841.24/235.

16. The original n. 16 has been deleted for security reasons.

17. Memorandum, Dunn to Berle, 23 Apr. 1940, RG 59, file 841.24/235.

18. U.S. Interdepartmental Intelligence Conference, minutes, 9 Apr. 1940, RG 165, file 9794-186A (L).

19. Ibid., meeting of 13 May 1940.

20. Ibid., file 9794-186A (2).

21. Ibid., file 9794-186A (9).

22. Ibid., file 9794-186A (12).

23. Hyde, QC, 25–26.

24. Letters, Tunney to Troy, 6 and 18 Aug., 18 Sept., 1969. The last two letters were signed by Tunney's secretary, K. M. Skallon.

25. Cuneo interviews, Washington, D.C., 27 Nov., 1 Oct. 1969.

26. Communication from FBI through CIA liaison, 15 Feb. 1968.

27. Minutes, Hemisphere Intelligence Conference, held in Hoover's office, 29 Jan. 1942, RG 59, file 800.20200/9.

28. Berle's memorandum of conversation, 10 Mar. 1942, RG 59, file 841.20211/36.

29. Sherwood, *Roosevelt*, 270.

30. Astor to Roosevelt, 14 Mar. 1941, Roosevelt Papers, PSF (Astor) (general 1933–1944).

31. Hyde, QC, 28.

32. Stephenson interview, Bermuda, 23 Oct. 1969.

33. Letter, SIS, n. 8, supra, para 6.

34. Hyde, QC, 34–35.

35. Stephenson interview, Bermuda, 12 Feb., 23 Oct., 1969.

36. Ibid., 12 Feb. 1969.

37. Ibid.

38. The original n. 38 has been deleted for security reasons.

39. Stephenson's memorandum (transcript), "Early Days" was recorded for Whitney H. Shepardson; a copy is in my files. The reference in QC is p. 36. The transcript, slightly edited for publication, has been reprinted in Hyde's *Secret Agent*, 247–61.

40. "The Two Bills," transcript of C. B. C. interview of Sir William S. Stephenson by Shaun Herron; others participating: Earl Mountbatten of Burma, Ernest Cuneo, Col. Charles H. Ellis, 4 (my pagination).

41. "British Relations with OSS," OSS Records, job 62-271, box 29, folder 2 (typescript, 1). Accompanying memoranda indicate it was written before 16 Oct. 1944.

42. Ibid. Accompanying memoranda are Conyers Read to Donovan, 16 Oct. 1944; O. C. D[oering], Jr. to Lt. Bane, 3 Nov. 1944; Lt. Charles A. Bane to Read, 7 Nov. 1944. That the writing in the margin is Donovan's has been confirmed by document analyst Dr. David A. Crown in a letter to me, 12 Feb. 1970.

43. Evidence not cited for security reasons.

44. Hyde, QC, 37.

45. Conyers Read, "Pre-COI Period," OSS Records, job 62-271, box 29, folder 4 (typescript, 5).

46. For this chronology see Goodhart, *Fifty Ships That Saved the World*, 121–90; and Sutphen, "The Anglo-American Destroyers-Bases Agreement, Sept. 1940," 14–84. Throughout June the President was unconvinced of the practicability, to say nothing of the legal feasibility, of a transfer of destroyers. According to naval historian Samuel Eliot Morison, it

was not until 24 July 1940 that an "agreement in principle" was reached on an exchange of destroyers and bases. See Sutphen, 87.

47. Donovan, an address delivered before the Union League of Philadelphia, 29 Apr. 1941, *The Union League of Philadelphia Annual Report*, 1941, 80–95.

48. Lord Lothian to F.O., no. 1311, 10 July 1940 (sent 11 July at 0210), F.O. Papers, A3542/90/45 (1940).

49. Hull to Kennedy, no. 1696, 10 July 1940 (noon), RG 59, fil 841.00N/9.

50. Hull to Kennedy, no. 1722, 11 July 1940 (1700), RG 59, file 841.00N/9.

51. Stimson diary, entries for 25 June, 9 July 1940. Hull "Desk Diary," 1940, Cordell Hull Papers, container 67B.

52. Knox to Beaverbrook, 11 July 1940, Donovan Papers, job 65-508, (vol. 34) box 70, item 3 (hereafter Donovan Papers, vol. 34).

53. John D. Biggers to Col. R. W. Weeks, 11 July 1940, ibid.

54. Knox to Mowrer, 18 Dec. 1941, Knox Papers, box 1.

55. Mrs. William J. Donovan to Troy, 20 May 1968. The information was taken from her diary, a "line-a-day."

56. *New York Times*, 15 July 1940, p. 28, col. 2.

Chapter 4: Donovan: To and from London

1. Mowrer, *Triumph*, 315.

2. Kennedy to Hull, no. 2113, 12 July 1940 (1700), RG 59, file 740.0011 EW 1939/4571 1/3. Kennedy wrote: "I had been advised this morning . . . Donovan was coming by Mr. Mowrer . . . [he] said he had been instructed to stay here and go back with [Donovan]."

3. Kennedy to Hull, no. 2133, 12 July 1940, RG 59, file 740.0011 EW 1939/4571 2/3.

4. See n. 2, supra.

5. Blum, ed., *From the Diaries of Henry Morgenthau, Jr.*, vol. 2, 96.

6. See n. 3, supra.

7. Welles to Roosevelt, 12 July 1940, and Roosevelt to Knox, 13 July 1940, Chief of Naval Operations, Central Files (classified) (hereafter CNO files), file A8-2EF13.

8. Kennedy to Hull, no. 2147, 13 July 1940, RG 59, file 841.00N/9 1/2.

9. Hull to Kennedy, no. 1776, RG 59, file 741.001 EW 1939/4571 1/3.

10. Hyde, QC, 37. The statement therein is repeated in Whalen, *Founding Father*, 303. For Kennedy's attitude see Krock, *Memoirs*, 335.

11. Telegram from Kirk, 12 July 1940, and telegram received by him, 14 July 1940, CNO files, Kirk Papers, series 1, 1939–41.

12. Swinton to Halifax, 15 July 1940, F.O. Papers, A3542/90/45 (1940), no. 231.

13. J. V. Perowne, 12 July 1940, in two comments on Lothian's telegram no. 1311, 10 July 1940, F.O. Papers, file A3542/90/45 (1940).

14. F.O. to Lothian, no. 1542, 16 July 1940, F.O. Papers, file A3542/90/45 (1940), no. 231.

15. Charles Peake, 15 July 1940, in a note on folder containing the related cable traffic.

16. Ibid.

17. Frank Darvall to T. N. Whitehead, 18 July 1940, F.O. Papers, file A3542/90/45 (1940), no. 234.

18. Lothian to F.O., no. 1395, 18 July, F.O. Papers, file A3542/90/45 (1940), no. 230.

19. Lothian's telegrams: no. 1311, 10 July; no. 1338, 13 July; and no. 1366, 15 July 1940. F.O. Papers, file A3542/90/45 (1940), nos. 227, 228, and 229, respectively.

20. Letter, Lady Astor's secretary to Donovan, 27 July 1940; telephone message from

same to him, 29 July 1940; Chief of Air Staff's program for WJD, 30 July 1940; and undated note by Donovan showing him "Lunch K[ing] Q[ueen]-Astor, 4 St. James Square 1:15," all in Donovan Papers, vol. 34.

21. Robert Vansittart to Churchill, 23 July 1940, Churchill Papers (Premier Three) hereafter Churchill Papers), box 145, folder 463/misc.

22. Telephone message, Lady Cooper to WJD, 25 July; letters, Kirk to WJD, 25, 27 July; letters, Lady Cooper to WJD, 27, 29 July; telephone message from Kennedy to WJD, 31 July 1940; all in Donovan Papers, vol. 34 (and Hyde; QC, 37).

23. Donovan to Menzies, 27 Aug. 1940, Donovan Papers, vol. 34.

24. Anderson to Donovan, 13 July; two letters, Kirk to Donovan, 22 July; the reference to "special line" is in Kirk to Donovan, 21 July 1940, Donovan Papers, vol. 34.

25. McLachlan, Room 39, 226–27.

26. The Anglo-American exchange of secret information, which was being developed in 1940–41, is a much larger subject than mine, and I suspect that Godfrey, in providing material to McLachlan years after the fact, may have confused discussions with Donovan with other discussions to which he was party.

27. Donovan to Godfrey, 27 Aug. 1940, Donovan Papers, vol. 34. Godfrey to Troy, 12 Dec. 1968.

28. Mowrer, Triumph, 315–17.

29. Details on the trip are found in letters from Donovan to J. C. Slessor, 5 Aug., to Brendan Bracken and Sir Cyril Newall, 27 Aug., and to Lee, 29 Aug. 1940. These and the Air Ministry's passenger list are in Donovan Papers, vol. 34. The plane's arrival was reported in the New York Times, 5 Aug. 1940, p. 1, col. 3. Donovan was "the only passenger" for New York.

30. Donovan to Slessor, 5 Aug. 1940, Donovan Papers, vol. 34. New York Times, 6 Aug. 1940, p. 3, col. 4.

31. Knox to A. R. Knox, 8 Aug. 1940, Knox Papers, box 3.

32. Stimson diary, 6 Aug. 1940.

33. Donovan to Lee, 28 Aug. 1940, Donovan Papers, vol. 34.

34. Elizabeth B. Drewry, Director of the Roosevelt Library, Hyde Park, N.Y., to Troy, 22 Nov. 1967.

35. These letters were written to Menzies, Godfrey, Bracken, and Newall on 27 Aug. and to Ronald Tree and Lee on 28 Aug. 1940, and are in Donovan Papers, vol. 34. The luncheon is described in a memorandum from Capt. W. D. Puleston to Secretary of the Treasury Henry Morgenthau, Jr., in the Henry Morgenthau, Jr. Diary (hereafter Morgenthau diary). This diary is not to be confused with Blum's From the Diaries of Henry Morgenthau, Jr.

36. Record of conversation of T. N. Whitehead with Donovan, 19 Dec. 1940, F.O. Papers, A5194/4925/45 (1940), no. 541.

37. Hyde, QC, 39.

38. For Stephenson's cables see Hyde, QC, 38–39. Donovan's cable is in Churchill Papers, box 145, folder 463/misc.

39. Speech given by Adm. Louis Mountbatten upon presentation to him of the Donovan Award in New York City on 21 Mar. 66, author's files.

40. Otto C. Doering, Jr., interviews, New York, 6, 8 Oct. 1969. Doering was a member of the firm before and after the war and worked closely with Donovan in COI and OSS.

41. In 1973 the firm, named Donovan, Leisure, Newton, and Irvine, moved uptown to 30 Rockefeller Plaza.

42. For Donovan to Bracken and Menzies see n. 35, supra.

43. Frankfurter to Knox, 27 Aug. 1940, Knox Papers, box 1.

44. J. C. Dunn to Herschel Johnson, 29 Sept. 1940. Klemmer's report, "The Fifth Column in Great Britain," 29 July 1940, was forwarded to Washington by Kennedy, 1 Aug. 1940. Even this, however, was described as of "no great value" by "REM" [Robert E. Murphy] of State's European Division, 2 Dec. 1940. All above items are in RG 59, file 841,00N/10.

45. Despatch 755, 26 Aug. 1940, from Lord Lothian. Perowne's note is dated 18 Sept. 1940, F.O. Papers, file no. missing.

46. Telegram from Sir Arthur Salter to Churchill, 17 Aug. 1940, F.O. Papers, A3542/90/ 45 (1940), no. 237.

47. All these documents are in Donovan Papers, vol. 34.

48. "Notes from WJD," 5 Apr. 1940; see n. 11, chap. 2, supra.

49. Minute by J. Balfour re: telegram to Lothian, 28 Nov. 1940, F.O. Papers, A4955/605/ 45 (1940).

50. Stimson diary, 6 Aug. 1940.

51. Letters, Donovan to Menzies, 27 Aug. to E. B. Stettinius, 10 Oct., and to Robert Van Sittart [sic], 26 Sept. 1940, Donovan Papers, vol. 34.

Chapter 5: Stephenson's British Security Coordination

1. Hyde, QC, 37.

2. Churchill to Sir Dudley Pound, First Sea Lord, 17 Feb. 1941, Churchill Papers, box 153, folder 489/4, serial M. 192/1.

3. Quoted in Cookridge, Set Europe Ablaze, 1.

4. Paget replaced Comdr. H. B. Taylor as PCO on 1 Aug. 1937. Aide-mémoire from British embassy, no. 238, 23 July 1937, RG 59, file 702.4111/1414. For move uptown see Hyde, QC, 28, 31–32, 50.

5. Stephenson interview, Bermuda, 17 Nov. 1969.

6. Letters, Astor to Roosevelt, 18, 20 Apr. 1940, Roosevelt Papers, PSF (Astor). Astor's role in intelligence and his relationship with FDR will be covered in chap. 7, as will the "club" mentioned by Astor.

7. QC, 228–29 on the recruitment, and 70–72 on Westrick. The Astor possibility is suggested by his acquaintance with Stephenson and by his full account of Westrick in a letter to FDR, 14 June 1940, Roosevelt Papers, PSF (Astor). Stephenson's Italian recruit was Max Salvadori, an antifascist intellectual.

8. For the Martinique episode and the Gulf affair, see Hyde QC, 111–12 and 56–58, respectively.

9. Memorandum, Donovan to AGO, War Department, 13 May 1943, CIA, W. S. Stephenson 201 file.

10. Stephenson, "Early Days," 7.

11. The BSC story is yet to be written. Surely much material lies in the FBI files, and there must be some in records of such agencies as the U.S. Customs, Coast Guard, and the New York City Police Department.

12. Hyde, QC, 61–62.

13. Stephenson interview, Bermuda, 16 Nov. 1969. The date of Ellis's arrival is found in U.S. Immigration and Naturalization Service form 1-404-A, a copy of which is in Stephenson's INS file A6 762 816.

14. Ellis, "Anglo-American Collaboration in Intelligence and Security," 20. This document deals with Stephenson and BSC, especially in 1940–41. The paper (hereafter Ellis,

"Notes") reflects Ellis's personal knowledge and experience but is not a memoir. For the Toronto school, see Hyde, *QC*, 227–28.

15. Ellis, "Notes," 36. *New York Times*, 23 Aug. 1940, p. 8, col. 6.

16. Ellis, "Notes," 36. Stephenson interview, Bermuda, 17 Nov. 1969.

17. Stephenson, "Early Days," 1, and Stephenson interview, Bermuda, 17 Nov. 1969. Stephenson's claim on the microdot referred to the Hemisphere Intelligence Conference at Hoover's FBI office, 29 Jan. 1942. At this conference Hoover discussed the dots and Stephenson stressed the "highly secret" character of their discovery. See minutes of the conference, RG 59, file 800/20200/9.

18. Ellis, "Notes," 37.

19. Ibid., 96.

20. 30 Oct. 1940, RG 59, file 102.31/168. This document is indexed but "not in the file."

21. E. S. Herbert to Donovan, 7 Mar. 1941, Donovan Papers, job 65-508, (vol. 3) box 83, item 6 (hereafter Donovan Papers, vol. 3).

22. This SIS is discussed in Chap. 7.

23. Memorandum, Sherman Miles to Sharp, 9 Oct. 1940, RG 165, file 51-901.

24. Stephenson interview, Bermuda, 23 Oct. 1969.

25. See n. 21, supra.

26. Ellis, "Notes," 38.

27. Cuneo interview, Washington, D.C., 27 Nov. 1969.

28. Stephenson, "Early Days," 1.

29. Sir Eric Holt-Wilson's story is treated in chap. 10.

30. Memorandum, R. B. Stewart, 28 Jan. 1941, RG 59, file 841.01B11/190. For Hoover's "suggestion" of "BSC" as the name, see *QC*, 52.

31. Memoranda, R. L. Bannerman, special agent, to Mr. Clark, special agent in charge, New York, 6 and 10 Feb. 1941, RG 59, file 841.01B11/191 and 192.

32. Hoover to Berle, 25 Feb. 1941, RG 59, file 841.20211/18.

33. Mentioned in a letter from Berle to Welles, 31 Mar. 1941, RG 59, file 841.20211/23.

34. Ibid.

35. Joseph C. Green to Berle, 1 Apr. 1941, RG 59 file 841.20211/27.

36. Berle to Hoover, 21 Apr. 1941, ibid., no. 49. Hoover to Berle, 30 Apr. 1941, RG 59, file 841.2011/25.

37. Memorandum of conversation, "Activities of British Intelligence Here," 5 Mar. 1942, and memorandum of conversation, 10 Mar. 1942, RG 59, filed with 841.20211/36. In the latter conversation Lord Halifax expressed the opinion that some of the problems under discussion had been "cleared" with Donovan. Berle did not understand how Donovan could be involved in what was essentially a domestic matter.

38. Dulles, *Secret Surrender*, 4.

39. The terminology and thought of this paragraph are taken from the work of the French medical doctor and biologist Claude Bernard and the French jurist Maurice Hauriou as discussed in Moorhouse F. X. Miller, S. J., "Hauriou, Suarez, and Chief Justice Marshall," *Thought* 6 (Mar. 1932):588–608.

40. Record of conversation of T. N. Whitehead with Donovan, 19 Dec. 1940, F.O. Papers, A5194/4925/45 (1940), no. 541.

Chapter 6: Donovan: In London and the Mediterranean

1. "British Relations with oss," oss Records, job 62-271, box 29, folder 2 (typescript, 1).
2. Hyde, *QC*, 43.
3. Read, "Pre-coi Period," 13.
4. Langer and Gleason, *Undeclared War*, 397.
5. Read, "Pre-coi Period."
6. Ibid.
7. Telegram, Lothian to F.O., no. 2926, 4 Dec. 1940, F.O. Papers, A4925/4925/45 (1940), no. 518.
8. Stimson diary, 2 Dec. 1940.
9. Telegram, no. 2829, 27 Nov. 1940, F.O. Papers, A4925/4925/45 (1940), no. 505.
10. Halifax to Beaverbrook, 29 Nov. 1940, F.O. Papers, A5029/4925/45 (1940), no. 526.
11. See n. 7, supra.
12. Cooper to Halifax 10 Dec. 1940, F.O. Papers, A5059/4925/45 (1940), no. 531.
13. Letters, Halifax to Eden and Sinclair, 5 Dec. 1940, F.O. Papers, A4925/4925/45 (1940), nos. 508, 509, and War Office to Under Secretary of State for Foreign Affairs, ibid., no. 510.
14. Sinclair to Halifax, 7 Dec. 1940, F.O. Papers, A5059/4925/45 (1940), no. 529.
15. Cadogan to Secretary of State, 17 Dec. 1940, F.O. Papers, A4925/4925/45 (1940), no. 535.
16. Notation on folder of F.O. Papers, A4925/4925/45 (1940).
17. Telegrams, Lothian to F.O. and F.O. to U.K. embassy, Lisbon, 5 Dec. 1940, F.O. Papers, nos. 519 and 517, respectively. Arrangements were made by Sinclair's private secretary.
18. *New York Times*, 7 Dec. 1940, p. 1, col. 2. Stephenson interview, Bermuda, 17 Nov. 1969.
19. Notation by J. Balfour, see n. 16, supra.
20. *New York Times*, 19 Dec. 1940, p. 5, col. 2.
21. Speech, Donovan to officers of the War Department, 17 [20] Mar. 1941 (hereafter Donovan, Officers speech), oss records, job 62-271, box 29, folder 8, p. 2. The date on the text is 17 Mar., but Donovan did not return until the eighteenth, and he did address army officers on 20 Mar.
22. Telegram no. 1608, 24 Dec. 1940, F.O. Papers, A5194/4925/45 (1940), no. 543.
23. Hyde, *QC*, 44. Godfrey wrote to me 12 Dec. 1968: "I had nothing to do with D[onovan]'s Mediterranean trip and sent nothing to Cunningham."
24. Record of conversation of T. N. Whitehead with Donovan, 19 Dec. 1940, F.O. Papers, A5194/4925/45 (1940), no. 541.
25. *New York Times*, 21 Dec. 1940, p. 1, col. 4.
26. Ibid., 27 Dec. 1940, p. 2, col. 5.
27. Donovan, Officers speech, 2.
28. Col. Dykes kept an excellent diary (hereafter Dykes diary), which appeared in oss records as sixty single-spaced typewritten pages. In 1990 it was edited by Alex Danchev and published under the title *Establishing the Anglo-American Alliance*. Unfortunately, Danchev deleted some entries of particular interest to Americans.
29. On Franco see telegram from U.S. Ambassador Weddell to Hull, no. 162, 1 March 1941, RG 59, file 740.00118 E.W. 1939/142. On Weygand see paraphrase of telegram from U.S. embassy, Vichy, France, no. 151, 3 Feb. 1941, cno files, file A8-2/EF13. See also Dykes diary,

37: "The Germans evidently dislike the very strong line he has been taking on our behalf in the Balkans recently."

30. Dykes diary, 37.

31. Donovan, Officers speech, 2–4.

32. Dykes diary, 15. "Y" referred to a naval wireless interception organization, and "M" was an SOE school.

33. Donovan, Officers speech, 8–9.

34. Ibid., 7.

35. Ibid., 4. With him at the time was "one of the British security fellows" whom U.S. Minister Earle wanted him to see.

36. The telegrams are in RG 165, file 2257-ZZ-331, nos. 2–4. Actually it was not a joke at the time; Dykes wrote: "When I returned I found him [Donovan] looking as worried as I have ever seen him . . . we made a frantic search through all his bags." Also, this time on the lighter side, the Bulgarian authorities were so understanding that crossing the border without a passport was "easier" than with one; Dykes diary, 27.

37. Langer and Gleason, *Undeclared War*, 398.

38. Ibid., 408. Donovan's "No" is written opposite the statement: "There is no doubt that it was entirely due to the line he took in Yugoslavia that General Simovic was persuaded to eject the then pro-German Government," which appears in "British Relations with OSS," OSS Records, job 62-271, box 29, folder 2 (typescript, 1).

39. Paraphrase of telegram no. 82, 20 Feb. 1941, from U.S. legation, Cairo, CNO files, A8-2/EF13.

40. Donovan, Officers speech, 9.

41. Telegram no. 87, 22 Feb. 1941, from U.S. legation, Cairo, A8-2/EF13.

42. Telegram no. 24, 7 Feb. 1941, from U.S. embassy, Ankara, ibid.

43. Telegram no. 81, 20 Feb. 1941, from U.S. legation, Cairo, ibid. The Dykes diary, 48–52, shows that Dykes wrote the first draft of this appreciation and Donovan "redraft[ed] it in his own words."

44. Donovan, Officers speech, 10.

45. Dykes diary, 20, 26, 28, 34, and 59. Grand was Lt. Col. (later Maj. Gen.) Laurence D. Grand, who headed the SIS division D (subversion), which became part of SOE. Division C handled espionage.

46. Telegram, Eden to Churchill, no. 361, 22 Feb. 1941, F.O. Papers, A1728/183/45 (1941).

47. Telegram no. 359, n.d., F.O. Papers, A1154/183/45 (1941). The following appears in Dykes diary, 52: "[On 21 February] I also drafted another telegram, as from Eden to the Foreign Office, regarding the publicity arrangements necessary for D. on his return to England. We had discussed these at considerable length, and he had pointed out to me that it was necessary that he should get a build up in the American Press if his report was to carry full weight." The second sentence in this diary entry was heavily blacked out in one text of the diary. None of this appears in Danchev's book.

48. For Balfour's comments see telegram no. 359, n. 47, supra.

49. The F.O. minute and Cadogan's comment are found in Eden's telegram no. 361, no. 46, supra.

50. Eden to Halifax, 5 Dec. 1940, F.O. Papers, A5059/4925/45, no. 521.

51. Donovan, Officers speech, 10–11.

52. Ibid., 11.

53. Ibid., 8.

54. Nelson to Dykes, 11 Mar. 1941, with attachments on "the system" and on the "Special Training Schools," Donovan Papers, job 65-508, box 83, item 5 (vol. 2) (hereafter Donovan Papers, vol. 2).

55. Herbert to Donovan, 7 Mar. 1941, with three attachments: "Note for Colonel Donovan"; aide-mémoire, 2 Dec. 1940; "Mail Communication with the Western Hemisphere"; Donovan Papers, vol. 2.

56. Swinton to Donovan, 7 Mar. 1941, Donovan Papers, vol. 2.

57. Memorandum, Miles to Marshall, "Coordinator for the Three Intelligence Agencies of the Government," 8 Apr. 1941, RG 319, Records of the Army Staff, file 310.11.

Chapter 7: Roosevelt and the Intelligence Agencies

1. Memorandum, FDR to Secretaries of State, Treasury, War, Navy, and Commerce, and to Attorney General and Postmaster General, 26 June 1939, CNO Files (SC), file A8-1/(A and N).

2. Memoirs, George S. Messersmith Papers, box 9, vol. 3, folder 5. Messersmith died in 1960; the mid-fifties is suggested by internal evidence as the date of dictation.

3. Memorandum of agreement on "Coordination of FBI, ONI, and MID," signed by Miles, Anderson, and Hoover, 5 June 1940, CNO files (SC), file A8-5.

4. Ibid. The signers found inadequate the section on cases directed from foreign countries and hence agreed to "study" the matter.

5. Minutes, Interdepartmental Intelligence Conference (IIC) meeting, 31 May 1940, RG 165, file 9794-186A/2.

6. Ibid.

7. Minutes, IIC, 3 June 1940, RG 165, file 9794-186A/3.

8. Memorandum and report on "Special Intelligence Service," 6 June 1940, RG 165, file 9794-186A/4.

9. Minutes, IIC, 11 June 1940, ibid.

10. Memorandum, Berle to Miles, Anderson, and Hoover, 24 June 1940, RG 165, file 9794-186B/2, 7.

11. Minutes, IIC, 2 July 1940, RG 165, file 9794-186A/7.

12. Memorandum, Miles to Anderson and Hoover, 23 July 1940, CNO files, further citation missing.

13. Minutes, IIC, meeting of 26 July, dated 29 July 1940, RG 165, file 9794-186A/12.

14. Letters, Hoover to Miles, 3 Aug., and Miles to Hoover, 7 Aug. 1940, RG 165, file 9794-186B/4; and Hoover to Miles, 15 Aug. 1940, RG 165, file 9794-186B/5.

15. Two letters, Miles to Hoover, 12 Oct., and one from Hoover to Miles, 10 Oct. 1940, RG 165, file 9794-186B (no separate filing).

16. Memorandum, Miles to Marshall, 1 July 1940, RG 165, file 10153-407/1.

17. Memorandum, Miles to Sharp, "Function and Scope of New York Office, M.I.D.," 2 Nov. 1940, ibid.

18. Memorandum, J. A. Lester to Miles, "Coordination with FBI Regards Major Sharp's Office in New York," RG 165, file 9794-186B/8.

19. Ibid. This memorandum details all of these exchanges.

20. Stimson diary, 12 Feb. 1941. On 14 Oct. 1941, Stimson had written: "General Miles came to me with reports of trouble with Edgar Hoover, who seems to be a good deal of a prima donna and has taken offense at some very innocent action of Miles. It only shows how

many little unnecessary troubles we have to keep the great machine from going to friction and trouble."

21. Ibid., 13 Feb. 1941.

22. These charges and MID's answers are found in "Charges Contained in Letter of February 10, 1941," RG 319, file 310.11.

23. Stimson diary, 13 Feb. 1941.

24. A draft of comment by or for Miles on an FBI memorandum of 3 Mar. 1941, RG 319, file 310.11.

25. Sharp to Miles, 10 Mar. 1941, RG 165, file 10153-423/5.

26. In June 1940 Roosevelt wrote Stark that he had asked Astor "to coordinate the Intelligence work in the New York area," but the origin and scope of this assignment are not fully known. Astor appears to have been coordinating the FBI and British intelligence but apparently had no formal connection with the other IIC agencies in New York until Mar. 1941, when Roosevelt named him "Area Controller" of the New York area. For more on Astor's job, see my *Donovan*, 46–51.

27. Minutes, IIC, meeting of 25 June, dated 1 July 1940, RG 165, file 9794-186A/4.

28. Anderson interview, New York, 7 Oct. 1969.

29. Memoranda, Miles to Marshall, 5 Sept. 1941, RG 319, file 310.11; and Stark to Knox, 25 Sept. 1941, CNO files (SC), file A8-5.

30. Anderson to Miles, 11 Dec. 1940, RG 165, file 10153-413/1.

31. Ibid.

32. Miles to Anderson, 12 Dec. 1940, RG 165, file 10153-413/2.

33. Anderson to District Intelligence Officer, Third Naval District, N.Y., 3 Jan. 1941, RG 165, file 10153-413/3.

34. Miles to Col. Frank K. Ross, 15 Jan. 1941, RG 165, file 10153-413/5.

35. Minutes, conference of ONI, G-2, and FBI, New York, 7 Mar. 1941, with "Addition to Major Sharp's Remarks," RG 165, file 10153-423/1.

36. Miles to Sharp, 13 Mar. 1941, RG 165, file 10153-423/2.

37. Astor to Marguerite LeHand, 31 Jan. 1941, Roosevelt Papers, PSF (Astor).

38. Sir William Wiseman had been British intelligence chief in the United States in World War I. His World War II activities, which brought him in touch with Stephenson, Astor, and Admiral Godfrey, and which involved him with the FBI and the State Department, especially in the case involving Fritz Wiedemann and Princess Hohenlohe, have not been well investigated. However, on the last subject see Costello, *Ten Days*, 399–403.

39. These responsibilities are discussed at the beginning of Chapter 8.

40. Astor to Roosevelt, 20 Apr. 1941, Roosevelt Papers, PSF (Astor).

41. Astor to Kirk, 22 Apr. 1941, Roosevelt Papers, PSF (Astor).

42. Rear Adm. Adolphus Andrews to Stark, 10 May 1941, CNO files, file A8-5.

43. Stark to Andrews, 20 May 1941, CNO files, file A8-5.

44. These biographical details are in a letter from Astor to Roosevelt, 23 June 1937, referring to a forthcoming *New Yorker Magazine* "Profile" of Astor. The remark on campaign contributions is the author's judgment.

45. *New York Times*, 4 Feb. 1959, p. 1, col. 3.

46. Astor to Roosevelt, 13 Jan. 1938, Roosevelt Papers, PSF (Astor).

47. Ibid., 5 Feb. 1940.

48. Ibid., 18 Apr. 1940.

49. Ibid., n.d.

50. Ibid., 1 June 1940.

51. Roosevelt to Stark, 26 June 1940, Roosevelt Papers, PPF 40.

52. Anderson interview, n. 28, supra.

53. Astor to Roosevelt, 26 Dec. 1940, Roosevelt Papers, PSF (Astor).

54. Memorandum of conversation by Berle, 7 Feb. 1941, in RG 59, Passport Office, file 138 Emergency Program/1459.

55. Usher's diary; and note, Kirk to Callaghan, 12 Mar. 1941, Roosevelt Papers, PSF (Astor).

56. Memoranda or notes of 14, 19, and 20 Mar. 1941, ibid.

57. The directive was undated, unaddressed, and forwarded to Miles by Berle in an undated letter and received by Miles on 22 Mar. 1941, RG 319, file 310.11.

58. Miles to Marshall, 24 Mar. 1941, ibid.

59. Stimson diary, 25 Mar. 1941.

60. Astor to Roosevelt, 3 Apr. 1941, Roosevelt Papers, PSF (Astor).

61. Sharp to Col. W. W. Cox, 1 Aug. 1942, RG 319, file 310.11.

62. Sharp to Brig. Gen. Hayes A. Kroner, 6 Nov. 1942, Roosevelt Papers, PSF (Astor).

63. Stimson diary, "Notes After Cabinet Meeting, April 4, 1941."

64. Miles to Marshall, 8 Apr. 1941, RG 319, file 310.11.

Chapter 8: A Green Light on COI

1. Memorandum, Donovan to Maj. Gen. W. B. Smith, 17 Sept. 1943. This memorandum was Exhibit W-18 in U.S. War Department, *War Report*, "Exhibits Illustrating the History of OSS."

2. Lecture, Donovan, "Office of Strategic Services," delivered at the Army and Navy Staff College, Washington, D.C., 1 Nov. 1943, OSS Records, Director's Office, Op. (hereafter Dir-Off-Op) 125, box 27, folder 1.

3. Roosevelt Papers, PPF 6558 (Donovan).

4. Composite presidential diary, Roosevelt Papers.

5. "As usual," wrote Ickes of another occasion, "[FDR] did a great deal of talking about unrelated matters." See Ickes, *Secret Diary* vol. 3, 533. Similarly Sherwood in *Roosevelt*, 265, referred to the usual "wildly irrelevant" talk at meetings with Roosevelt.

6. Sherwood, *Roosevelt*, 282.

7. Deuel, "History of the OSS," 103, Donovan Papers, job 62-271, box 29, folder 5.

8. Ickes, *Secret Diary*, vol. 3, 470.

9. Stimson diary, 19 Mar. 1941.

10. Ibid., 20 Mar. 1941; Donovan, Officers speech, 14.

11. Morgenthau diary, bk. 384, 23–25.

12. Marshall to Miles, 22 Mar. 1941 and Miles's undated reply RG 165, file 2257-22-341.

13. Memorandum, Miles to Marshall, "Joint Intelligence Committee," 15 Apr. 1941, RG 319, file 350.05.

14. Stimson diary, 25 Mar. 1941.

15. MacLeish to Donovan, 24 Mar. 1941, Donovan Papers, vol. 34.

16. *New York Times*, 26 Mar. 1941, p. 1, col. 4.

17. The Ankara, Madrid, and London items are in Donovan Papers, vol. 2.

18. Deuel, "History of the OSS," 107.

19. Miles to Marshall, 8 Apr. 1941, RG 319, file 310.11.

20. Stimson correspondence, box 35.

21. Donovan to Knox, 26 Apr. 1941, Donovan Papers, job 66–595, box 1, folder 22.

22. Stephenson interview, Bermuda, 13 Feb. 1969. See also Doering interviews, New York, 6, 8 Oct. 1969, for Doering who said Donovan would have pushed the idea of COI but not himself.

23. Stimson diary, 12, 20 May 1941.

24. Ibid., 12 May 1941.

25. Langer and Gleason, *Undeclared War*, 514–15.

26. Ickes, *Secret Diary*, vol. 3, 510.

27. U.S. Bureau of the Budget, *U.S. at War* (Washington, D.C.: Bureau of the Budget, 1947), 15.

28. Ibid., 521–35 for a complete list of these agencies and their dates of establishments.

29. Harold D. Smith Papers, Conferences with the President, 1941-1942, vol. 13, 4 Apr. 1941.

30. Ibid., 17 Apr. 1941.

31. Stimson diary, 17 Apr. 1941.

32. Memorandum, Brig. Gen. Reymond E. Lee to Marshall, 27 Mar. 1941, RG 319, file 350.05.

33. See n. 13, supra.

34. Memorandum, George A. Gordon to Welles, 22 May 1941, RG 59, file 102.2/3434.

35. Letters, Miles to each committee member, 17 June 1941, RG 319, file 350.05.

36. Letters, Miles to each committee member, 7 July 1941.

37. British Military Mission in Washington, "Formation of a Joint Intelligence Committee (Washington)," 12 June 1941, CNO files (SC), file A8-2/EF13.

38. The recommendations were made in separate letters of 14 July and are cited in a memorandum from the Joint Planning Committee to the Joint Board, 10 Sept. 1941, CNO files (SC), file A8-1 (A and N).

39. Montague, "Intelligence Service," memorandum for record, 1 Dec. 1969, 6.

40. All in this paragraph is in RG 319, file 310.11.

41. Miles to Marshall, 22 May 1941, ibid.

42. "Report on Coordination of the three Intelligence Services [FBI, MID, and ONI]," 29 May 1941, CNO Files, file A3-1/A8-5 (5-29).

43. Letter, SIS to U.S. embassy, London, no. YP/81/1 (Historian), 10 Nov. 1969, paras. 10 and 12. The telegram is in Hyde, QC, 152.

44. Stephenson, "Early Days," 7–8.

45. Ibid., 8. Until I read and pondered the italicized portion of this quotation, I remained puzzled by the stylistic and material dichotomy of Donovan's 26 April memorandum to Knox. Here are two sample paragraphs that suggest separate authorship: "I think it should be read with these considerations in mind. Intelligence operations should not be controlled by party exigencies. It is one of the most vital means of national defense. As such, it should be headed by someone appointed by the President directly responsible to him and to no one else. It should have a fund solely for the purpose of foreign investigation and the expenditures under this fund should be secret and made solely at the discretion of the President." And then, "Reports received from representatives abroad go first to Central Registry, when, after going through the process of carding and attachment of files, they are stamped with the number of the Production section concerned and passed to it, a copy of each report (submitted in quadruplicate) being passed to the D. section to whom the reporting representative belongs. (This is done in order that the D. section can keep a record of representatives' activities; all

correspondence other than reports goes direct to D. sections.)" Surely Donovan did not write the second paragraph!

46. Stephenson interview, Bermuda, 13 Feb. 1969.

47. Medlicott, *Economic Blockade* vol. 2, 502.

48. Astor to Roosevelt, 9 May 1941, Roosevelt Papers, PSF (Astor). Eliot's article appeared on 8 May.

49. Knox to Frankfurter, 22 May 1941, Knox Papers, correspondence, box 1.

50. Donovan to Roosevelt, 28 May 1941, Roosevelt Papers, PPF 6558 (Donovan).

51. Transcript of telephone conversation, 2 June 1941, Morgenthau diary, bk. 403, 85.

52. Morgenthau to Donovan, 5 June 1941, ibid., bk. 405, 204.

53. Stephenson interview, Bermuda, 23 Oct. 1969.

54. Sharp to Miles, 18 June 1941, RG 165, file 10153-423. The quotation continues: "I heard the other day that Col. Wild Bill Donovan is behind a movement to combine MID, ONI, & FBI: That Col. D spent Monday with Mr. Astor trying to sell him the idea so that he in turn could sell it to the President. That Secy [sic] Knox was for the plan: That Mr. Hoover was dead against it."

55. Stephenson, "Early Days," 7.

56. Sherwood to Morgenthau, 16 June 1941, Morgenthau diary, bk. 410, 221.

57. Sherwood to Donovan, 16 June 1941, U.S. War Department, *War Report*, "Exhibits."

58. Usher's diary.

59. Ibid., and Winant, *Letter*, 195.

60. Usher's diary and Presidential diary.

61. Deuel, "History of OSS," 108.

62. For a fuller account of this 10 June memorandum and ensuing developments, see my "Donovan's Original Marching Orders."

63. A photostat of the original memorandum is in U.S. Bureau of the Budget, Records, folder 211. The original has not been located.

64. Charles H. Ellis to Troy, 13 Nov. 1969. I talked about the matter with Ellis and Stephenson at the same time, 11 Feb. 1969. Ellis was particularly unhappy that promised changes in *Room 39* were never made.

65. David K. E. Bruce interview, Washington, D.C., 11 Dec. 1969.

66. Pearson, *Fleming*, 96–97. *New York Times*, 26 May 1941, p. 8, col. 3.

67. Godfrey interview, Eastbourne, Eng., 4 Nov. 1969.

68. McLachlan, *Room 39*, 229. Usher's diary.

69. McLachlan, *Room 39*, 234.

70. Pearson, *Fleming*, 101. The first quotation is from Fleming's letter to Col. Rex Applegate, n.d. Mar. 1957. The second is in a letter to Cornelius Ryan, 8 May 1952.

71. Fleming, "Memorandum to Colonel Donovan," 27 June 1941, OSS Records, Dir-Off-Op, 125.

72. Otto C. Doering, Jr., interviews, New York, 6, 8 Oct. 1969.

73. Memorandum, Miss Roberta Barrows to General Watson, Roosevelt Papers, PPF 6558 (Donovan).

74. The 13 June conversation is in Morgenthau diary, bk. 408, 4; the note to Mrs. Klotz is in bk. 413, 14; and the conversation with Donovan is in bk. 409, 151–52.

75. The appointment appears in Presidential diary. The "in totem" is from a transcribed telephone conversation with Morgenthau in his diary, bk. 411, 67–71. For FDR's note see n. 63, supra.

76. Letter, Donovan to Whitney, 19 Aug. 1941, OSS Records, job 62-271, box 29, folder 8.

77. Morgenthau diary, bk. 413, 14.

78. Security deletion.

79. The medal was awarded to Stephenson by Donovan, on behalf of President Truman, on 30 Nov. 1946. The text of the citation and a photograph of the award ceremony appeared in *New York Times*, 1 Dec. 1946, p. 54, col. 3.

Chapter 9: A Postscript

1. Stephenson, "Early Days," 12.

2. Memorandum, Morton to Col. E. I. Jacob, 18 Sept. 1941, Churchill Papers, box 145, folder 463, item 2. This comment was brought on by Admiral Stark's wish "to take over the Security System in the West Indies." The answer, in short, was that his cooperation in maintaining physical security was welcome but control of the "internal domestic security of our Colonies" was out of the question.

3. Morton to Sir David Scott, 1 Apr. 1942, F.O. Papers, A3874/2487/45 (1942). Morton had been asked to comment on a British paper, George F. Todd's "U.S. Information Services," 1 Dec. 1941.

Chapter 10: The FBI: Run by the British?

1. Mowrer and his wife, having fled Paris ahead of the conquering Germans, reached London on 10 July.

2. Memorandum, Lord President of the Council (Neville Chamberlain), 27 May 1940, doc. W. P. (40)172, Churchill Papers, box 138, folder 418/1. An "executive" committee reported not to the ministers but to the prime minister. Churchill's instruction is in Andrew, *Secret Service*, 478.

3. H. R. S. Philpott, *Daily Herald* (London), 16 Aug. 1940, p. 5, col. 5.

4. Swinton to Halifax, 15 July 1940, F.O. Papers, A3542/90/45 (1940), no. 231.

5. Harvey Klemmer interview, Silver Spring, Md., 24 Apr. 1978. He wrote *Harbor Nights* (1937), about the merchant seaman's days and nights ashore, and *They'll Never Quit* (1941), an account of Britain during the blitz.

6. Letter, Holt-Wilson to Herschel V. Johnson, 19 July 1940, RG 59, file 841.00N/10.

7. Sir Eric's curriculum vitae, Sept. 1940, is a seven-page "Note on the work of Sir Eric Holt-Wilson in the creation and development of the IMPERIAL SECURITY SERVICE, 1912 to 1940," an enclosure in Johnson to Dunn, 16 Oct. 1940, in RG 59, file 841.00N/14. Novelist MacKenzie's account of his MI-6 (then M.I.1.c.) World War I service in Athens was published in Nov. 1932, immediately banned, republished—less 130 pages—in 1939, and in 1987 was published in its original, complete form.

8. West, *MI5*, 152–54. For "purge" see Deacon, *British Secret Service*, 392; "butcher" comes from Page, Leitch, and Knightley, *Philby*, 141.

9. Stephenson interview, Bermuda, 23 Oct. 1969.

10. Kennedy to Hull, 1 Aug. 1940, enclosing (1) Klemmer's "Report on Fifth Column Activities and Counter Measures in Great Britain," (2) Holt-Wilson's letter to Johnson, 19 July, and (3) attachment from Holt-Wilson listing the documents made available to Klemmer and to Mowrer. The first enclosure is cited hereafter as Klemmer, "Report."

11. Klemmer, "Report," 19.

12. For "Imperial Security Service" see Holt-Wilson's vita in n. 7, supra; the term occurs

there five times. Other names encountered elsewhere are "Imperial Security Intelligence Service" and "Imperial Intelligence Service."

13. Klemmer, "Report," 22.

14. Ibid.

15. Ibid., 25.

16. Berle, *Navigating Rapids*, 253–54. Berle said Wiseman had come to his office to solicit his help in interpreting American opinion for Ambassador Lothian. The request reminded Berle of what he considered the Machiavellian role played by both Wiseman and Lothian in Washington in World War I. See his views later in this chapter.

17. Berle to Moffat, 18 Apr. 1940, RG 59, file 841.24/235.

18. Dunn to Johnson, no. 3966, 30 Dec. 1940, RG 59, file 841.00N/11; Johnson to Dunn, no. 423, 4 Feb. 1941, RG 59, 841.00N/12.

19. For "cooperation" see Dunn to Berle, 23 Apr. 1940, RG 59, file 841.24/235. Otherwise, all in the paragraph is in Dunn to Johnson, 29 Sept. 1940, RG 59, 841.00N/10. On FDR's 1939 action on coordination see Chap. 7.

20. For readying the country, see *New York Times*, 22 May 1940, p. 1, col. 1.; for Clegg, ibid., 2 June 1940, p. 15, col. 3.

21. Dunn to Johnson, n. 18, supra. Turrou was dismissed from the FBI with prejudice. The Gustave Rumreich case centered on the operation of a German espionage ring in the U.S. Army; see my *Donovan*, 11.

22. Dunn to Johnson, n. 18, supra.

23. Stewart to Dunn, 7 Oct. 1940, RG 59, file 841.00N/10. Johnson to Dunn, 16 Oct. 1940, RG 59, file 841.00N/14.

24. Dunn to Berle and Sumner Welles, 16 Nov. 1940, RG 59, file 841.00N/14.

25. Berle to Dunn, 18 Nov. 1940, RG 59, file 841.00N/14.

26. Ibid. Berle, *Navigating Rapids*, 11. The "twisted policy" is in his article "The Betrayal at Paris." For "the easiest mark" see *Navigating Rapids*, 253–54. See also n. 16, supra.

27. Berle to Dunn, n. 25, supra.

28. Murphy to Berle, 2 Dec. 1940, RG 59, file 841.00N/10. On Murphy and for a photograph of him, see my article "'Ah, Sweet Intrigue!'"

29. Hoover to Fletcher Warren, 17 Mar. 1941, RG 59, file 841.00N/13; Johnson to Dunn, no. 423, 4 Feb. 1941, RG 59, file 841.00N/12.

30. Murphy to Berle, n. 28, supra. The Berle diary entry was read to me at an interview in New York, 7 Oct. 1969, but it was not printed in *Navigating Rapids*.

31. On Wiseman and Lothian see the Wiseman Papers, serial 2, box 13, folder 8. For Churchill and Halifax see Costello, *Ten Days*, 399. The negotiations involved Wiseman; Capt. Fritz Wiedemann, the German consul general in San Francisco; and Princess Stephanie von Hohenlohe-Waldenburg, a friend of Hitler. Wiseman, however, had apparently been commissioned by Lothian and Stephenson to undertake the discussions and was subsequently saved by the latter from deportation.

32. Hall and Peaslee, *Three Wars*, 236–38 and 243.

33. Ibid., 258.

34. Berle Papers, diary, box 212, folder "Oct.–Dec. 1940." Hull to Jackson, 14 Dec. 1940, RG 59, file 841.00N/10.

35. Jackson to Hull, 31 Dec. 1940, and Dunn to Johnson, 10 Jan. 1941, RG 59, file 841.00N/11.

36. Report of Visas issued under Section 3(1) "during the fortnight ending March 30,

1940," London embassy despatch 4981, 2 Apr. 1940, RG 59, file 811.111 diplomatic/15254. Lothian to Hull, 15 June 1940, RG 59, file 702.4111/1608.

37. BSC *History*, 11. E. A. Tamm, "Memorandum for the Director (Hoover)," 13 Aug. 1940, FBI files (file no. not legible).

38. Berle to B. Hatha, ca. 19 Feb. 1941, RG 59, file 841.01B11/185 PS/JHS.

Chapter 11: Three Books: From Obscurity to Fame

1. Memorandum, Troy to DTR, "Report on Interview with . . . Stephenson . . . 11–15 February 1969," 13 Mar. 1969, Troy Papers, box 7, folder 66.

2. Evidence of this publicity appears later in this chapter.

3. Naftali, "Deception," 74–75.

4. In its day the center was known as "the camp" or "Camp X." In official records it was, and is, referred to as the National Defence File S25-1-1. For the history project, see David Stafford's *Camp X*, 251–57, and Naftali, "Deception," 75–76. The "hidden" description will be found in an untitled, undated eleven-page exposition of *A Man Called Intrepid* in the William Stevenson Papers (hereafter WSP). WSP, Intrepid 801.4.

5. Stafford, *Camp X*, 251–57, and WSP, Intrepid 801.4.

6. Naftali, "Deception," 75; Stafford, *Camp X*, 255.

7. Stafford, *Camp X*, 255–57.

8. Stephenson's foreword to the book is dated 31 Dec. 1945. I never found any copy in CIA. For Stevenson's account of the number of copies of the history, see n. 13, infra.

9. Stafford, *Camp X*, 257.

10. The substance of the marginalia and the handwriting testify to Stephenson as their author. Thus, the first two notes show Stephenson's known dislike of Lord Halifax and his contempt for his MI-6 superior, Stewart Menzies.

11. Hyde, *QC*, x. Sir William's "Point of Departure: A Foreword by Intrepid," in Stevenson, *AMCI*, xiv.

12. Stevenson's announcement appeared in a letter to Toronto's *Globe and Mail*, 2 Dec. 1983. On the resultant flurry and disappointment see my article "Stevenson Papers." Sir William's objection is found in Stevenson's letter to me, 14 May 1989. On 7 Jan. 1984 Stevenson told me that in his *Globe and Mail* letter he had written "loosely," that he meant to say that he would make the history available to a few persons only.

13. For Stevenson's story see "Claim Intrepid's Secrets Are Going to Be Published," *Royal Gazette* (Bermuda), 31 Mar. 1989. When I told Sir William, 6 Jan. 1984, that I had a copy, he said he "didn't know how that was possible," "would get right on to it," and would not permit its publication. As for my ability to publish the book, I had it—subject to my publisher—as the founding general editor of the "Foreign Intelligence Book Series," published by University Publications of America, Frederick, Md.

14. Ignatius, "Britain's War in America." The story consumed almost two pages in the "Outlook" section. Bryden, *Best-Kept Secret*, 272.

15. For a list of published books on OSS, see George C. Constantinides, "The OSS: A Brief Review of Literature." Stevenson wrote Sir William (17 Mar. 1973, WSP, Intrepid 801.3-1): "Harcourt Brace do not know, of course, that there has been such a bumpy ride for previous attempts at [writing your] biography."

16. Porter, "Private Eye." Stephenson to Ellis, 24 Aug. 1959, Hyde Papers.

17. Hyde to Stephenson, 4 Dec. 1960, Hyde Papers. Hyde recalled that he was then in

New York on a parliamentary mission but that later as a professor he had more time for writing.

18. Stephenson had been impressed by Ellis's article "Operations in Transcaspia 1918–19 and the Commissars Case," which Ellis sent him. Ellis, who had been in the operations, rebutted an often repeated Soviet charge of British complicity in the massacre of the commissars in Baku. Ellis probably also sent Sir William a copy of his article "The Transcaspian Episode: Operations in Central Asia, 1918–1919." These articles were followed by Ellis's *Transcaspian Episode*.

19. Stephenson to Ellis, 24 Aug. 1959, Hyde Papers. For Stephenson's promise and Ellis's comment thereon, see Ellis to Hyde, 26 Dec. 1960, ibid.

20. Memorandum, Troy to DTR, "Report on TDY in London . . . 22 October–22 November 1969 . . . Report on the Donovan Project," 5 Dec. 1969, Troy Papers, box 7, folder 58.

21. Hyde to Ellis, 4 Dec. 1960, Hyde Papers. Ellis to Hyde, 10 Dec. 1960, ibid., 1/5.

22. Ibid. Ellis to Hyde, [14] Jan. 1963, Hyde Papers, 1/10.

23. Ellis to Hyde, 10 Dec. 1960, Hyde Papers, 1/5. The obstructionists Stephenson had in mind apparently included SOE, PWE, and SE, and his own MI-6 leadership. The operations Stephenson had in mind related to "Vichy and the Spaniards," and he thought "we should say quite openly how certain things were carried out in Bermuda, Trinidad, etc.," Ellis to Hyde, 26 Dec. 1960, ibid.

24. Ellis to Hyde, 10 [18] June 1963, ibid. Ellis attributed Stephenson's remarks about Hyde and Ellis's clearance to a Stephenson letter to him 17 Nov. 1960.

25. Ellis to Hyde, 12 Dec. 1960, Hyde Papers, 1/5. The "famous secret report" is in Ellis to Hyde, June [1961], ibid.

26. Hyde to Stephenson, 20 Sept. 1961; Stephenson to Hyde, 25 Sept. 1961. Both in Hyde Papers.

27. Hyde to Stephenson, 20 Sept. 1961, Hyde Papers, on Hyde's "borrowing freely" see Naftali, "Deception," 79, 94, n. 50, where he speaks of Hyde's "massive" borrowing. On the other hand, Ellis said that "75% of the book" was material already mentioned by other writers in some fashion; see Ellis to Hyde, 5 Nov. 1962, Hyde Papers, 1/9. For Sherwood on the title see Stephenson to Ellis, 24 Aug. 1959, Hyde Papers.

28. For "forthright" see Ellis to Hyde, 26 Dec. 1960, and for "fierce" and the remainder of the sentence see Ellis to Hyde, 23 June 1962. The "meat" quotation is in Ellis to Hyde, 9 Jan. [1963]. The next sentence is in Ellis to Hyde, [14] Jan. 1963, 1/10. All above in Hyde Papers.

29. Morrell's comments are in Ellis to Hyde, 9 Jan. [1963]. Stephenson's "unalterably opposed" is in his cable to Hyde, 13 Feb. 1963. Stephenson said he had received "shocking information" that Farrar Straus intended to provoke controversy in order to increase sales. He also thought Hyde "not sufficiently concerned" about the adverse effect on British relations. Hyde, trying to disabuse Stephenson of his fears, emphasized David Bruce's favorable opinion of the book. On Iceland Stephenson's unhappiness with Hyde's opposition to holding up publication caused Sir William to cable that he was "beginning to regret the whole thing," in Stephenson-Hyde, 13 Mar. 1963, Hyde-Stephenson, 14 Mar. 1963, and Stephenson-Hyde, 15 Mar. 1961 [1963], 1/11. All above in Hyde Papers.

30. For Morrell's comments see Ellis to Hyde, [14] Jan. 1963. Ellis's comment is in his letter to Hyde, 18 Feb. 1963. Cuneo is quoted by Ellis writing Hyde, 14 Oct. 1963. The remainder of the paragraph is from Hyde to Straus, 22 Feb. 1963. All above in Hyde Papers.

31. Hyde Papers. Bruce, a close friend and former colleague of both Stephenson and Ellis, had often been in contact with them and Hyde during the writing of the book. Hyde informed Stephenson (4 June 1962, Hyde Papers) that after he and Ellis had met with Bruce on

1 June, Hyde had rewritten ten thousand words and made many "minor corrections, omissions [deletions], and additions." Bruce's foreword to the QC's British edition (pp. 11–12) speaks eloquently of his personal indebtedness, as a Donovan subordinate, to Stephenson and Ellis and of the "permanent debt of gratitude and respect" owed to Stephenson by the United States.

32. The "official blessing" claim was made by Ian Fleming in his foreword to Hyde's *Room 3603*, xi. While Rome was protesting the apparent use of official documents, the Lais family was protesting the entire story and eventually successfully sued Hyde. As for Ellis, he had cleared the first draft of the manuscript with an MI-6 security officer and offered to clear the final draft, but the offer was left to his good judgment. As for "Cynthia," Lovell's *Cast No Shadow* is the fullest account of her life, career, and amours. For my review of it see "Cynthia in Living Color."

33. After his retirement, Ellis apparently had two jobs with the government, but they are not easily differentiated. He worked at one time or another with both the Home and the Foreign Offices, and the latter may have been cover for an MI-6 job. Financially he needed both jobs. The "weeding" job was winnowing MI-6 files. That he was on "the suspended list" (Ellis to Hyde, 12 Nov. 1962) he attributed to the "official blessing" matter. As for the termination news he could not explain it; Ellis to Hyde, 22 Nov. 1962. The "douceur" is in Ellis to Hyde, 26 Dec. [1962]. All in Hyde Papers.

34. For the £600 refund see Hyde to Stephenson, 30 July 1963. The remainder of the paragraph is in Hyde to Miss Green, 22 Mar. 1966. Both in Hyde Papers.

35. Intrepid to Bison [Herbert L. Rowland], n.d. Dec. 1972, WSP, Intrepid 801.8.

36. Stevenson said that, returning some lend-lease planes in Apr. 1945, he "reported to OSS and in this way became attached to yourself [Intrepid] with the title of ADO [Assistant Director for Operations] to regularise what was really a minor historian's role with the winding down of your organisation. It's not something about which I want to chatter, anyway," Stevenson to Intrepid, 22 Mar. 1976, WSP, Intrepid 801.3-2.

37. Memorandum of conversation with Stevenson, 4 Dec. 1972, Troy Papers, box 7, folder 1. Stevenson said Intrepid, because of ill health, had long resisted the idea but finally relented in mid-1972. On the "one pair of eyes," see, e.g., Stevenson to Intrepid, 7 Sept. 1972 and 4 June 1973, WSP, Intrepid 801.3-1. On the "cans of film," see Stevenson to Intrepid, 3 Aug. 1973, WSP, Intrepid 801.3-1.

38. Stevenson, *Bormann Brotherhood*. "Intrepid," which had been BSC's cable address, was used by Sir William as his own as early as 1953.

39. Ibid., xviii. Stevenson to Intrepid, 17 Mar. 1973, WSP, Intrepid 801.3-1.

40. The words "The Two Bills" were part of the subtitle, but they were used more than the title "Mission Accomplished."

41. Sir William's criticisms of Ellis are found in two cables to Rowland, ca. Oct. and Dec. 1972, WSP, Intrepid, 801.8.

42. Stevenson to Intrepid, 9 Aug. 1974, WSP, Intrepid 001.4; 4 June 1973, Intrepid 801.3-1; 5 Oct. 1973, ibid.; 11 Aug. 1974, WSP, Intrepid 801.3-2.

43. Stevenson to Sir Colin Gubbins, 7 Aug. 1973, WSP, Intrepid 801.6. Stevenson to Intrepid, 9 Aug. 1974, WSP, Intrepid 801.4.

44. For the sentence containing "enormously helpful" and the one following, see Stevenson to Intrepid, 3 Aug. 1973, WSP, Intrepid 801.3-1. For "on my own authority" see Stevenson to Intrepid, 3 Sept. 1974, WSP, Intrepid 801.3-2.

45. For civilization resting in Intrepid's hands see Stevenson to Intrepid, 16 Oct. 1973, WSP, Intrepid 801.3-1. The rest of the paragraph is in Stevenson to Intrepid, 11 Aug. 1974, WSP, Intrepid 801.3-2.

46. *SIS*, Mar. 1977.

47. Among the reasons given for long denying him the Companion of the Order of Canada, which he received in 1980, were his long absence from Canada, his knighthood, and his strong anti-communist stance. Fewer than twenty persons attended his private funeral service on 2 Feb. 1989 at St. John's Church in Pembroke, Bermuda. He was laid to rest beside his wife Lady Mary, whom he had married sixty-five years earlier.

Chapter 12: Donovan: A British Agent During World War I?

1. Memorandum, Troy to DTR, "Report on Interview with . . . Stephenson . . . 11–15 February 1969," 13 Mar. 1969, Troy Papers, box 7, folder 66.

2. Harry B. Lake interview, New York, 27 Mar. 1969.

3. George S. Leisure interview, New York, 27 Mar. 1969. Leisure to Troy, 31 Mar. 1969. Leisure said that Donovan's secretary, Jane Smith, also had never heard of the case.

4. Stephenson cabled me 1 Apr. 1970: "First met Bill [Donovan] in 1931 [sic]. He was representing Ed Bud[d] Co . . . and at lunch in my office dining room he mentioned desire meet Beaverbrook to whom he had letter from Frank Knox. I forthwith phoned Max, upshot was dinner with Max at his house Stornoway next door my office. Churchill and few other leaders present including Rothermere and Billy Hughes prime minister Australia. Bill and I in frequent contact thereafter."

5. Memorandum, Troy to DTR, "Report of Consultation with . . . Stephenson in Bermuda," 17-22 Sept. 1974, Troy Papers, box 7, folder 1.

6. Ibid.

7. Ibid.

8. Doering would not have denied Donovan's handling of the Pressed Steel case if he knew it to be a fact.

9. Stevenson, *AMCI*, 5-6.

10. Shepardson's son, John W., who is writing his father's biography, gave me the "7 August" date on 14 June 1994. For "1 November" see Shepardson to Lawrence R. Houston, 1 Nov. 1961, in Donovan Papers (Carlisle Barracks), box 1, folder 8. On "no access" the reader will have to accept my assurance that no writer outside CIA could have had access to the Donovan Papers without my knowing it, especially in the early 1970s when Stevenson was writing *AMCI* and I was busily using those and other papers in writing my *Donovan* book.

11. Here are the "thirteen days": although Donovan reached Southampton 26 Mar., he was not able to land until 27 Mar.; he left London 9 Apr. For his landing see A. C. Brown, *Last Hero*, 31. The 9 Apr. departure is in Donovan to Warwick Greene, 1 July 1916, Rockefeller Foundation Archives, RG 1.1, ser. 100, box 61, folder 604. For "a brief stay," see Richard Dunlop, *Donovan*, 43. He was in Berlin 1 July, was wanted there until 8 July, took about eight days steaming home, must have visited his family briefly, was "on active duty" 15 July, was "mustered into Federal Service on 19 July," and some time in July or August was in Texas with his unit. He could hardly have had a week in London. The 8 July date is in Greene's cable to Donovan, n.d. June 1916, Rockefeller Foundation Archives, RG 1.1, ser. 100, box 58, folder 575; the 15 July date appears on Donovan's post-World War II "Application for Retirement Benefits under . . . PL810—80th Congress." The 19 July date appears in his AGO 201 file, 15 July 1943.

12. I have seen only one piece of primary evidence attesting to Stephenson's pre-RFC service. It is a photostat of a page of his war record. While it does not show his name, I think it authentic. It was given to me 8 Sept. 1994 by William MacDonald, who is writing a Stephen-

son book. It reads: "App. Act/Sgt with Pay of Clerk" in Aug. or Sept. 1916. No writer has cited any primary documents on this pre-RFC service or gassing and recuperation. All of this, however, is laid out generally plausibly enough in the works of Porter, Hyde, and Stevenson. Sir William laid it out in cables to Stevenson 29 Aug. 1972, WSP, Intrepid 801.1-2, and 21 Aug. 1975, WSP, Intrepid 801.1-1. As for RFC service, he was "appointed to a Commission in the Royal Flying Corps. on 11 Sept. 1917," W. A. B. Douglas (Director, Directorate of History, National Defence Headquarters, Ottawa) to Troy, 5 Apr. 1984.

13. Surprisingly enough, in 1981 Sir William seemed to have forgotten this alleged 1916 meeting. Instead, he returned to his original Lake and Donovan story of 1930. He did this in a long cable on 6 June in which he took issue with my remarks (in my *Donovan*, vi) about his "claim to a long-standing pre-1940 friendship with Donovan." It was a much more plausible account than that quoted in n. 4, supra. While the evidence is against him, Stephenson died convinced, I am sure, of the truth of his "claim."

14. Brown, *Last Hero*, 30–36; my article "For Years the Brits Ran One of America's Best, says Anthony Cave Brown," 1. The later comment was made in a TV interview on WTTG, 11 Jan. 1983.

15. Brown, *Last Hero*, 31–32.

16. Ibid., 32.

17. Ibid.

18. Ibid., 32–33.

19. Ibid., 33.

20. Ibid., 33–35.

21. My article cited in n. 14, supra. For "intelligence master" see Brown, *Last Hero*, 33. In the TV interview Brown said the British "supported" Donovan "in his aspirations to become head of the first American Secret Service."

22. Sir William's account of his mother is in a cable to Stevenson, 23 July 1973, WSP, Intrepid 801.8 and in AMCI, 4. The earliest date that I can find of Stephenson's service in the RFC is 6 June 1917; it appears in the MacDonald document cited in n. 12, supra.

23. Both Donovan and his wife were natives of Buffalo and inevitably had contacts and interests in neighboring Canada. Troy, *Donovan*, 53 and 488, n. 31.

24. The fifteen-page report is Donovan's letter to Greene, n. 11, supra.

25. No sooner did Brown make that allowance, however, than he returned five lines later to his fantasizing about Donovan coming to the "attention" of British intelligence. Incidentally, in making that allowance Brown had Donovan "still in London" on 24 Apr. (p. 33) when by Brown's own account Donovan was in Holland on 10 Apr. and never shown as returning to London.

26. Donovan to Prof. Dr. Ludwig Stein, 7 June 1916, Rockefeller Foundation Archives, no further citation available.

27. "Proclamation of August 1, 1914, with regard to the war between Austria-Hungary and Servia," U.S. Department of State, *Papers Relating to the Foreign Relations of the United States, 1914*, 550.

28. CIA, "The Ceremony and Exhibit: 'With the Fighting Sixty-Ninth: Donovan in World War I' June 1986." William M. Henhoeffer, "Donovan's Allies in World War I." Henhoeffer's article is a commentary on the exhibit. The words "Donovan's Allies" in the article's title show how deeply Brown's insinuations had permeated the thinking of Henhoeffer, a friend of mine now deceased; those so-called allies were not Donovan's or America's allies in 1915–16; and after the United States entered the war, they were only "associated powers."

29. Henhoeffer, "Donovan's Allies," 47.

30. Sullivan, "Intelligence Career of William J. Donovan," 4. Sullivan's suggestion about "an espionage assignment" for Cardinal Mercier recycled Cave Brown's odd query: "*Is it possible* wjd had become a spy for Christ?" [My emphasis.]. This was brought on by Brown's musing about Donovan's interest in reconstructing Louvain as cover for those "odd perambulations" on the eve of the battle of the Somme. "Whatever his purpose" in raising the query, Brown went to strange lengths to tell his readers that "from now on" Donovan grew "increasingly close to the Catholic hierarchs of the United States and was later made "by Pius XII a Knight Grand Cross of the Order of St. Sylvester, the oldest and most prized of papal decorations, awarded only to 100 knights who 'by feat of arms, or outstanding deeds, have spread the Faith, and have safeguarded and championed the Church'—the so-called Golden Militia," *Last Hero*, 35. Since Donovan was also honored by Belgium, Denmark, France, Great Britain, Greece, Italy, Netherlands, Norway, Poland, Serbia, and Siam, "is it possible" he also carried out "an espionage mission" for each of them?

Chapter 13: Churchill's "Personal Representative"

1. My personal (and now unedited) note at the time reads: "As to two visits in spring '40 WSS today not clear—to me, that is. At first seemed to say that W. C.—before becoming PM—asked him to go to USA. This was when WC was 1st Lord of the A. Later stressed that WC as PM asked him to go as '*pers rep*' [orig. emphasis]." In my trip report and for whatever reason, I did not mention that request, despite my emphasis in "*pers rep.*" See memorandum, Troy to DTR, "Report on Interview with . . . Stephenson . . . 11–15 February 1969," 13 Mar. 1969, Troy Papers, box 7, folder 66.

2. In my trip report of 11 Oct. 1974, I wrote that Stephenson "said he had read every word of it overnight. He made several marginal notes, each of which he initialed." See memorandum, Troy to DTR, "Report of Consultation with . . . Stephenson in Bermuda," 17–22 Sept. 1974, Troy Papers, box 7, folder 1.

3. Porter, "Private Eye," 7, 70. Hyde, QC, 2, 28–30.

4. Colville, *Churchill*, 83–84.

5. Kimball, "World War II's 'Intrepid'."

6. A characterization made to me at a conference in Annapolis, Md., by a Canadian scholar, Wesley K. Wark, 30 Sept. 1983.

7. Gilbert, *Finest Hour*, 990.

8. Kimball, n. 5, supra.

9. Sherwood, *Roosevelt*, 270. Dahl, wsp, Intrepid 500.1-4. Bruce to Julian P. Muller, 22 Sept. 1975, wsp, Intrepid 801.17-1. Sweet-Escott, transcribed interview, roll 1, p. 7, wsp, Intrepid 500.1-4.

10. Coit is mentioned in Hyde, QC, 181, as one of ten English businessmen and financiers who served in bsc. He "headed Stephenson's soe section," according to George Merten, another little known bsc agent, writing me 3 Mar. 1972. Coit was instrumental in placing Merten's anti-German cartel material in American papers in 1941. On Merten see my article "'George': oss's fbi Secret." The traitors, briefly mentioned, are Burgess, Fuchs, Maclean, Philby, and Pontecorvo.

11. The two quotations are in the bsc History, xi and 13, respectively. The occasion for the second one was Donovan's trip to the Middle East in Dec. 1940.

12. Porter, "Private Eye," 70. For Porter's sources, see Chap. 14.

13. On the two trips, see U.S. Department of Justice, Immigration and Naturalization Service, form 1-404-A, Stephenson, William S., New York, 21 June 1940 (ins file A6 762816);

and "Weekly Report of Visas Issued . . ." U.S. embassy, London, despatch 4981, 2 Apr. 1940, RG 59 (State decimal file 1940–42), file 811. 111 dip/15254.

14. Hyde, QC, 30.

15. Sir William's response to Colville is in his foreword to Hyde's *Secret Agent*, xiv–xv. For another response see my article "Where Was Churchill?" Hunt's response to Stephenson is in "A Tepid Intrepid," a review of Hyde's *Secret Agent*. On the date of the dinner, strangely enough, Sir William on 25 Oct. 1973 had cabled Stevenson: "The date required was probably May twelfth 1940," WSP, Intrepid 801.1-1. Later Stevenson wrote vaguely about the date: "It was a fine evening, with the washed-blue skies that come in late May or early June," in AMCI, 99.

16. For the concept of a hero in search of a role see Gamal Abdul Nassar, *Egypt's Liberation*, 87. Nasser's line is a modification of Luigi Pirandello's *Six Characters in Search of an Author*.

17. Stevenson, AMCI, 7, 10, 14–15, 28, 30.

18. Cruickshank's SOE, 33–36, offers a brief account of Stephenson's role in the attempted sabotage of the Swedish port of Oxelösund. See also West, MI6, 121–23.

19. Lord Dacre (Hugh Trevor-Roper) is quoted in Andrew's *Secret Service*, 461–62. Andrew calls Dacre's judgment not "charitable" but "understandable" in light of the attempt made in the SIS to have him dismissed from the service because of his alleged pro-German contacts. Andrew also thinks Dacre's "overall judgment on the wartime SIS is probably too harsh." David Bruce interview, Washington, D.C., 11 Dec. 1969. Bruce also said he himself "cared little" for Menzies but liked Godfrey. On "my representative" see *Letter*, SIS to U.S. embassy, London, no. YP/81/1 (Historian), 10 Nov. 1969.

20. Kim Philby, My *Silent War*, 90. The "unpaid representative" comment was made by Walter Bell in an interview in Dublin, N.H., 20 Aug. 1983. Bell was assigned to the New York office in 1935 and remained there until Oct. 1940 when he went to Mexico "to watch the ships."

21. The "wide-ranging brief" is in Hyde, *Secret Agent*, 59. See also Taylor, "Daddy, What Was Winston Churchill?" and West, MI6, 122–23.

22. Conyers Read, "Pre-COI Period."

23. For Bruce's comment see n. 19, supra.

24. Porter, "Private Eye," 68. Cuneo, "The British and Sir William Stephenson," 6. On the same subject see Cuneo's letter in Bermuda's *Royal Gazette*, 24 Sept. 1981.

25. Cuneo, "Take It or Leave It: Donovan of O.S.S." Idem., "The British and Sir William Stephenson," 7. For "through wire" see the first paper, 3.

26. James R. Murphy interview, Washington, D.C., 5 Jan. 1976. Sir R. B. Lockhart, *Diaries* 2: 479. Maurice Buckmaster, "The Back Rooms," a review of AMCI; on SOE and "Baker Street" itself, see Berkeley, A *Spy's London*, 164–83. Gubbins to Ellis, 16 Aug. 19[72], WSP, Intrepid, 801.6.

27. According to Irving (*Churchill's War*, 525), it was Stephenson's deputy, Colonel Ellis, who "was sitting with Hoover and Donovan, and reporting directly to the president." Irving cites no proof for the statement, and reason renders it untenable: if a British officer were so positioned vis-à-vis Hoover, Donovan, and FDR, that officer would surely have been not a deputy but a chief.

28. See Foot, SOE, 19. On Morton's handling secret affairs, West (MI6, 123) describes Morton as having taken on "the role of Churchill's unofficial intelligence adviser."

29. Hyde, *Secret Agent*, xvi.

30. Hoover wrote Attorney General Francis Biddle 31 Dec. 1941: "At the beginning of the World War in 1940 the FBI was instructed to establish an informal but close relationship

with the British . . . and Canadian intelligence," in Griffith (FBI) to Troy, Troy Papers, box 8, folder 60. This relationship must have been established by early July since FBI records make clear that Hoover and Stephenson were in very frequent contact by that time. Sherwood, *Roosevelt*, 270.

31. This sentence has a sourcing problem. As it stands, with the quoted portion, it is a faithful rendering of lines in Hinsley's *British Intelligence* 1: 312–13. It is similar to, but slightly different from, lines in Gilbert's *Finest Hour*, 990. Both authors give the same source: a naval attaché report from Washington to London, 14 Jan. 1941, Admiralty Papers "233/84." The Public Record Office discovered, in response to my queries, that "233/84" was "out of range for this class" and was actually "223/84." Even so, the document never mentions any Rooseveltian assurance to "C's representative," though it mentions the attaché's "very good understanding" with "Stephenson" of "the Passport Control Office." While it supports nothing in Gilbert's book, it does support Hinsley's comment about British disappointment in the quality of American intelligence and American difficulties in obtaining information. Now, what is the point of this pedantry? First, I have never found any primary source for FDR's alleged assurance to "C's representative," though I think such assurance quite credible. Second, who characterized Stephenson as "C's representative"? The original source? Hinsley? Certainly not FDR, inasmuch as that term was then British and not American usage, as is evident in Berle's references to Stephenson cited in nn. 32, 34, and 36, infra.

32. For Astor see Chap. 7, 84. The 3 Sept. statement is in a "Memorandum," which has no addressee or signature, in Berle Papers, diary, box 13, folder "July–September 1941." On this code situation see Berle's message to Roosevelt on 9 Oct., infra.

33. On James Roosevelt see Hyde, *QC*, 213 and Costello, *Days*, 30.

34. Memorandum, Berle to Hull and Welles, 31 Mar. 1941, RG 59, file 841.20211/23. Berle said Stephenson's "operatives" were "in fact spies," whose activities could cause the United States much trouble if, for instance, the information they gathered fell into enemy hands as a result of "a British defeat or a change of [the British government's] attitude towards a negotiated peace." Jackson's attitude was reported by Ickes in his *Secret Diary* 3: 474.

35. Memorandum, 18 Sept. 1941. Memorandum, Berle to Welles, "Re: your memorandum of September 27 . . . and enclosures," 27 Sept. 1941. Both in Berle diary, box 213, folder "July–September 1941." Memorandum, Berle to Roosevelt, 9 Oct. 1941, citation missing.

Twice, on 3 Sept. and 9 Oct., Stephenson has been quoted as saying the code carrying Roosevelt-Churchill messages could not be given to U.S. authorities without FDR's permission. Now Christopher Andrew, on the basis of apparently contradictory hearsay evidence from Lord Halifax and "a report" from Hoover (Andrew, *Eyes Only*, 101, 130), has saddled Stephenson with the "fraudulent claim" of having provided a communication channel for secret messages. What Andrew apparently has not seen is FDR's response to Berle's 9 Oct. memorandum, namely a note to Donovan: please "look into" and "handle" this "matter" with Berle, Hoover, and "the British Intelligence," FDR to Donovan, 13 Oct. 1941, Troy Papers, box 9, folder 20. Stephenson's emphasis was not on sending messages but on needing FDR's permission to reveal the code. Before charging Stephenson with fraud, one must know whether Stephenson did send such messages. Also, one must ask: why would Stephenson tell Berle, and surely Hoover, that he was doing so if he were not? In any case, we know now only that the matter was left in Bill Donovan's hands.

36. For "taken in" and "deceived," see Andrew, *Eyes Only*, 100, 102, 130. On the map, see, inter alia, my article "Ex-British Agent Says . . . Map Faked," and Naftali, "Deception," 91, n. 26.

37. BSC *History,* xiii–xiv.

38. Hyde, *Secret Agent,* 252.

39. Churchill's comment was first publicized in Porter, "Private Eye," 75. He probably learned of it from Stephenson's friends who, like Stephenson himself, heard of it from Churchill or some high ranking person such as Lord "Top" Selborne, who succeeded Hugh Dalton as minister of economic warfare, SOE's cover. Sir William cabled Stevenson the following unedited message on 11 Sept. 1974: "The good man 'Top' Selborne Earl of Selborne said at the end quote I can testify that when Winston wrote himself alongside Intrepids name in the prime ministers list recommendations to the crown quote this one is dear to my heart unquote he meant it most sincerely unquote stop," WSP, Intrepid 801.1-4. As for verifying the comment's authenticity, Whitehall's Management and Personnel Office informed me, 22 Aug. 1983: "The confidentiality of honours papers extends to the recipient and continues after the death of the person concerned."

40. William MacDonald to Troy, 8 Sept. 1994. He wrote: "I find it hard to believe that each man, obviously both intelligent, independent thinkers, would abruptly put seemingly unconditional trust in a stranger during a time of crisis. This may have occurred, but I find it more likely that they knew each other beforehand."

41. Letter from Ms. Moira MacKay, Churchill College Archives Center, n.d. July 1994.

Chapter 14: Thirty-Seven Years of Deception

1. For "apotheosis" see Naftali, "Deception," 74. Reinforcing the idea of "apotheosis" is Naftali's use of such words as myth, mythology, and hagiography.

2. The launching in 1991 was Naftali's reading of his paper at an intelligence conference in Toronto. In 1992 the paper was acclaimed by the National Intelligence Study Center in Washington as the "best student paper" of 1991. It was published in 1993 in *Intelligence and National Security.* The *Post* article is Ignatius's "Britain's War . . . Pearl Harbor." Ignatius based his story on a reading of the BSC *History.* For Naftali, however, the story was old hat, because it had already been substantially told by Hyde and Stevenson. Hence the *Post* was a "deceived party," the victim of what Naftali chose to call "media manipulation," i.e., Sir William's decades-long "deception." The story was timeworn; what was new in it, and what Ignatius did not fully appreciate, was his "scoop" in fully and publicly identifying the history for the first time. The "last deception," according to Naftali, was Sir William's own self-deception, inasmuch as he died believing his false claims. Bryden, *Best-Kept Secret,* 335.

3. Naftali, 78, 79, and 78 for making money; and 73 and 74 for the "mess" and "thicket."

4. Ibid., 73–74, 77.

5. Ibid., 76–77.

6. Ibid., 77. Naftali says Stephenson's breaking silence came abruptly and may have been caused by the "serious stroke that he suffered in 1950." If so, why had that fact not become known to Porter, whose article was published 1 Dec. 1952? For "collaborated," "sensational," "brimmed," and "bluster," see 77. For "deciphering," see 78. The Heydrich assassination is on p. 73. Not mentioned by Porter, it was spun out in AMCI.

7. The four places are in Naftali, 77, 78, and 95, n. 27. Porter's answer is found in his "Private Eye," 68, 69. Stephenson's comment on Porter is in Chap. 11.

8. The "created a sensation," which was in Naftali's paper as read in Toronto, was not retained in the published article. For the other "sensations" see Naftali, 72, 85; for press reaction see 78, 93, n. 39. Since the *Post* story gave me considerable play, I naturally looked in

vain for those letters. David Ignatius sent me a few that were obviously not publishable and were not published.

9. Porter, "Private Eye," 7, 70. Naftali wrote: "The tone of the article could be dismissed as a product of the time and of the magazine. . . . *Maclean's* was then [1952] in the habit of using breathless titles and includ[ing] fiction alongside its general articles, inviting readers to move from fact to fiction and in the process blurring the line between the two," 78.

10. Porter, "Private Eye," 7, 73. Naval History Division, *United States Submarine Losses*. This publication was reissued with an appendix of Axis submarine losses. The verdicts by Kahn and Rohwer were given to me in conversation on 25 Apr. 1992. Tordella's "science fiction" comment was made a few weeks earlier. Tordella also doubted that BSC had any coast watchers in Uruguay and said BSC had no Enigma capability.

11. Naftali, 78; 80; 94, n. 51; 80; and 78, respectively. Winterbotham, *Ultra Secret*.

12. Ellis, "Mission Accomplished," 9. There Ellis wrote: "With the outbreak of war . . . Churchill turned to those who stood by him in the pre-war years, among whom Stephenson had been . . . a close friend, whose mature judgment and energy had already been manifested."

13. On Stephenson wanting Ultra discussed see Naftali, 94, n. 51, where he says that Hyde refused to comply because he intended to reside in Britain where he would be subject to the Official Secrets Acts. See Naftali, 79, for changing "BSC" to "Stephenson."

14. Naftali, 78. Ellis, writing Hyde, contested Stephenson's creation of BSC "ex nihilo," on the grounds of a preexisting prewar MI-6 and FBI connection. From Stephenson's point of view, and in view of what BSC became, this connection was truly nothing.

15. Bryden, *Best-Kept Secret*, 68; see p. 164 for "extravagant" and "exaggerated or impossible" claims and p. 335 for the "liar" summation.

16. Ibid., 375, n. 16; 272; 345, n. 30.

17. Ibid., 345, n. 30, and 272.

18. For "spy thriller" to "cleverly written" see Naftali, 77, and see 77–78 for the "evolution" sentence. Incidentally, if the history is part "spy thriller," "remarkably eloquent," and "strikingly dramatic," so is the *Encyclopaedia Britannica*.

19. The four allegations are in Bryden, *Best-Kept Secret*, 110, 164, 118, and 269–74.

20. Ibid., 274.

21. For "romantically exaggerated claims," see Hunt, "Tepid Intrepid." For "old men" see Stafford's review of Stevenson's *Intrepid's Last Case*. For "decent modesty" see Le Carre, "England's Spy in America." For "delusions" and "hallucinations" see Trevor-Roper, "Superagent." The "one critic" is Chapman Pincher, author of "Who Really Remembers Why So Many Men Died?"

22. For "prodigious memory" see Stevenson to Intrepid, 3 Aug. 1973, WSP, Intrepid 801.3-1. Sir William often referred to recent books, but he never cited any book or document as proof of a point.

23. For the stroke evidence see Naftali, 77; 81; 82; 85; 86; 87; 95, n. 59; and 96, n. 64.

24. Ibid., 83.

Chapter 15: Too Much Gratitude?

1. McLachlan, review of Ransom, *Intelligence Establishment*; source missing.

2. Thomas Gray, *Ode for Music*, chorus, line 5, as quoted in John Bartlett, *Familiar Quotations*, 10th ed. (New York: Blue Ribbon Books, 1919), 383.

3. For OSS literature see Constantinides, "The OSS: A Brief Review of Literature."

Donovan's tribute to Stephenson first appeared in Porter, "Private Eye," 67 and then as an epigraph in Hyde, *QC*, vi. Stephenson said in his "Early Days" (reprinted as an appendix in Hyde's *Secret Agent*, 248) that Porter's source was Gen. W. B. Smith. Perhaps, but Porter only attributed it to Donovan.

4. Jeffreys-Jones, *CIA*, 11-23.

5. Ibid., 11, 15-16, 17.

6. The Donovan-Mowrer articles, which ran in the *New York Times* 20-23 Aug. 1940, were released to the press by Secretary Knox. The first installment was headlined "U.S. Survey of Hitler Conquests Reveals '5th Column' Spearhead." A subtitle said "Evidence is Held Warning to America." For letters to Menzies and also Bracken on the administration's interest in the articles see Donovan Papers, vol. 34.

7. "Cousins" is my term, not Jeffreys-Jones's. Another term, often used as security language in intelligence relationships, is "our friends." Muggeridge remembered new OSS arrivals in London as "*jeune filles en fleur* straight from a finishing school, all fresh and innocent, to start work in our frowsty old intelligence brothel," quoted by Jeffreys-Jones, 256, n. 19, from Smith, *OSS*, 163. Jeffreys-Jones also footnotes my paper "CIA's British Parentage—and the Significance Thereof."

8. Jeffreys-Jones, *CIA*, 17. See his *CIA*, 256, n. 20 for the exchange between critics and defenders. It all takes place in Kirkpatrick's *Intelligence Community*, 173-74, where Mumford is quoted accusing "the American machine" of taking over "the most regressive features of the Czarist-Stalinist system." On the borrowing bit Kirkpatrick's response consisted of five words: "the models have been British." Those words have been somewhat enlarged upon in Jeffreys-Jones's line linking CIA and the British service.

9. Jeffreys-Jones, *CIA*, 17, 256, n. 21. This last note indicates that Cline, in his *CIA*, 21, called OSS's success "almost a miracle."

10. In reviewing Jeffreys-Jones's *American Espionage*, I called it "a confused and confusing book" but one rich in interesting material.

11. The 1921 situation is in State's departmental order no. 223, 30 Aug. 1921. It lists the following offices and their occupants: U-1, Harrison; U-2, Hurley; U-3, Bannerman; U-4 MacEachran; and U-5, Miles; RG 59, State decimal file, 1910-29, file 111.16/106, box 1014.

12. For the Wilson action see Lansing's two letters to Wilson, 20 Nov. 1915, with the second one's enclosure titled "Memorandum," in *Lansing Papers* 1: 218-21. On Wilkie see Jeffreys-Jones, *American Espionage*, 16-17, 29-41. On State and Frank Polk see Jeffreys-Jones's *CIA*, 13, 73.

13. For Lansing to Wilson, and the "trustworthy stenographer" and "a filing clerk," see the memo in n. 12, supra. For the remainder of the paragraph, see McAdoo to Wilson, 16 Apr. 1917, McAdoo Papers, container 522; Jeffreys-Jones, *American Espionage*, 158.

14. State's departmental order no. 415, 17 June 1927, RG 59, State decimal file, file 111.16/107. On Kelley and Murphy see Murphy to Berle, 2 Dec. 1940, RG 59, file 841.00N/10.

15. Jeffreys-Jones, *CIA*, 14, 13. On "internal cohesion" see his *American Espionage*, 171.

16. On FDR's "coordinating" the services and their "coordinating" themselves see my *Donovan*, 11-14, 51. See also Chap. 7. Jeffreys-Jones on Berle is in the former's *CIA*, 15. Truman's instruction to State is in his letter to Secretary of State James F. Byrnes, 20 Sept. 1945, in my *Donovan*, 463. On Moynihan see his Senate bill 126, introduced 4 Jan. 1995.

17. For Stimson's dictum see Fischel, "Mythmaking." Jeffreys-Jones quotes Marshall and Eisenhower, *American Espionage*, 113 and 173, respectively. The other "credible witnesses" are Acheson, *Present at the Creation*, 16; Strong, in Bidwell, *History*, 271; Russell, memo to John C.

Ross, 18 Dec. 1944, State Department Central Files, lot A, Intelligence Office, Jan.–Mar. 1945; Thayer, *Diplomat*, 165, 172; Stuart, *American Practice*, 51.

18. Jeffreys-Jones, CIA, 21.

Chapter 16: Twenty-Five Years Later

1. Stephenson to Donovan, 15 Nov. 1944. I have a copy of the letter but no citation for it.

2. Stafford, *Camp X*, 252.

··–·–··

Bibliography

Archives and Papers

This bibliography includes many materials to which I had access twenty-five years ago. For various reasons I cannot now list their present location. While some may still be stored in CIA in Langley, Virginia, most are probably in the National Archives and Records Administration in Washington or the Donovan Papers in Carlisle, Pennsylvania. In any case, such materials are marked below by an asterisk. *The Foreign Intelligence Literary Scene* and *Studies in Intelligence* are abbreviated below as *FILS* and *SII*, respectively.

Auxier, George, W., comp. "Historical Manuscript File: Materials on the History of Military Intelligence in the U.S., 1884-1944." Office of the Chief of Military History, U.S. Department of the Army. Washington, D.C.*

Churchill, Winston S. Papers (Premier Three). Historical Section, Cabinet Office. London, Eng.*

Cuneo, Ernest L. Papers. Franklin D. Roosevelt Library. Hyde Park, N.Y.

Donovan, William J. Personal Papers. Central Intelligence Agency. Langley, Va.*

———. Papers. U.S. Army Military History Institute. Carlisle, Penn.

Hull, Cordell. Papers. Manuscript Div. Library of Congress. Washington, D.C.

Hyde, H. Montgomery. Papers. Churchill Archives Centre, Churchill College. Cambridge, Eng.

Kirk, Alan G. Papers. Naval Historical Center, Washington Navy Yard, Washington, D.C.

Knox, Frank. Papers. Manuscript Div., Library of Congress. Washington, D.C.

Messersmith, George S. Papers. University of Delaware Library, Newark, Del.

Morgenthau, Henry, Jr. Papers, diary. Franklin D. Roosevelt Library, Hyde Park, N.Y.

Roosevelt, Franklin D. Papers. Roosevelt Library. Hyde Park, N.Y.

Smith, Harold D. Papers. Roosevelt Library. Hyde Park, N.Y.

Spaatz, Carl T. Papers. Manuscript Div., Library of Congress. Washington, D.C.

Stevenson, William. Papers. University of Regina Library. Regina, Saskatchewan.

Stimson, Henry L. Papers. Sterling Memorial Library, Yale University. New Haven, Conn.

Troy, Thomas F. Papers. Record Group 263, Records of the Central Intelligence Agency. National Archives. Washington, D.C.

U.K. Foreign and Commonwealth Office, American Department. "Telegrams and Papers, 1940–1942." London.

U.S. Bureau of the Budget. Records of oss, Units 209–13. Washington, D.C.*

U.S. Central Intelligence Agency. Records of coi and oss. Langley, Va.*

———. *Studies in Intelligence.* Record Group 263, Records of the cia. National Archives. Washington, D.C.

U.S. Secretary of the Navy, Chief of Naval Operations. Central Files (classified). "Telegrams and Memoranda 1940–1942." Naval Historical Center, Washington Navy Yard, Washington, D.C.

U.S. Department of State. "Telegrams and Memoranda 1940–1942." Record Group 165, Records of the State Department. National Archives, Washington, D.C.

U.S. War Department General Staff, Military Intelligence Division. "Correspondence, Minutes, and Memoranda 1940–1942." Record Group 165, Records of the War Department. National Archives. Suitland, Md., and Washington, D.C.

Interviews and Letters

The name of a city or other location in the list below distinguishes an interview from a letter.

Anderson, Vice Adm. Walter Stratton (Ret.). New York. 12 Feb. 1968 and 7 Oct. 1969.

Bannerman, Robert L. Washington, D.C. 3 Oct. 1969.

Bard, Ralph A., Sr. 6 Jan. 1968.

Bergin, Adm. John H. (Ret.). New York. 8 Oct. 1969.

Berle, Adolf A. New York. 7 Oct. 1969.

Bruce, David K. E. Washington, D.C. 11 Dec. 1969.

Cavendish-Bentinck, Victor F. W. London. 13 Nov. 1969.

Cohen, Benjamin V. Washington, D.C. 8 Dec. 1969.

Cuneo, Ernest L. 13 Nov. 1968 and numerous letters thereafter.

———. Washington, D.C. 27 Nov. 1968 and numerous interviews thereafter.

Doering, Otto C., Jr. New York. 6 and 8 Oct. 1969 and numerous meetings thereafter.

Donovan, Mrs. William J. 20 May 1968.

Drewry, Elizabeth B. 22 Nov. 1967.

Ellis, Col. Charles H. 13 Nov. and 10 Dec. 1969.

Godfrey, Rear Adm. John H. (Ret.) 12 Dec. 1968.

———. Eastbourne, Eng. 4 Nov. 1969.

Goodfellow, Col. M. Preston. Washington, D.C. 19 Aug. 1969.

Lake, Harry B. New York. 27 Mar. 1969.

Landon, Alfred M. 20 June and 8 July 1969.

Leisure, George S., Sr. New York. 27 Mar. 1969.

———. 31 Mar. 1969.

Lyon, Frederick B. Washington, D.C. 5 Dec. 1969.

Murphy, James R. Washington, D.C. 10 Jan. 1969.

Shepardson, John W. 4, 14, and 23 June 1994.

Spaatz, Gen. Carl T. (Ret., USAF). Chevy Chase, Md. 11 June 1969.

Stephenson, Sir William S. 16 Nov. 1968 and numerous letters and telegrams thereafter.

———. Bermuda. 11–15 Feb. 1969 and several visits thereafter.

Tunney, Gene. 6, 18 Aug. and 8 Sept. 1969.

Published and Unpublished Writings

Acheson, Dean G. *Present at the Creation: My Years in the State Department.* New York: Norton, 1969.

Albion, Robert G. and Robert H. Connery. *Forrestal and the Navy.* New York: Columbia University Press, 1962.

Alsop, Stewart, and Thomas Braden. *Sub Rosa: The oss and American Espionage,* 2d ed. New York: Harcourt, Brace and World, 1964.

Andrew, Christopher. *Her Majesty's Secret Service: The Making of the British Intelligence Community.* New York: Viking, 1986.

———. *For the President's Eyes Only: Secret Intelligence and the American Presidency from Washington to Bush.* New York: Harper Collins, 1995.

Ashley, Maurice P. *Churchill as Historian.* New York: Scribner's, 1968.

Beesly, Patrick. *Very Special Admiral: The Life of Admiral J. H. Godfrey, C. B.* London: Hamish Hamilton, 1980.

Berkeley, Roy. *A Spy's London.* Foreword by Nigel West. London: Cooper, 1994.

Berle, Adolf A. *Navigating the Rapids 1918–1971: From the Papers of Adolf A. Berle.* Edited by Beatrice Bishop Berle and Travis Beal Jacobs. New York: Harcourt Brace Jovanovich, 1973.

———. "The Betrayal at Paris." *The Nation,* 9 Aug. 1919, 170–71.

Bidwell, Bruce W. *History of the Intelligence Division of the Army General Staff: 1775–*

1941. Frederick, Md.: University Publications of America, 1986. When first used, this volume was titled "History of the Military Intelligence Division, Department of the Army General Staff." 8 vols., typescript, ca. 1957–58.

Blum, John Morton, ed. *From the Diaries of Henry Morgenthau, Jr.* Vol. 2: *Years of Urgency, 1938–1941.* Boston: Houghton Mifflin, 1965.

Bouverie, [Lt.] Col. [Pleydell-]. "British Relations with oss." Washington, D.C., 1944. Mimeo, 12 pp.*

British Security Coordination. *British Security Coordination (bsc): An Account of Secret Activities in the Western Hemisphere 1940–1945.* A top secret document published in 1945 but otherwise unidentified.

Brown, Anthony Cave. *Wild Bill Donovan: The Last Hero.* New York: Times Books, 1982.

Brown, J. J. *The Inventors: Great Ideas in Canadian Enterprise.* The Canadian Illustrated Library. Toronto: McClelland and Stewart, 1967.

Brownlow, Louis. *A Passion for Anonymity: The Autobiography of Louis Brownlow.* Chicago: University of Chicago Press, 1958.

Bryden, John. *Best-Kept Secret: Canadian Secret Intelligence in the Second World War.* Toronto: Lester Publishing, 1993.

Buckmaster, Maurice. "The Back Rooms." *Spectator,* 10 Apr. 1976, 20.

Butler, J. R. M. *Lord Lothian* [Phillip Kerr]. London: Macmillan, 1960.

Casey, William J. "The Clandestine War in Europe (1942–1945)." *sii* 25 (spring 1981): 1–7.

Central Intelligence Agency. "The Ceremony and Exhibit 'With the Fighting Sixty-Ninth: Donovan in World War I,' June 1986." Washington, D.C.: cia, 1986.

Chadwick, Mark Lincoln. *The Hawks of World War II.* Chapel Hill: University of North Carolina Press, 1968.

Claussen, Martin P. "Who Thought Up CIA?" 2 Aug. 1977, 3 pp.*

Cline, Ray S. *The CIA Under Reagan, Bush and Casey.* Washington, D.C.: Acropolis, 1981.

Colville, John. *Winston Churchill and His Inner Circle.* New York: Wyndam, 1981.

Colvin, Ian. *Vansittart in Office.* London: Gollancz, 1965.

Constantinides, George C. *Intelligence and Espionage: An Analytical Bibliography.* Boulder, Colo.: Westview, 1983.

———. "The oss: A Brief Review of Literature." In *The Secrets War: The Office of Strategic Services in World War II,* edited by George C. Chalou. Washington, D.C.: National Archives, 1992, 109–17.

Cookridge, E. H. *Set Europe Ablaze.* New York: Crowell, 1967.

Cooper, Duff [Viscount Norwich]. *Old Men Forget: The Autobiography of Duff Cooper.* New York: Dutton, 1954.

Costello, John. *Days of Infamy: MacArthur, Roosevelt, Churchill—The Shocking Truth Revealed.* New York: Pocket Books, 1994.

———. *Ten Days to Destiny: The Secret Story of the Hess Peace Initiative and British Efforts to Strike a Deal with Hitler.* New York: Morrow, 1991.

Crozier, Emmet. *American Reporters on the Western Front 1914–1918.* New York: Oxford University Press, 1959.

Cruickshank, Charles. *SOE in Scandinavia.* Oxford and New York: Oxford University Press, 1986.

Cuneo, Ernest L. "The British and Sir William [Stephenson]." Typescript, n.d., 13 pp. This and the next entry are probably now in the Cuneo Papers in Hyde Park.

———. "Take It or Leave It: Donovan of O.S.S." Typescript, 2/9/70 [sic], 4 pp.

———. Letter, Bermuda's *Royal Gazette,* 24 Sept. 1981.

Dalton, Hugh. *The Fateful Years 1931–1945.* London: Muller, 1957.

Danchev, Alex. *Establishing the Anglo-American Alliance: The Second World War Diaries of Brigadier Vivian Dykes.* London: Brassey, 1990. This book includes most of the original text of Dykes's diary, which is now in the Donovan Papers, U.S. Army Military History Institute, Carlisle, Penn.

Darling, Arthur B. *The Central Intelligence Agency: An Instrument of Government to 1950.* With introductions by Bruce D. Berkowitz and Allan E. Goodman. University Park: Pennsylvania State University, 1990.

———. "Origins of Central Intelligence." *SII* 8 (summer 1964): 55–94. This is now included in the entry above.

Deacon, Richard. *A History of the British Secret Service.* London: Muller, 1969.

Deuel, Wallace R. "History of the OSS." Draft manuscript, 1944.*

Dulles, Allen W. *The Secret Surrender.* New York: Harper & Row, 1966.

———. "William J. Donovan and the National Security." *SII* 3 (summer 1959): 35–41.

Dunlop, Richard. *Donovan: America's Master Spy.* Chicago: Rand McNally, 1982.

Edwin, Frederick [The Earl of Birkenhead]. *Halifax: The Life of Lord Halifax.* London: Hamish Hamilton, 1965.

Ellis, Charles Howard. "Anglo-American Collaboration in Intelligence and Security: Notes for Documentation." Typescript, ca. 1963, 205 pp.

———. "Mission Accomplished." Typescript, 1972. 209 pp.

———. *The Transcaspian Episode 1918–1919.* London: Hutchinson, 1963.

Farley, James A. *Jim Farley's Story: The Roosevelt Years.* New York: Whittlesy House, 1948.

Fischel, Edwin C. "Mythmaking at Stimson's Expense." *FILS* 4 (Oct. 1985): 4–6.

Foot, M. R. D. *SOE: An Outline History of the Special Operations Executive 1940–46.* London: BBC, 1984.

Ford, Corey. *Donovan of OSS.* Boston: Little Brown, 1970.

Gilbert, Martin. *Finest Hour: Winston S. Churchill 1939–1941.* London: Heinemann, 1983.

———. *Winston Churchill: The Wilderness Years.* Boston: Houghton Mifflin, 1982.

Goodhart, Phillip L. *Fifty Ships That Saved the World.* London: Heinemann, 1965.

Gretton, Vice Adm. Sir Peter. *Former Naval Person: Winston Churchill and the Royal Navy.* London: Cassell, 1968.

Hall, Adm. Sir W. Reginald, and Amos J. Peaslee. *Three Wars with Germany.* New York: Putnam's, 1944.

Hammond, Paul Y. "The Secretaryships of War and Navy: A Study of Civilian Control of the Military." Ph.D. diss., Harvard University, 1953.

Henhoeffer, William M. "Donovan's Allies in World War I." *SII* 30 (winter 1986): 47–53.

Hinsley, F. H., E. E. Thomas, C. F. G. Ransom, and R. C. Knight. *British Intelligence in the Second World War: Its Influence on Strategy and Operations.* Vol. 1. London: HMSO, 1979.

Hunt, David. "A Tepid Intrepid." *Times Literary Supplement*, 3 Sept. 1982.

Hyde, H. Montgomery. *Cynthia.* New York: Farrar, Straus and Giroux, 1963.

———. *The Quiet Canadian: The Secret Service Story of Sir William Stephenson.* Foreword by David Bruce. London: Hamish Hamilton, 1962. Published in the United States as *Room 3603: The Story of the British Intelligence Center in New York During World War II.* Foreword by Ian Fleming. New York: Farrar, Straus and Giroux, 1963.

———. *Secret Intelligence Agent.* Foreword by Sir William S. Stephenson. New York: St. Martin's, 1983.

Ickes, Harold L. *The Secret Diary of Harold L. Ickes.* 3 vols. New York: Simon and Schuster, 1953, 1954, 1954.

Ignatius, David. "Britain's War in America: How Churchill's Agents Secretly Manipulated the U.S. Before Pearl Harbor." *Washington Post*, 17 Sept. 1989, C1–2.

Irving, David. *Churchill's War: The Struggle for Power.* Perth, Australia: Veritas, 1987.

Janeway, Eliot. *The Struggle for Survival: A Chronicle of Economic Mobilization in World War II.* Vol. 53 of *The Chronicles of America Series*, edited by Allan Nevins. New Haven: Yale University Press, 1951.

Jeffreys-Jones, Rhodri. *American Espionage: From Secret Service to CIA.* New York: Free Press, 1977.

———. *The CIA and American Democracy.* New Haven: Yale University Press, 1989.

Kimball, Warren F. *Churchill and Roosevelt: The Complete Correspondence.* Edited with commentary by Warren F. Kimball. 3 vols. Princeton: Princeton University Press, 1934.

———. "World War II's 'Intrepid' and the Pitfalls of Popular History." Letter, *New York Times*, 5 Aug. 1981, A22.

Kirkpatrick, Lyman B., Jr. Review of Hyde's *The Quiet Canadian. SII* 7 (summer 1963): 122–25.

———. *The Real CIA.* New York: Macmillan, 1968.

———. *The U.S. Intelligence Community: Foreign Policy and Domestic Activities.* New York: Hill and Wang, 1973.

Klemmer, Harvey. *Harbor Nights.* Philadelphia: Lippincott, 1937.

———. *They'll Never Quit.* Sydney and London: Angus and Robertson, 1941.

Krock, Arthur. *Memoirs: Sixty Years on the Firing Line.* New York: Funk and Wagnalls, 1968.

Langer, William L. and S. Everett Gleason. *The World Crisis and American Foreign Policy.* Vol. 1: *The Challenge to Isolation, 1937–1940.* Vol. 2: *The Undeclared War, 1940–1941.* New York: Harper, 1952, 1953.

Lansing Papers. See U.S. Department of State. *Papers Relating to the Foreign Relations of the United States: The Lansing Papers*.

Le Carre, John. "England's Spy in America." *New York Times Book Review*, 29 Feb. 1976, 1.

Lobdell, George Henry. "A Biography of Frank Knox." Ph.D. diss., University of Illinois, 1954.

Lockhart, Sir Robert Bruce. *The Diaries of Sir Robert Bruce Lockhart*. Vol. 2: 1939–1965. Edited by Kenneth Young. London: Macmillan, 1980.

Lovell, Mary S. *Cast No Shadow: The Life of the American Spy Who Changed the Course of World War II*. New York: Pantheon, 1992.

Mackenzie, Compton. *Greek Memories*. Frederick, Md.: University Publications of America, 1987. First published in London, 1932.

Mahl, Thomas Earl. "'48 Land': The United States, British Intelligence and World War II." Ph.D. diss., Kent State University, 1994.

Maschwitz, Eric. *No Chip on My Shoulder*. London: Herbert Jenkins, 1957.

Mayer, George H. *The Republican Party 1854-1966*. 2d ed., New York: Oxford University Press, 1967.

McCoy, Donald R. *Landon of Kansas*. Lincoln: University of Nebraska, 1966.

McLachlan, Donald. *Room 39: A Study in Naval Intelligence*. New York: Atheneum, 1968.

Medlicott, William N. *The Economic Blockade*. 2 vols. London: HMSO, 1952.

Montague, Ludwell Lee. *General Walter Bedell Smith as Director of Central Intelligence October 1950–February 1953*. Introduction by Bruce D. Berkowitz and Allan E. Goodman. University Park: Pennsylvania State University, 1992.

———. "Intelligence Service, 1940–1950." Memorandum for the Record, typescript, 1969, 68 pp.*

Morison, Elting E. *Turmoil and Tradition: A Study of the Life and Times of Henry L. Stimson*. Boston: Houghton Mifflin, 1960.

Moscow, Warren. *Roosevelt and Wilkie*. Englewood Cliffs, N.J.: Prentice-Hall, 1968.

Mountbatten, Lord Louis. Address given upon receipt of the William J. Donovan Medal from the Veterans of OSS, 21 Mar. 1966, in New York City. Typescript, 13 pp.*

Mowrer, Edgar Ansel. *Triumph and Turmoil: A Personal History of Our Times*. New York: Weybright and Talley, 1968.

Naftali, Timothy J. "Intrepid's Last Deception: Documenting the Career of Sir William Stephenson." *Intelligence and National Security* 8 (July 1993): 72–92.

"Newfoundland: Development Boss." *Time*, 21 Apr. 1952, 41.

Overstreet, Harry, and Bonaro Overstreet. *The FBI in Our Open Society*. New York: Norton, 1969.

Page, Bruce, David Leitch, and Phillip Knightley. *Philby: The Spy Who Betrayed a Generation*. London: Andre Deutsch, 1968.

Pawle, Gerald. *The War and Colonel Warden*. New York: Knopf, 1963.

Pearson, John. *The Life of Ian Fleming*. New York: McGraw-Hill, 1966.

Philby, Kim [Harold Adrian Russell]. *My Silent War*. Introduction by Graham Greene. London: MacGibbon and Kee, 1968.

Pincher, Chapman. *Their Trade Is Treachery*. London: Sidgewick and Jackson, 1981.

———. "Who Really Remembers Why So Many Men Died?" *Daily Express* (London), 19 Mar. 1976.

Porter, McKenzie. "The Biggest Private Eye of All." *Maclean's Magazine*, 1 Dec. 1952, 7.

Read, Conyers. "Pre-COI Period." Draft manuscript, n.d.*

Richards, Denis. *The Royal Air Force 1939–1945*. Vol. 1: *The Flight at Odds*. London: HMSO, 1953.

Sherwood, Robert E. *Roosevelt and Hopkins: An Intimate History*. New York: Harper, 1948.

Smith, R. Harris. *OSS: The Secret History of America's First Central Intelligence Agency*. Berkeley: University of California Press, 1972.

Stafford, David. *Camp X*. Toronto: Lester and Orpen, 1986.

Stephenson, Sir William S. "Early Days of OSS (COI)." Transcribed dictation, ca. 1960; now incorporated in Hyde's *Secret Intelligence Agent*, 247–61.

———. "Foreword," Hyde's *Secret Intelligence Agent*, xiii–xviii.

———. "Point of Departure: A Foreword by Intrepid," Stevenson, *A Man Called Intrepid*, xi–xvi.

Stevenson, William. *A Man Called Intrepid: The Secret War*. New York: Harcourt Brace Jovanovich, 1976.

———. *The Bormann Brotherhood*. New York: Harcourt Brace Jovanovich, 1973.

Stickle, Warren F. "New Jersey Politics—1940: An Acid Test of the Roosevelt Coalition." Master's thesis, Georgetown University, 1967.

Strong, Maj. Gen. Sir Kenneth. *Men of Intelligence: A Study of the Roles and Decisions of Chiefs of Intelligence from World War I to the Present Day*. London: Giniger, 1970.

Stuart, Graham H. *The Department of State: A History of Its Organization, Procedure, and Personnel*. New York: Macmillan, 1949.

———. *American Diplomatic and Consular Practice*. 2d ed. New York: Irvington, 1952.

Sudaplatov, Pavel, and Anatoli Sudaplatov. *Special Tasks: The Memoirs of an Unwanted Witness—A Soviet Spymaster*. With Jerold L. and Leona P. Schecter. Foreword by Robert Conquest. Boston: Little, Brown, 1994.

Sullivan, Brian P. "The Intelligence Career of William J. Donovan." *Rockefeller Archive Center Newsletter* (fall 1993): 4–6.

Sutphen, Harold J. "The Anglo-American Destroyers-Bases Agreement, September 1940." Ph.D. diss., Tufts University, 1967.

Swinton, the Earl of [Phillip Cunliffe-Lister], in collaboration with James D. Margach. *Sixty Years of Power: Some Memories of the Men Who Wielded It*. London: Hutchinson, 1966.

Taylor, A. J. P. "Daddy, What Was Winston Churchill?" *New York Times*, 28 Apr. 1974, 6:30.

Thayer, Charles. *Diplomat*. New York: Harper, 1959.

Trevor-Roper, H. R. "Superagent." *New York Review of Books*, 13 May 1976, 3–4.

Troy, Thomas F. " 'Ah, Sweet Intrigue!' Or, Who Axed State's Prewar Soviet Division?" FILS 3 (Oct. 1984): 1–2.

———. "An Inventory of Papers at the Franklin D. Roosevelt Library [Hyde Park, N.Y.] of William J. Donovan, of the Coordinator of Information, and of the Office of Strategic Services." Typescript, 7 pp.

———. "CIA's British Parentage—and the Significance Thereof." Paper delivered at the tenth annual meeting of the Society for Historians of American Foreign Relations, George Washington University, Washington, D.C., 3 Aug. 1984. Typescript, 17 pp.

———. "Cynthia in Living Color." FILS 11 (June 1992): 3–4.

———. *Donovan and the CIA: A History of the Establishment of the Central Intelligence Agency.* Washington, D.C.: CIA, 1981; and Frederick, Md.: University Publications of America, 1981.

———. "Donovan's Original Marching Orders." SII 17 (summer 1973): 39–69.

———. "Ex-British Agent Says FDR's Nazi Map Faked." FILS 3 (Dec. 1984): 3–4.

———. "For Years the Brits Ran One of America's Best, Says Anthony Cave Brown." FILS 2 (Feb. 1983): 1–3.

———. Review of Jeffreys-Jones, *American Espionage.* SII 23 (fall 1979): 61–64.

———. Review of Stevenson, *A Man Called Intelligence.* SII 21 (spring 1977): 71–73.

———. "Stevenson Papers at University of Regina—But No BSC Papers." FILS 3 (June 1984): 1.

———. "U.S., Canada, and OSS Vets Honor Bill Stephenson." FILS 2 (Oct. 1983): 1,3.

———. "Where Was Churchill on the Night of May 10, 1940?" FILS 3 (Feb. 1984) 1,5.

U.S. Chief of Naval Operations. Naval History Division. *United States Submarine Losses World War II.* Reissued with an appendix of Axis submarine losses, fully indexed. Washington, D.C.: CNO/NID, 1963.

U.S. Congress. House Committee on Military Affairs. *Selective Compulsory Military Training and Service. Hearings on.* H. R. 10132, 10–11, 24–26, 30–31 July and 2, 12–14 Aug. 1940. Washington, D.C.: GPO, 1940.

———. Senate Committee on Military Affairs. *Compulsory Military Training and Service. Hearings on S 4164,* 3, 5, 10–12 July 1940. Washington, D.C.: GPO, 1940.

U.S. Department of State. *Papers Relating to the Foreign Relations of the United States, 1914.* Supplement: *The World War.* Washington, D.C.: GPO, 1928.

———. *Papers Relating to the Foreign Relations of the United States: The Lansing Papers 1914–1920.* Vol. 1. Washington, D.C.: GPO, 1939.

U.S. War Department. Strategic Services Unit. *War Report: Office of Strategic Services (OSS).* 2 vols. Washington, D.C.: GPO, 1949.

Vansittart, Lord Robert Gilbert. *The Mist Procession.* London: Hutchinson, 1958.

West, Nigel. *MI5: British Security Service Operations 1909–1945.* New York: Stein and Day, 1982.

———. *MI6: British Secret Intelligence Operations 1909–1945.* London: Weidenfield and Nicolson, 1983.

Whalen, Richard. *The Founding Father*. New York: The New American Library, 1964.

Wheatley, Ronald. *Operation Sea Lion: German Plans for the Invasion of England 1939–42*. Oxford: Clarendon, 1958.

Whitehouse, Arch. *Heroes of the Sunlit Sky*. New York: Doubleday, 1967.

Winant, John Gilbert. *Letter from Grosvenor Square*. Boston: Houghton Mifflin, 1947.

Winterbotham, F. W. *The Ultra Secret*. New York: Harper and Row, 1974.

Wright, Peter. *Spycatcher: The Candid Autobiography of a Senior Intelligence Officer*. New York: Viking, 1987.

Index

Acheson, Dean G., 208
Aldrich, Winthrop, 106
Alsop, Stewart, 20
Ames, Aldrich Hazen, 210
Amouroux, Edward B., 47
Anderson, Sir John, 138
Anderson, Rear Adm. Walter S., 54, 56, 60, 96–97, 102, 107
Andrew, Christopher, 238n35
Andrews, Admiral, 104–5
Angleton, James Jesus ("Jim"), 13, 155
Astor, Lady, 52
Astor, Vincent: and British intelligence, 40, 64–65, 149, 225n38; and Stephenson, 41, 63, 121, 123–24, 148; and Westrick, 66; as intelligence coordinator, 101, 106–8, 112, 122; and Phillips, 103–5; and Roosevelt, 103–8, 112, 121–24, 142, 148, 187, 225n26, 228n54; and Norden, 106
Auchincloss, Gordon, 206
Augustine (Saint), 19

Balfour, Earl of, 87–88
Ballantyne, Charles T., 36, 142, 143, 146, 149
Bane, Frank, 118
Bannerman, Robert C., 206
Beaverbrook, Lord, 7, 46, 79, 234n4
Bell, Edward, 206

Bell, Walter, 64–65, 237n20
Bellairs, Adm. R. M., 63, 114
Benson, Col. Rex, 8
Bergin, Jack, 30
Berle, Adolf A.: on British intelligence, 36–38, 40, 74–75, 145–49, 187–90, 238n34; and the IIC, 36–37, 95; on FBI's SIS, 97; and Astor, 107; and Wiseman, 142, 230n16; and Holt-Wilson, 145–49; anger at British, 185; and Stephenson, 31, 187–90, 238n34; and Donovan, 221n37
Bermuda: and Stephenson, 8, 69–70, 72, 80, 164, 189; strategic location of, 69, 89; Donovan in, 80; Astor in, 107; author meets Stephenson in, 167, 178
Bermuda Development Company, 8
Bernard, Claude, 221n39
Best-Kept Secret (Bryden), 192, 197–99
Biddle, Francis, 75
Blandford, John B., Jr., 129
Bodard, Jean, 47
Boris, King of Bulgaria, 84, 85
Bormann, Martin, 159–60
Bowes-Lyon, David, 189
Bracken, Brendan, 55, 59, 179, 186
Braden, Thomas, 20
Breckman, Christina, 173
British Information Center, 68

British Intelligence Service, 172
British Passport Control Office, 63–66, 181–82
British Purchasing Commission, 38, 60, 68, 95
British Security Coordination (BSC): and Stephenson, 20, 33, 61, 67–76; and Canada, 68–69, 72; and Latin America, 69–72; and FBI, 71, 148–49; focus of, 72–73, 188–89; and State Department, 73–76; as parent of COI, 132; Stephenson's history of, 150–54, 156, 180–81, 189, 193, 197–99, 231n8; and "Cynthia" and Lais, 158; and Lake, 166; Hyde on, 196; Ellis on, 240n14
Brown, Anthony Cave, 165, 171–77, 182, 213–214n13, 235n25
Brownlow, Louis, 22, 23, 28
Bruce, David K. E., 102, 158, 180, 183, 185, 204, 205, 232–33n31
Bryden, John, 153, 192, 197–99
BSC. See British Security Coordination (BSC)
BSC History, 150–54, 156, 180–81, 189, 193, 197, 198, 199, 231n8
Buckmaster, Maurice, 186
Budd, Edward G., 64, 71
Bullitt, William C., 26, 118
Buxton, Edward, 7

Cadogan, Sir Alexander, 79–80, 88
Callaghan, Captain, 106, 107
Camp X, 151–52, 231n4
Campbell, Sir Ronald, 74, 75
Canadian intelligence services, 68–69, 209–10
Caribbean Cement Company (CCC), 8, 9
Carrel, Alexis, 86–87
Casey, William J., 3, 4, 176, 202
CCC. See Caribbean Cement Company (CCC)
Central Intelligence Agency (CIA): origin of, 3–4, 19–20, 95, 149, 202; establishment of, 19, 132, 205; Studies in Intelligence in, 137, 163; Historical Intelligence Collection in, 169; Donovan exhibit in, 176; Jeffreys-Jones on, 203–5; Donovan's role in establishing, 210; checkered career of, 210–11
Central Intelligence Group, 132
Chamberlain, Neville, 62
Churchill, Winston: and Stephenson, 5, 15, 20, 33, 40, 41, 121, 142, 152, 160–61, 166, 178–91, 194–96, 236n1, 239n39, 240n12; coalition cabinet of, 23; and Donovan, 44, 52–53, 81, 87, 184–85, 186; and World War II, 55, 62–63, 189–90; fires Kell and Holt-Wilson, 140; and Wiseman, 147; and BSC History, 152, 153; and Roosevelt, 179, 185, 188, 238n35
CIA. See Central Intelligence Agency (CIA)
Clark, Grenville, 28

Clegg, Hugh P., 71, 97, 144
Cohen, Ben, 127–28
COI. See Coordinator of Information (COI)
Coit, Richard, 180, 236n10
Colby, William E., 4
Colville, Sir John, 179, 180, 182
Coolidge, Calvin, 25, 52
Cooper, Lady Diana, 53
Coordinator of Information (COI): Donovan's role in establishing, 3–4, 19–20, 76, 90, 92, 109–10, 115, 120–30, 202–3; origin of, 3–6, 19–20, 132–33, 202; Stephenson's role in establishing, 4–6, 20, 67, 120–30, 149; and Roosevelt, 5, 116, 122–25, 127–30, 132; Donovan as, 20, 128, 130; and Phillips, 105; Donovan on establishment of, 111; opposition to, 118–20, 228n54
Cord, B. E. L., 34, 36
Coward, Noel, 7
Craig, Gen. Malin, 27
Crane, Lt. Col. William C., 98
Crozier, Emmet, 173
Cumming, Comdr. Sir Mansfield, 139
Cuneo, Ernest: on Stephenson's stroke, 10, 157, 214n19; and Stephenson, 39, 64, 181; and BSC, 72; on Churchill-Stephenson relationship, 185; on British intelligence, 204, 214n19
Cunliffe, Geoffrey, 55, 56
Cunliffe-Lister, Phillip. See Swinton, Lord
Cunningham, Adm. Andrew, 81, 84

Dacre, Lord, 183, 237n19
Dahl, Roald, 151, 161, 180, 198
Danchev, Alex, 222n28
Danckwerts, Capt. Victor, 114
Darling, Arthur B., 5, 20
De Valera, Premier Eamon, 84
Defense Savings Program, 123
Dill, Gen. Sir John Greer, 84, 85, 88
Dobbie, General, 84
Doering, Otto C., Jr., 167–68, 171, 219n40, 227n22, 234n8
Donovan, William J.: Casey on, 3; and establishment of COI, 3–4, 19–20, 76, 90, 92, 109–10, 120–30, 228n54; 1940 trip to London by, 3–5, 29, 30, 42, 44–61, 76, 137–38; and Stephenson, 5, 6, 40–44, 67, 87, 120–24, 130–31, 165, 186, 189, 190, 203, 209; death of, 6, 167–70; and Stephenson's award, 7, 229n79; and Bermuda Development Company, 8; appointed COI, 20, 128, 130; in World War I, 21, 41, 165–77, 234n11; and World War II, 21, 61, 116, 182, 215n5; and Knox, 23–29; and Roosevelt, 25, 123; con-

gressional testimony by, 29, 45; Knox and
Stimson in cabinet, 29; first meets Stephenson, 41, 166-77, 190, 234n4, 235n13; and
Churchill, 44, 52-53, 81, 87, 184-85, 186;
reports on London trip, 56-61; law firm
of, 59, 167, 219n41; inspects Pearl Harbor,
61; 1940-41 trip by, 77-82, 88-92, 112-16,
184-85, 223n36; first paper on intelligence,
115-16, 121-22, 227-28n45; suggested as
coordinator of countersubversion cases,
115; seen as Defense Savings administrator,
123, 128, 130; memo on COI by, 125, 126;
military blocks promotion, 131; articles on
Fifth Column by, 144, 203-4, 241n6; as
British agent in World War I, 165-77; on
Stephenson-Churchill relationship, 184-
85; and CIA's establishment, 210; home of,
216n32; honored, 236n30
Donovan, Leisure, Newton, and Irvine, 59,
167, 219n41
Douglas, Lewis, 27, 28
Duff Cooper, Alfred, 51, 79
Dulles, Allen W., 3, 4, 20, 76, 202, 210
Dunn, James Clement, 37-38, 143-48
Dykes, Lt. Col. Vivian, 81, 87, 89, 222n28,
223n36, 223n43, 223n47

Early, Stephen T., 24, 112, 123
Eden, Anthony, 23, 85, 87, 88, 113, 223n47
Edison, Charles, 23
Eisenhower, Dwight D., 169, 208, 210
Eliot, Maj. George Fielding, 122
Ellis, Col. Charles H. ("Dick"): author's meetings with, 10-13; physical appearance of,
10-11; intelligence activities of, 11, 14-15, 68,
125, 180, 237n27; on Room 39, 12, 228n64;
Stephenson manuscripts by, 14, 154-58,
160-61, 193, 195-96, 233n32; as Nazi and
Soviet agent, 14, 160; articles on Transcaspia, 232n18; on Hyde's Quiet Canadian,
232n27; and Bruce, 232-33n31; jobs after retirement, 233n33; on Churchill-Stephenson
relationship, 240n12; on BSC, 240n14

Fairey, C. R., 56
Farouk, King of Egypt, 84
Federal Bureau of Investigation (FBI): and
British intelligence, 33, 34, 36-40, 61, 64-
66, 71, 74-75, 106, 142, 145-46, 225n38,
237-38n30; Special Intelligence Service of,
36, 71, 95-99, 102, 105, 120, 121, 143; and
Mowrer's trip to London, 51; foreign operations of, 71-72, 95, 97; and coordination
of intelligence, 93-95, 99, 107-9; and G-2,
97-101, 116; and Norden, 106; and Astor,

106, 107; and Lazarus, 114; and civil defense,
118; British interest in running, 137-49; and
Holt-Wilson, 140-49; General Intelligence
Division of, 143-44; compared with British
system, 144
Fifth Column: and Donovan's trips, 45, 47, 60,
76, 114, 203; Mowrer's investigation of, 45-
46, 138-40; Klemmer's investigation of, 49,
138-39, 143, 146; Mowrer-Donovan articles
on, 59, 204, 241n6; Eliot on, 122; Churchill
on, 138
Fleming, Ian, 7, 12, 20, 125, 127, 159, 233n32
Forrestal, James, 30, 56, 60
Foxworth, P. E., 97, 99
Franco, Gen. Francisco, 84
Frankfurter, Felix, 28, 59, 122-23

G-2: and Stephenson, 34; and British Purchas-
ing Commission, 38; and coordination of
intelligence, 93, 95, 97-101; and Donovan,
108-10; and FBI, 116, 117; and Berle, 145;
prewar intelligence of, 208
Gardner, Max, 118
George VI, King of Greece, 20, 84, 185
Gilbert, Martin, 179
Gleason, S. Everett, 85
Godfrey, Adm. John H.; author's meeting
with, 12-13; and Room 39, 12, 202, 203,
219n26; in World War II, 13; and Donovan,
54-55, 81, 125, 127, 222n23; and Wiseman,
225n38
Goetz, Charles C., 47
Gort, Lord, 55
Gouzenko, Igor, 199
Graham, Katharine, 216n32
Grand, Lt. Col. Laurence D., 223n45
Graves, Harold, 123
Gubbins, Sir Colin, 186
Guthrie, Sir Connop, 68

Hale, Nathan, 6
Halifax, Lord, 75, 79, 87, 88, 138, 147, 221n37,
231n10, 238n35
Hall, Adm. Sir William Reginald ("Blinker"),
139, 147, 182-83
Harrison, Leland, 206
Hauriou, Maurice, 221n39
Helms, Richard, 4
Henhoeffer, William M., 176, 177, 235n28
Herbert, E. S., 89-90
Heydrich, Reinhard, 194, 195-96
Highet, Gilbert, 151, 198
Hill, Thomas W., 151, 152, 198
Hitler, Adolf, 85, 230n31

Hohenlohe-Waldenburg, Princess Stephanie
   von, 225n38, 230n31
Holt-Wilson, Sir Eric, 138–49, 189
Hoover, Herbert, 23, 25, 28
Hoover, J. Edgar: and Stephenson, 33, 34, 36,
   39–40, 64, 66, 71, 73–75, 143, 148, 181, 187–
   90, 237–38n30; on foreign agents in U.S.,
   38; and Paget, 65, 145–46; and Messersmith,
   94–95; and FBI-MID conflict, 97–101, 116,
   224–225n20; and Astor, 106; and coordination of intelligence in New York, 108; and
   opposition to COI, 119–20, 228n54; and
   British offer to help run FBI, 137, 146; and
   Klemmer's report, 146
Hopkins, Harry, 112, 113, 117
Hull, Cordell, 45–46, 48–49, 58, 75, 81, 88, 121,
   148, 188
Hunt, David, 182
Hurley, William L., 206
Husseini, Mufti Haj Amin al, 84
Hyde, H. Montgomery: *Quiet Canadian* by, 4,
   5, 16, 20, 39, 41–42, 53, 130, 150, 151, 153–59,
   165, 178, 196, 197, 203; on Stephenson, 157,
   181, 182; and Ellis's manuscripts on BSC,
   161; in Parliament, 231–32n17

Ickes, Harold, 23, 112, 117–18, 226n5
Ignatius, David, 153, 240n8
IIC. *See* Interdepartmental Intelligence Con-
   ference (IIC)
Immigration and Naturalization Service, 144
Industrial Security Division, 68
Interdepartmental Intelligence Conference
   (IIC), 36–38, 64–66, 95, 97, 101, 108, 119–20
Ismay, Maj. Gen. Sir Hastings ("Pug"), 121,
   187, 189

Jackson, Robert, 100, 112, 116, 117, 148, 188,
   189
Jacob, Lt. Col. Ian, 186, 187, 188
Jamaica, 7, 8, 9, 69, 70, 72, 189
Jeffreys-Jones, Rhodri, 203–8, 241n10
JIC. *See* Joint Intelligence Committee (JIC)
Johnson, Herschel V., 143–47
Johnson, Louis, 23, 24
Joint Intelligence Committee (JIC), 118–19
Justice Department, 38, 74, 144, 148

Kahn, David, 195
Kell, Sir Vernon, 139–41, 145
Kelley, Robert F., 207
Kellogg, Frank B., 207
Kennedy, Joseph: and Mowrer-Donvan trip,
   45–46, 48–50, 53, 55, 57, 61, 218n2; and

Klemmer's investigation, 49, 138–39, 143;
   and Holt-Wilson, 140, 148
Kimball, Warren, 179, 180
King, Mackenzie, 199
Kirk, Alan G., 50–54, 57, 103, 104, 107, 108,
   119–20
Kirkpatrick, Lyman B., Jr., 5, 20, 205, 241n8
Klemmer, Harvey, 49, 59, 138–44, 146, 148,
   229n5
Knickerbocker, H. R., 124
Knox, Frank: appointed secretary of the
   navy, 21, 22–31; supports Donovan, 23–29;
   and Donovan's trip to London, 42, 44–47,
   48–51, 59, 139; and Donovan's report on
   London trip, 56, 57, 58; and Fifth Column,
   59; inspects Pearl Harbor, 61; and Donovan's report on 1940–41 trip, 78–80, 112,
   114; Donovan's influence with, 79–81, 87–
   88, 121; and FBI-MID conflicts, 100; and
   Phillips, 105; receives Donovan's paper on
   intelligence, 115–16, 121–22, 227–28n45; and
   World War II, 117–18; and JIC, 119; wants
   Donovan in FDR administration, 122–23;
   supports COI idea, 228n54

LaGuardia, Fiorello, 118
Lais, Adm. Alberto, 158
Lake, Harry B., 64, 166–67
Land, Adm. Emory S., 60
Landon, Alfred M., 22, 23–24, 26–27
Lane, Lee, 114
Langer, William S., 85
Lansing, Robert, 205–7
Last Hero: Wild Bill Donovan (Brown), 171
Lazarus, Isidore, 114
Leach, Paul, 26
Lee, Col. Raymond E., 55, 57, 118, 119
Leisure, George S., 166–67, 234n3
Lend-Lease Act, 117
Lester, Lt. Col. J. A., 99
Lockhart, Sir Robert Bruce, 186
Lodge, Henry Cabot, 23
Lothian, Lord: and Donovan's trips, 44–46,
   50, 51, 58–61, 78–79, 184, 185; and Wiseman,
   147, 230n16; and Stephenson, 149, 187
Lucas, Scott, 29
Luce, Henry, 154
Lyons, Leonard, 6–7

MacDonald, William, 239n40
MacFall, Capt. Roscoe C., 101, 103, 104
MacKenzie, Compton, 139, 229n7
MacLeish, Archibald, 114
Man Called Intrepid, A (Stevenson): Stephen-

son's role in writing of, 11–12, 162–63, 168; content of, 159–64; reviews of, 163, 168; Stephenson-Churchill relationship in, 179, 182; Naftali on, 193, 196, 200–201

Manitoba Economic Advisory Board, 9

Marshall, Gen. George C.: and coordination of intelligence, 90, 92, 107, 109, 118, 120; and Donovan, 61, 90, 92, 109, 113–15; and FBI-MID conflict, 98–100; on American prewar intelligence, 208

Martin, H. H., 147

Martin, Joe, 23

McAdoo, William G., 207

McCloy, John J., 115

McCoy, Gen. Frank R., 27

McIntire, Dr., 112

McKinley, William, 206

McLachlan, Donald, 12, 20, 202–4, 219n26

Meloney, Mrs. William Brown, 27, 216n23

Menzies, Col. Stewart: and Stephenson, 33, 40, 41, 179–84, 190; and Donovan, 44, 53–55, 79, 87, 120, 204; criticisms of, 157, 160, 183–84, 189, 231n10; and Gouzenko case, 199

Mercier, Cardinal, 172, 174, 177, 236n30

Merten, George, 236n10

Messersmith, George S., 94–95, 101, 108

Metaxas, Ioannis, 84

MI-5, 138–41, 143, 144, 147, 189

MI-6: and Wiseman, 142; Ellis in, 154, 158; Menzies as chief of, 160, 179; Donovan's purported link with, 171; and Stephenson, 183, 189, 232n23

MID. See Military Intelligence Division (MID)

Miles, Gen. Sherman: and Hoover, 38, 65, 95–102, 107, 224–25n20; and Donovan, 56, 57, 60, 90, 92, 109, 114–16; and Stephenson, 71; and Astor, 107–8; and Lee, 118–19; on coordination of intelligence, 120

Military History Institute, 169

Military Intelligence Division (MID), 93, 95, 97–101, 103, 107–8, 116, 119, 143. See also G-2

Miller, Douglas, 124

Mitchell, Hamish, 36, 37, 64, 68, 73, 142, 143, 146, 149

Morgenthau, Henry, 113, 123–25, 128, 130

Morison, Samuel Eliot, 217–218n46

Morrell, Sydney, 157

Morris, Gen. E. L., 114

Morton, Sir Desmond, 121, 132–33, 183, 186–91

Mountbatten, Lord Louis, 59, 219n39

Mowrer, Edgar Ansel: Fifth Column investigation by, 45–56, 137–40, 218n2, 229n1; Fifth Column articles by, 59, 204, 241n6; and COI, 124

Mowrer, Paul Scott, 47

Moynihan, Daniel P., 176, 208

Muggeridge, Malcolm, 204, 241n7

Muller, Julian, 162, 163, 200

Mumford, Lewis, 205, 241n8

Murphy, James R., 185–86

Murphy, Raymond L., 146, 148, 207

Naftali, Timothy J.: on Stephenson's strokes, 9, 10, 214n19, 239n6; on Stephenson as liar, 151–53, 192–96, 198, 200–01, 239n2, 240n9

Nasser, Gamal Abdel, 21, 215n7, 237n16

Nelson, Sir Frank, 89

Newall, Sir Cyril, 55

Newfoundland and Labrador Corp., Ltd., 8–9

Norden, Carl L., 106

Office of Civil Defense, 118

Office of Naval Intelligence (ONI), 38, 90, 92, 93, 95–97, 101–5, 107–9, 143, 145

Office of Strategic Services (OSS), 3–5, 19–20, 69, 132, 202, 209

Ogilvy, David, 157–58

O'Keefe, John, 56

"Olds" intelligence network, 15, 16, 209

ONI. See Office of Naval Intelligence (ONI)

OSS. See Office of Strategic Services (OSS)

Paget, Comdr. Sir James Francis, 63–65, 73, 106, 142, 145–46, 148, 149, 184

Patterson, Robert P., 28, 56

Paul, Prince Regent, 84

Pearson, Drew, 64

Pearson, John, 20

Peaslee, Amos, 147

Pepper, John A. R., 155, 180, 181

Perowne, J. V., 59–60, 80

Pforzheimer, Walter, 13

Philby, Kim, 184, 186–87

Philips, Sir Frederick, 41

Phillips, Wallace B., 101–5

Pincher, Chapman, 14, 160

Pirandello, Luigi, 215n7, 237n16

Playfair, Giles, 152, 198

Polk, Frank L., 206

Porter, McKenzie, 154, 178, 181, 182, 185, 190, 193–96, 239n6, 240n9

Powers, Francis Gary, 205

Pressed Steel Company, 33, 166–67, 183, 184

Purvis, Arthur, 41, 60, 68

Quiet Canadian, The (Hyde): author's use of, 4; title of, 4, 156; content of, 16, 20, 39, 41–42, 53, 130, 153–59, 165, 178; documenta-

Quiet Canadian (continued)
tion for, 150; Naftali's critique of, 193, 196,
197, 232n27; reviews of, 203; Stephenson's
response to, 232n29

Read, Conyers, 184
Rocca, Raymond, 13, 155
Rockefeller Foundation, 173–77
Rohwer, Jürgen, 195
Room 39 (McLachlan), 12, 20, 202, 228n64
Roosevelt, Eleanor, 27, 127
Roosevelt, Franklin D.: establishes COI, 3,
20; and COI, 5, 116, 122–25, 127–30, 132;
and Stephenson, 5, 39, 64, 120–21, 143, 148–
49, 152, 161, 185, 187–89; forms coalition
cabinet, 21, 22–29; on Donovan, 25; and
Donovan's trips, 46, 52, 57–59, 78, 87; and
Kennedy, 49, 50; and the FBI's SIS, 71;
Donovan's relationship with, 79–81, 87–88,
121, 187; and coordination of intelligence,
93–110, 120, 122, 144, 207, 225n26; and
Astor, 103–8, 112, 122–24, 142, 148, 187,
225n26; and Donovan's report on 1940–41
trip, 112; and Miles, 116; and establishment
of war agencies, 117; and World War II,
117–18; and Donovan as Defense Savings
administrator, 123; proclaims national
emergency, 123; and Wiseman, 127; and Im-
migration and Naturalization Service, 144;
and Churchill, 179, 185, 188, 238n35; and
destroyers-bases agreement, 217–218n46;
Ickes on, 226n5
Roosevelt, James, 105, 187–88
Roskill, Capt. Stephen, 13
Ross, Alec, 87
Ross, Col. Frank, 101–3
Royal Canadian Mounted Police, 68
Rumreich spy case, 144, 230n21
Russell, Francis, 208

Sackett, D. E., 101
Salter, Arthur, 41
Schiaparelli, Mme. Elsa, 127
Scotland Yard, 138, 139, 144
Secret Intelligence Service (SIS), 5, 14, 34, 36,
40, 68, 177
Selborne, Lord "Top," 239n39
Sharp, Maj. Frederick D., 71, 98–103, 108
Shearer, Brigadier, 84
Shepardson, John W., 234n10
Shepardson, Whitney H., 6, 150, 168–70,
234n10
Sherwood, Robert E.: Stephenson as a "quiet
Canadian," 4, 156, 180; and award for
Stephenson, 7; on Stephenson and FBI, 40;

and Stephenson's contact with FDR, 64,
121, 123, 187; on Hopkins, 112; and COI,
124; and Porter, 181
Simmons, Mary French. *See* Stephenson, Lady
Mary
Simovic, General, 223n38
Sinclair, Sir Archibald, 79
SIS. *See* Secret Intelligence Service (SIS);
Special Intelligence Service (SIS)
Slessor, Air Comdr. J. C., 55, 114
Smith, Harold D., 118
SOE. *See* Special Operations Executive (SOE)
Somerville, Adm. Sir James, 84
Spaatz, Col. Carl T., 57
Special Intelligence Service (SIS), 36, 71,
95–99, 102, 105, 120, 121, 143, 190
Special Operations Executive (SOE), 89, 189
Spycatcher case, 14
Stafford, David, 152
Stark, Adm. Harold, 56, 105–7, 114, 119,
225n26, 229n2
State Department: and British intelligence
in U.S., 40, 64–66, 73–76, 106, 137, 142–
49, 188; and FBI, 40, 71; and Kennedy on
Mowrer-Donovan trip, 49–50; German
information sent to, 64; and coordination
of intelligence, 93, 95, 97, 107; and Norden,
106; and Donovan, 78, 114; and Lee's proposal, 119; U-1 in, 205–9; and Wiseman,
225n38
Stephenson, Elizabeth, 9, 214n17
Stephenson, Lady Mary, 7, 11, 34, 63, 157, 178,
234n47
Stephenson, Sir William: and establishment of
COI, 3–4, 19–20, 67, 76, 90, 92, 109–10, 115,
120–30, 142–43, 149; Hyde's biography of,
4, 16, 20, 39, 41–42, 53, 130, 150, 151, 153–59,
178, 196–98, 232n29; intelligence activities
of, 4–6, 15–16, 73–74, 180; and Churchill, 5,
15, 20, 33, 40, 41, 121, 142, 152, 160–61, 166,
178–91, 194–96, 236n1, 239n39, 240n12; as
intelligence professional, 5, 15, 20, 33–44,
63–76, 181–91, 209–10, 232n23; and Roosevelt, 5, 39, 64, 148–49, 152, 161, 185, 187–89;
British and American honors for, 6–7, 10,
20, 67, 131, 154, 164, 190, 229n79, 234n47;
retirement of, 6, 9–11; business activities
of, 7–9, 33, 166, 182, 183, 184; strokes suffered by, 9–10, 157, 214n17, 214n19, 239n6;
author's meetings with, 10–11, 13–15, 150–
51, 167, 178; Stevenson's book on, 11–12,
159–64, 168, 179, 193, 196, 198, 200–201; on
Ellis's loyalty, 14; and "Olds," 15, 16, 209; in
World War I, 15, 31, 41, 166, 168–71, 234–
35n12; and BSC, 20, 33, 61, 67–76, 148–54,

159, 166, 188–89, 196, 197, 240n14; photo
of, 32; and Hoover, 33, 34, 36, 39–40, 64, 66,
71, 73–75, 143, 148, 181, 187–90, 237–38n30;
travels to United States, 33–44, 181–82;
and first meeting with Donovan, 41, 166–
77, 190, 234n4, 235n13; and Donovan's 1940
trip, 41–44, 52, 58, 186; as passport control officer, 63–66, 181–82; Latin American
responsibilities of, 69–72; and Donovan's
1940–41 trip, 72, 77, 79–80, 87, 184–85, 186;
on JIC, 119; and Donovan as COI, 120–
30; on Swinton, 140; and Wiseman, 147,
225n38; and *BSC History*, 150–54, 156, 180–
81, 189, 193, 197, 198, 199, 231n8; death of,
190, 193–95, 234n47; called liar, 192–201;
alleged deciphering of German messages by,
193, 194–95
Stettinius, Edward R., Jr., 8, 60
Stevenson, William: *Man Called Intrepid*
by, 11–12, 159–64, 168, 179, 182, 193, 196,
198, 200–01, 234n10; on Camp X, 151;
literary papers of, 153, 231n12; on Donovan-
Stephenson friendship, 165, 168–71, 173; and
BSC History, 197, 231nn12–13; meets
Stephenson, 233n36; and Stephenson-
Churchill relationship, 237n15, 239n39
Stewart, Robert B., 73, 144
Stimson, Henry L.: appointed secretary of war,
21, 23, 25, 28–29; and Stephenson, 42, 44;
and Donovan's trips, 46, 56–58, 78, 112–13;
Donovan's influence with, 61, 81, 121; and
G-2, 98–100, 224–25n20; on coordination of
intelligence in New York, 107–8; and Dono-
van as coordinator in countersubversion
cases, 115, 116, 118; and FBI's relationship
with G-2, 116, 117; as war activist, 117–18;
and World War II, 117–18; on not reading
other people's mail, 208
Straus, Roger, 157, 158
Strong, Brig. Gen. George V., 208
Stuart, Graham, 208
Studies in Intelligence (CIA), 137, 163
Sudaplatov, Anatoli, 14–15
Sudaplatov, Pavel, 14–15
Sullivan, Brian P., 176–77, 236n30
Sullivan, John, 30
Sulzberger, Arthur Hays, 127
Sweet-Escott, Bickham, 180
Swing, Raymond Gram, 124
Swinton, Lord, 50, 90, 114, 138–40, 144, 148

Taft, Robert A., 23
Taft, William Howard, 28
Tamm, Edward A., 37, 99

Taylor, A. J. P., 184
Taylor, Edmond, 124
Tedder, Arthur William, 84
Thayer, Charles, 208
Thomson, Sir Basil, 139
Tordella, Louis W., 195, 240n10
Trend, Sir Burke, 12
Truman, Harry S., 7, 8, 20, 205, 207–8, 210,
229n79
Tully, Grace, 104, 127
Tunney, Gene, 31, 33, 39, 40, 64, 216n2
Turrou, Leon G., 144, 230n21
Tweedy, Bronson, 13

U-1, 205–8
U-2 reconnaissance aircraft, 205
Ultra, 180, 195, 240n13

Vandenberg, Arthur H., 23
Vansittart, Robert, 52, 55, 61
Vining, Arthur C. M., 209

Wallace, Henry, 118
Wark, Wesley K., 179, 236n6
Watson, Gen. Edwin "Pa", 100, 112, 120, 123,
127
Wavell, Gen. Archibald Percival, 84, 85, 88,
113
WCC. *See* World Commerce Corp. (WCC)
Welles, Sumner, 49, 119, 188
West, Nigel, 184
Westrick, Dr. Gerhard Alois, 66
Weygand, Gen. Maxime, 78, 84
White, Harry Dexter, 113, 117
Whitehouse, Arch, 161
Whitney, William D., 130
Wiedemann, Fritz, 225n38, 230n31
Wilkie, John E., 206
Williams, Valentine, 55
Wilson, Gen. "Jumbo," 84
Wilson, Woodrow, 175, 205, 206
Winant, Ambassador, 64, 121, 123–25
Winchell, Walter, 64
Winslow, L. Lanier, 206
Winterbotham, F. W., 180, 195
Wiseman, Sir William: in Jamaica, 7; intelli-
gence activities of, 103–4, 146–47, 225n38,
230n16, 230n31; and Phillips, 103–04; and
Godfrey, 127; in World War I, 142, 225n38,
230n16; and Berle, 146–47; and Porter, 181;
health of, 214n18
Woodring, Harry, 23, 24
World Commerce Corp. (WCC), 7–8
Wright, Peter, 14, 160

Young, Philip, 113